VELLEIUS PATERCULUS

THE ROMAN HISTORY

VELLEIUS PATERCULUS

THE ROMAN HISTORY

From Romulus and the Foundation of Rome
to the Reign of the Emperor Tiberius

Translated, with Introduction and Notes, by
J. C. Yardley and Anthony A. Barrett

Hackett Publishing Company, Inc.
Indianapolis/Cambridge

15   14   13   12   11   1   2   3   4   5   6   7

For further information, please address:
   Hackett Publishing Company, Inc.
   P.O. Box 44937
   Indianapolis, IN 46244-0937
   www.hackettpublishing.com

Cover design by Listenberger Design & Associates
Text design by Meera Dash
Map by William Nelson
Composition by Agnew's, Inc.
Printed at Edwards Brothers, Inc.

Library of Congress Cataloging-in-Publication Data

Velleius Paterculus, ca. 19 B.C.–ca. 30 A.D.
   [Historiae Romanae libri II. English]
   The Roman history : from Romulus and the foundation of Rome
to the reign of the Emperor Tiberius / Velleius Paterculus ; translated,
with introduction and notes, by J.C. Yardley and Anthony A. Barrett.
       p. cm.
   ISBN 978-1-60384-591-5 (paper)—ISBN 978-1-60384-592-2 (cloth)
   1. Rome—History.   I. Yardley, John, 1942–   II. Barrett, Anthony,
1941–   III. Title.
   DG207.V4413 2011
   937—dc22

                                                            2011014041

Contents

Preface

This book is intended to make Velleius Paterculus' account of Roman history available to as wide a range of readers as possible. To that end, we have made a number of compromises. First, the title: we are aware that whatever title Velleius might have given to the history he completed almost two thousand years ago, he almost certainly did not call it a *Roman History*. His aim was far more comprehensive. In its original published form his work had a broad geographical range, embracing Greeks as well as Romans (and possibly other peoples, too), and a broad chronological range, beginning in the mythical past with the Trojan War and ending in AD 30, during the reign of Tiberius. The title often attached to his work, *Historia Romana,* has no ancient pedigree and seems to have been coined by Velleius' first editor in the early sixteenth century. But the passage of time has not been kind to Velleius' original all-embracing and wide-ranging text. Only a very small fragment of the "Greek" portion of the complete history has survived, so that less than 3 percent of the surviving text deals with Greek matters; the other 97 percent or more deals almost exclusively with Rome. It is on this latter "Roman" section that we place our focus, and we feel therefore that it is in no way misleading for us to appropriate the traditional name of *The Roman History* in the case of our particular book, especially since the term that Velleius himself uses, *opus* ("work"), conveys little or no useful information. For the sake of completeness, however, we have also provided a translation of the surviving small fragment dealing with Greek matters, in an appendix. We feel that this arrangement of the material, while not preserving the order that has come down from the first edition of Velleius and, safe to assume, the manuscript, now lost, on which it is based, will make the text much clearer and far more coherent.

We have allowed ourselves certain licenses with Roman names. These can be confusing at the best of times, and Velleius can be particularly baffling, not least because of his practice of referring to the emperor Tiberius and to his predecessor, Octavian/Augustus, in the latter case both before and after the accession, as "Caesar," inviting a head-spinning confusion with one another or with Julius Caesar. After much deliberation, we have put loyalty to the reader before loyalty to terminological exactitude, so that the first mention of the name in any given chapter will be Caesar Octavian, Caesar Augustus, or Tiberius Caesar, as the case may be, then we follow Velleius in using "Caesar" alone for the remainder of the chapter. Also in the

service of clarity, we have dropped the "Nero" element from the name Tiberius Nero when the reference is to the future emperor Tiberius (it is preserved in the case of his father). Other Roman names are generally given in
their Latin versions, except that famous individuals like Pompey and Mark
Antony are called by their familiar nomenclature. Iulius and Iunius are rendered as Julius and Junius (and the same principle is applied to their female
counterparts), but the less familiar Iullus and Iuncus retain their Latin
forms. Velleius occasionally inverts the normal order of names, as do other
Roman writers. In such cases we have remained faithful to Velleius' order in
the text but use the "correct" order in the notes. Also, Velleius does not always use the most familiar spellings of the names of people who appear in
his narrative. We have retained his spellings for the people he mentions.
Otherwise we have adopted the more familiar spellings. We generally use
the standard English names for very familiar geographical and topographi-
cal features, such as Rome or the Rhine, and have kept the Latin forms for
the less well known (we concede that the borderline is somewhat arbitrary).

In the same spirit, we have tended to add a "BC" or "AD" (whichever is
applicable) to the first date or date range mentioned in any given note, and
thereafter also if it seems useful and appropriate. For events close to the turn
of the era, we have assigned a "BC" or "AD" to every date where the intention is not self-evident. We have also provided information in the Glossary
that at times is already available in the text but perhaps not always readily
accessible.

This translation of Velleius, and indeed every study of Velleius, is derived
ultimately from the first printed edition of his work and at times reflects the
corrupt state of the now lost manuscript on which that edition is based. We
have, except in a small number of places, followed the text of the Teubner
edition of W. S. Watt, and for the sake of simplicity we have limited ourselves to one set of symbols where the translation of any given passage is
affected by a serious textual problem. Angled brackets < > are used to show
that the Latin version as transmitted is corrupt or that some of the text is
missing.

Velleius tends to write in long and often convoluted sentences. We have
not tried to emulate him in this. To have preserved his sentence structure
would no doubt have produced an English version that in some ways could
claim to be more authentic, but the end result would have been largely
unreadable, especially for those not already conversant with the subject
matter.

In preparing this book we have benefited from the generous support of
family, friends, and colleagues. Chris Kelk and Doreen Barrett read through
the proofs. Alexander Puk of the University of Heidelberg was ever willing
to share his thoughts on Velleius. At various stages of the work's evolution

Ann-Cathrin Harders and John Jacobs gave us the benefit of their historical and linguistic expertise by reading the whole manuscript. Any errors that might have slipped in since their perusal are exclusively our own responsibility. The anonymous reader for Hackett Publishing also saved us from a number of errors that we had not noticed. The excellent library resources and collegial atmosphere in Toronto, Oxford, and Heidelberg have made our task much lighter than it would otherwise have been. Finally, we wish to express our gratitude to Deborah Wilkes and Meera Dash for their professionalism, patience, and affability while helping us to put the manuscript through the complicated process of going to press.

Abbreviations of Ancient Authors and Works

App. *BC*	Appian, *Bellum Civile* (*Civil War*)
Caes. *BC*	Caesar, *Bellum Civile* (*Civil War*)
Cat. *Carm.*	Catullus, *Carmina*
Cic. *Brut.*	Cicero, *Brutus*
Cic. *Fam.*	Cicero, *Ad Familiares* (*Letters to His Friends*)
Cic. *Mil.*	Cicero, *Pro Milone*
Cic. *Orat.*	Cicero, *De Oratore*
Cic. *Phil.*	Cicero, *Philippics*
Cic. *Pis.*	Cicero, *In Pisonem*
Cic. *Sest.*	Cicero, *Pro Sestio*
Cic. *Tusc.*	Cicero, *Tusculan Disputations*
Diodorus	Diodorus Siculus, *Bibliotheca Historica* (*Library of History*)
Florus	Florus, *Epitome*
Epit. de Caes.	(Anonymous) *Epitome de Caesaribus*
Hor. *AP*	Horace, *Ars Poetica* (*Art of Poetry*)
Hor. *Ep.*	Horace, *Epistles*
Hor. *Od.*	Horace, *Odes*
Hor. *Sat.*	Horace, *Satires*
Jos. *Ant.*	Josephus, *Antiquities*
Jos. *BJ*	Josephus, *Bellum Judaicum* (*Jewish War*)
Just. *Epit.*	Justin, *Epitome*
Liv. *Per.*	Livy, *Periochae* (*Summaries*)
Livy	Livy, *Ab Urbe Condita* (*From the Founding of Rome*)
Macr. *Sat.*	Macrobius, *Saturnalia*
Mart. *Ep.*	Martial, *Epigrams*
Nep. *Att.*	Nepos, *Atticus*
Nic. Dam. *Aug.*	Nicolaus of Damascus, *Life of Augustus*
Ovid *Am.*	Ovid, *Amores*
Pliny *NH*	Pliny, *Natural History*
Plut. *Ant.*	Plutarch, *Antony*
Plut. *Brut.*	Plutarch, *Brutus*
Plut. *Caes.*	Plutarch, *Caesar*
Plut. *Cic.*	Plutarch, *Cicero*

Plut. *Crass.*	Plutarch, *Crassus*
Plut. *Mar.*	Plutarch, *Marius*
Plut. *Marc.*	Plutarch, *Marcellus*
Plut. *Pomp.*	Plutarch, *Pompey*
Plut. *Quaest. Rom.*	Plutarch, *Quaestiones Romanae*
Plut. *Sull.*	Plutarch, *Sulla*
Plut. *Ti. Gr.*	Plutarch, *Tiberius Gracchus*
Priscian *Inst.*	Priscian, *Institutiones Grammaticae*
Quint. *Inst.*	Quintilian, *Institutio Oratoria*
RG	*Res Gestae Divi Augusti* (*The Achievements of the Deified Augustus*)
Sall. *Cat.*	Sallust, *Conspiracy of Catiline*
Sall. *Jug.*	Sallust, *Jugurthine War*
Sen. *Ben.*	Seneca, *De Beneficiis*
Sen. *Brev. Vit.*	Seneca, *De Brevitate Vitae* (*Shortness of Life*)
Sen. *Clem.*	Seneca, *De Clementia*
Sen. *Contr.*	Seneca, *Controversiae*
Sen. *Ep.*	Seneca, *Epistles*
Sen. *Marc.*	Seneca, *Consolatio ad Marciam*
Sen. *NQ*	Seneca, *Quaestiones Naturales*
Sil. *Pun.*	Silius Italicus, *Punica*
Strabo *Geog.*	Strabo, *Geography*
Suet. *Aug.*	Suetonius, *Augustus*
Suet. *Cal.*	Suetonius, *Caligula*
Suet. *Jul.*	Suetonius, *Julius Caesar*
Suet. *Nero*	Suetonius, *Nero*
Suet. *Tib.*	Suetonius, *Tiberius*
Tac. *Ann.*	Tacitus, *Annals*
Tac. *Dial.*	Tacitus, *Dialogus*
Val. Max.	Valerius Maximus, *Memorable Deeds and Sayings*
Virg. *Aen.*	Virgil, *Aeneid*
Virg. *Ecl.*	Virgil, *Eclogues*
Vir. *Ill.*	(Anonymous) *De Viris Illustribus* (*On Famous Men*)

Introduction

I. Velleius' Life and Career

Awareness of Velleius Paterculus is currently enjoying something of a renaissance, and he is now starting to be regarded as a useful and interesting historical source, especially for the period of the early Roman empire and for the events that he himself witnessed. But, for all that, it would still be fair to say that even his most fervent admirers would hesitate to place him in the first rank of Roman historians. What modest reputation he enjoys as a recorder of the past is almost totally eclipsed by such historical giants as Sallust, Livy, and Tacitus. It is somewhat ironic, then, that there are few Roman writers whose family backgrounds and whose own careers are so well documented. The explanation for this paradoxical circumstance is a simple one. Velleius did not belong to an established and distinguished Roman family. His forebears were manifestly "provincial" (in the modern, rather than the Roman, sense of the word): he belonged, on both his father's and his mother's side, to those representatives of Italian municipal aristocracies who had been consistently loyal to Rome and had done very well out of that loyalty, to the extent that their descendants could eventually aspire to membership in the Roman senate. Velleius was unashamedly, and often engagingly, proud of his laudable ancestors, eager to record their exploits and never reluctant to extol their achievements, or his own contributions to the stature of the family name.

Velleius could trace his family back some two hundred years, to the time of Hannibal. He speaks with considerable affection of one of his maternal forebears, Decius Magius of Capua, some fifteen miles north of Naples, a leading figure of Campania, "a man of great fame and reliability," whose exploits are known to us from a detailed account in Livy.[1] After the battle of Cannae in 216 BC, Decius was singled out among the Capuans and arrested by Hannibal, then placed on a ship bound for Carthage. When a storm drove the vessel to Cyrene, he escaped to Egypt, where he obtained his freedom and where he may have died. One of Decius' descendants, Magius Minatus, was no less stalwart in his support of Rome. When, in 91 BC,

---

1. 2.16.2; Livy 23.10; Sil. *Pun.* 11.157–258, 377–84, 13.280; see also Cic. *Pis.* 24. Velleius calls himself the great-great-great-grandson of Decius. Sumner (1970, 259) argues for an extra generation.

much of Italy rose against Rome in the Social War, he remained steadfastly loyal. The family was by this time the leading one of Aeclanum, a town of the Hirpini in central Italy. Minatus recruited an army, helped the Romans take Herculaneum, aided the future dictator Sulla in the siege of Pompeii, and, on his own initiative, occupied Compsa. He was rewarded with Roman citizenship, and his sons were granted the praetorship at some point before 81.[2] To judge from Velleius' silence, his Magian connections perhaps failed to achieve major distinction from that point on, but the family did not disappear. The name of Velleius' brother Magius Celer Velleianus suggests that the brother was adopted by a Magian relative, an unlikely development had the Velleii not considered the renewed connection to be to its social and political advantage.[3]

On his father's side Velleius is most likely descended from the Velleii long attested in Capua in Campania.[4] We can only speculate on this, since he limits himself to recording his paternal family line from his grandfather's time on. Velleius Paterculus' grandfather Gaius Velleius was one of the 360 judges chosen by Pompey in 52 BC to deal with disorder and corruption. Then he held the rank of *praefectus fabrum*, the officer in charge of military engineers, under Pompey, when the civil war first broke out in 49 and he later held the same position under Marcus Brutus, one of the assassins of Caesar, although we do not know where he served. He appears in that same military rank for a third time in 41 BC, on this occasion under the command of Tiberius Claudius Nero. This Tiberius was the first husband of Livia (later to become Augustus' wife) and the father of the future emperor Tiberius. Velleius notes that Tiberius Nero had a bond of "close friendship" (*singularis amicitia*) with Gaius. They both opposed Octavian and supported Antony's cause in the Perusine War (41–40), and both were on the losing side. Tiberius Nero and his family, along with his son, the infant Tiberius, fled from Naples and made for Sicily. Gaius Velleius, a man "second to none" (2.76.1), according to his grandson, but now worn out by old age and illness, took his own life.

This period could be likened to that of the American civil war, in that bitter political rifts within families were a common occurrence. The next generation of the Velleii were on the "other side" and unequivocal in their adherence to Octavian, even while their pro-Antonine father was alive.

---

2. 2.16.3. Velleius mentions that the sons were elevated when the number of praetors stood at six. The number was raised to eight by Sulla in 81 BC.

3. 2.115.1, 2.121.3, 2.124.3; Sumner (1970, 261–2) argues that Marcus Magius Maximus, prefect of Egypt under Augustus, had a family link with Velleius.

4. *Corpus Inscriptionum Latinarum* 10. 3037 (=8184), 3898, 3924; elsewhere in Campania: 1154, 1403, 1612.

There were two sons. One of them, Capito, the historian's uncle, was co-signer, with Agrippa in 43 BC, to the proceedings that the latter initiated against the tyrannicide Gaius Cassius, when Caesar's assassins were tried in their absence. Capito, either at this point or later, held senatorial rank (2.69.5). The other brother, the father of the historian, remained equestrian (the distinction between these ranks is discussed in section III). We are given only one piece of information about him, that in AD 4 our Velleius succeeded his father as *praefectus equitum* (cavalry commander) on the Rhine (2.104.3). The father's commander, in charge of the legions stationed in Germany, was, until the future emperor Tiberius' arrival there in that same year, Marcus Vinicius (he had held that position since about AD 1 or 2).[5] The relationship of superior/subordinate between Marcus Vinicius and Velleius' father continued, although in a different form, in the descendants of both men.

Velleius' pride in the achievements of his family is more than matched by the immense satisfaction that he took in the progress of his own career, which he describes in similar detail. On the basis of the offices he later held we can assume that he was probably born in the late 20s BC.[6] Ironically, despite the relative abundance of information on his life and family, we cannot be certain of his praenomen (given name), Gaius, Marcus, or Publius, or perhaps none of the above.[7] By convention Velleius Paterculus is always referred to as such, without praenomen. He and his brother Magius followed their father into a military career, and Velleius' first recorded service was as a tribune in Thrace and Macedonia, in about 2 BC. He served there under Publius Vinicius, the son of his father's commander, Marcus, in Germany, and also under Publius Silius (2.101.3). Gaius Caesar, the grandson and adopted son of Augustus, visited the Balkans when Velleius was serving there.[8] Whether or not he and Velleius became acquainted then we have no way of telling, but, when Gaius was sent in 1 BC on a mission to the east,

---

5. 2.104.2; see Hanslik (1961), 116.

6. Sumner (1970, 275 n. 111) suggests a birth in about 20–19 BC; Syme (1986, 423) suggests 23 BC.

7. Priscian (*Inst.* 6.63) calls him "Marcus" (see Appendix B), citing an "M. Velleius Paterculus," but Sumner (1970, 278 n. 124) notes that there is no other certain case (there is a dubious one, at 9.47) of Priscian using all three elements in the name in a citation and suggests that the "M." might be intrusive. The first editor, Beatus Rhenanus (see Note on the Text), gave him the name Publius in his frontispiece, perhaps identifying Velleius with the Publius Vellaeus mentioned by Tacitus (*Ann.* 3.39.1). In the dedicatory section to Frederick, prince-elector of Saxony, Beatus refers merely to "Velleius Paterculus." In the *Vita* section at the beginning of his *editio princeps* he calls him "Gaius," perhaps an analogy with his grandfather; in Amerbach's copy (see Note on the Text) there is no praenomen.

8. Dio 55.10.17 (2/1 BC).

Velleius joined him, at the same rank of tribune. It may also be significant that Sejanus, the future commander of the praetorian guard, for whom Velleius later expresses manifest—though, some have argued, muted—admiration, was probably on Gaius' staff during the same eastern enterprise (2.127–8). Velleius is able to provide us with a vivid eyewitness account of the meeting between Gaius and the Parthian king Phraates, and the delicate protocol involved, as Roman and king met on an island in the middle of the Euphrates with their forces arrayed on either bank, then celebrated their agreement by dining first on the Roman side of the river, then on the Parthian. Velleius seems to have looked back on this time as a sort of gilded age, when he traveled throughout Achaea and Asia and all the eastern provinces, standing on both sides of the Black Sea and its outlet. We do not know if he remained with Gaius until the latter's death in Lycia on February 21, AD 4. In any case, his five years' service terminated, Velleius was in Rome by June 26 of that year and was able to witness the enthusiastic popular reaction to Augustus' adoption of Tiberius (2.103).

Tiberius took over command of Roman troops on the Rhine from Marcus Vinicius later in the same year, AD 4, and Velleius joined him, succeeding his father as *praefectus equitum*. He was an eyewitness to military events in the region for the next nine years, and he provides detailed accounts of campaigns that saw Tiberius advance to the Elbe. In AD 6 Velleius had completed his *equestris militia* (equestrian military service) and was now ready to embark on a senatorial career, with his election as quaestor. He no doubt had powerful backing and may have benefited from the help of his father's old commander, Marcus Vinicius, or of his own, Publius Vinicius, or even of Tiberius himself (2.101.3, 2.113–14). At this point a crisis arose, when a rebellion erupted in Illyricum, creating a desperate need for troops in the area. Velleius was not yet a senator, being only quaestor-designate, but, presumably because of his considerable military experience, he was given a special appointment to command a relief army to be sent to Tiberius. Once the troops were delivered, Velleius returned to Rome, presumably before December 5, when quaestors traditionally took office. On assuming the quaestorship, instead of being sent to a province, as might have been expected, he rejoined Tiberius, with command of a legion.[9] In the winter of AD 7/8 Velleius was in command of part of the army (2.113.3). The weather was very severe, and he may well have been ill; at any rate he expatiates at length about the excellent medical services that Tiberius had established (2.114.1–2). At the end of AD 8, Tiberius turned his attention

---

9. 2.111.4. Velleius held the rank of *legatus Augusti*, which in this period applied to a legionary commander. Later such an officer would be a *legatus legionis*, the other title being reserved for governors of imperial provinces; see Saddington (2003).

to Dalmatia, where Velleius' brother Magius Celer Velleianus served as his legate and received commendations from both him and Augustus (2.115.1, 2.121.3). Tiberius assigned command in Pannonia to Marcus Lepidus; Velleius has high praise for Lepidus and presumably stayed with him in Pannonia, marching with him to join up with Tiberius in AD 9 (2.114.5, 2.115.2–3).

Five days after the conclusion of the campaigns in Pannonia, word arrived of the catastrophic defeat suffered by Quintilius Varus in the Teutoburg Forest. Tiberius was dispatched to Germany to rectify the situation. Since we know that Velleius served with him for nine seasons, he presumably must have accompanied Tiberius there, although he makes no mention of his own activities. By AD 12 Velleius and his brother were back in Rome, and on October 23 they were honored with a prominent role in the triumph celebrated in that year for Tiberius' earlier Illyrian campaign, postponed because of Varus' tragedy.[10]

After this interruption, Velleius was free to resume his senatorial career. In AD 14, the year of Augustus' death and Tiberius' accession, Velleius and his brother were elected to the praetorship. They were among the *candidati Caesaris,* candidates specifically nominated by the emperor, which guaranteed election. By a historical fluke they were in a sense nominated by two emperors, since their names were provided by Augustus and then after his death confirmed by Tiberius (2.124.3). We have no record of further office. It has long been claimed that our Velleius is to be identified with Publius Vellaeus, a legionary legate whose outstanding service in Thrace in AD 21 is recorded in a single passage of Tacitus but who is otherwise unknown.[11] Certainly Velleius shows considerable interest in contemporary Thracian events. Otherwise it is hard to pin down specific details about his later life. He describes a fire on the Caelian Hill in AD 27 as if he might have been on the spot (2.130.2). He was still alive when Marcus Vinicius, grandson of his namesake, assumed the consulship in AD 30. The last specific event recorded by him is the death of Livia in AD 29, probably early in the year (2.130.5).

Apart from the emperors Augustus and Tiberius, one further individual appears to play a dominating role in Velleius' life during the first third of the century. Velleius addresses Vinicius throughout his work. He almost certainly published his history during his consulship and often uses that consulship as a reference point for dates. It would not be misleading to describe Vinicius as Velleius' "patron," provided we use that term in the modern

---

10. 2.121.3; the date is provided by the *Fasti Praenestini* (*Inscriptiones Italiae* 13.2.135, 524–5).

11. Tac. *Ann.* 3.39; the identification was first made by Beatus Rhenanus in 1520; see Sumner (1970), 277.

rather than in the technical Roman sense; he would be someone of standing and prestige, able to give encouragement and general support to his acquaintances. In return, it is fairly safe to assume that Velleius would have dedicated his work to him, the dedication presumably appearing in a preface, which along with the first chapters is now lost from the beginning of the history.[12]

Marcus Vinicius belonged to a Campanian family that came to prominence as a result of Augustus' ascendancy. His grandfather Marcus Vinicius senior, who became consul in 19 BC as a "new man" (*novus homo*), was one of Augustus' most able commanders and also his close personal friend. Our Marcus' father, Publius Vinicius, commanded Velleius when the historian began his military career. Publius was consul in AD 2 and later proconsul of Asia, and a highly regarded orator.[13] Publius' son Marcus Vinicius would, to judge from his later career, have been about fifteen or so years younger than Velleius; his consulship in AD 30 suggests he was born not much before 2 BC. He seems to have been a person of considerable charm and tact. Tacitus describes him as a man of gentle disposition, and Dio observes that he survived by minding his own business and keeping quiet.[14] We know nothing of his early years. He presumably held a series of offices leading up to the praetorship, which he would have attained in the 20s, sometime before his consulship. A powerful indication of his standing is his marriage to Julia Livilla, daughter of Germanicus and hence, by adoption, the granddaughter of Tiberius. He was thus Caligula's brother-in-law, and although Caligula banished his sisters Julia Livilla and Agrippina the Younger, on the supposed grounds of adultery, in AD 39, Vinicius, at this time proconsul of Asia, survived unscathed.[15] His name came forward as a possible successor to Caligula on the latter's assassination, but he pragmatically accepted the accession of Claudius.[16] As a consequence of the change of emperor, Julia Livilla was recalled from exile (as was her sister) but banished again very soon afterward, on the grounds of adultery with the philosopher Seneca. Vinicius survived these upheavals and remained in imperial favor, possibly accompanying Claudius on his British expedition in 43, and held a second consulship in 45.[17] He died in 46 and received a state funeral.[18] He clearly

---

12. Woodman (1975), 273.

13. 2.101.3; Sen. *Contr.* 7.5.11.

14. Tac. *Ann.* 6.15.1; Dio 60.27.4.

15. Suet. *Cal.* 24.3; Dio 59.22.6, 8.

16. Jos. *Ant.* 19.251.

17. For Vinicius in Britain, see Syme (1933), 143.

18. Dio (60.27.4) claims that Vinicius was poisoned by Messalina, wife of the emperor Claudius, for refusing to grant her sexual favors.

possessed remarkable diplomatic skills that enabled him to stay in high
favor through a succession of three emperors.
Vinicius looms large throughout Velleius' history. But we must bear in
mind that, for all the references made by Velleius to him, we know only one
definite fact about their relationship, that Velleius began his military career
under Vinicius' father Publius (2.101.3).
After the consulship of Vinicius in AD 30, Velleius disappears from the
historical record. The next two years were among the most turbulent in
Roman history. The ambitious and powerful commander of the praetorian
guard, the notorious Sejanus, reached the acme of his power when he assumed the consulship in January of 31. In October of that same year he was
denounced in the senate, imprisoned, and put to death (as were his children
somewhat later). Although Velleius places great emphasis on speed and
brevity through his history, he devotes two chapters to the praise of Sejanus
(2.127–8). Having described the boons of Tiberius' reign, Velleius observes
that great figures of history made use of great lieutenants. Many of these
helpers were "new men," and Velleius draws a parallel between Augustus
and Agrippa, and Tiberius and Sejanus. He also adds for good measure that
although Sejanus was an equestrian, he could boast, on his mother's side, of
connections to eminent senatorial families, and he had relatives who were
of consular rank. Velleius could no doubt speak about Sejanus from personal contacts going back a number of years (both had probably served on
the staff of Gaius Caesar). His praise of the praetorian commander gives us
a fascinating insight into the attitude of ambitious Romans toward this
towering figure, second in the Roman state only to the emperor.[19] It is important not to view these chapters with excessive hindsight. We know that
Sejanus was to be brought down in spectacular fashion, and that he would
be vilified by his contemporaries and his character assaulted by writers such
as Tacitus. But this would not have been known in AD 30. Many were no
doubt hostile to him and resented his success, but few would have anticipated
that his fall would be so precipitous. Moreover, it has been suggested that
Velleius is in fact less than enthusiastic about Sejanus. Sumner considers
Velleius' eulogy "tense, uneasy, and ambivalent" and "shaded with reservations and insinuations," and Woodman on different grounds reaches essentially the same conclusion, arguing that his praise of Sejanus displays an
"awkwardness and incongruity which testify to their author's discomfort."[20]
It is difficult to know how much to read into Velleius' reservations. It is true,

---

19. Apart from the power that Sejanus exercised, Velleius admired men who made their way
in the world by their personal energy and achievements; see Newbold (1988).
20. Sumner (1970), 293–4; Woodman (1975), 304; the observation was initially made by Steffen (1954, 191–201).

as Woodman is right in pointing out, that on two occasions where Sejanus played a positive role in events, the quelling of the mutinies in Illyricum and the action in fighting the fire at Pompey's theater in 22, his name is in fact omitted by Velleius. But note that similar gaps appear in Velleius' account of Tiberius, such as his failure to mention Tiberius' role in the restoration by Phraates in 20 BC of the standards taken at Carrhae, where there can hardly have been any hidden agenda behind the historian's silence.[21] If Velleius does curb his enthusiasm in extolling Sejanus, it could be because of the need to ensure that his praise will not run the risk of eclipsing his eulogy of Tiberius, which follows shortly afterward.

The regard that Velleius expresses for Sejanus, combined with the silence of the record about Velleius after AD 30, has led to an assumption that Velleius was brought down in the aftermath of Sejanus' fall. This assumption is unwarranted. We must remember that while the sources are indeed silent on Velleius after 30, they are no more so than they were before then, in that for practical purposes our only source of information on Velleius' life is in fact his own history. It is only the chance survival of the manuscript of that history, published in 30 or thereabouts, that gives us any information about Velleius up to that date. Without his *opus* he would have vanished from the record, apart from the passing reference to a single line of his in the late fifth-century grammarian Priscian, and two mentions in medieval commentaries (scholia) on the poet Lucan.[22] The clues we have to his later family fortunes indicate no such disgraceful end, since he seems to have left two sons, Gaius and Lucius, whose careers suggest that his family standing survived intact and that his family fortunes did so, too, allowing them to maintain senatorial status. The Gaius Velleius Paterculus recorded in an inscription as *legatus* of Legio III in Africa cannot be the historian.[23] The inscription must date to 39 at the very earliest; up to that point Legio III had been commanded not by a *legatus* but by the proconsul of Africa, a public province (Caligula transferred command to an imperial legate). This Gaius is probably to be identified with a Gaius Velleius Paterculus who served as suffect consul in about 60.[24] He may well be the historian's son. The other possible son, Lucius Velleius Paterculus, is recorded as suffect consul in 61. Clearly the fate of Velleius after AD 30 must remain an open question.

21. Woodman (1975), 247. On mutinies, see Tac. *Ann.* 1.24.1–2; on fire, Tac. *Ann.* 3.72.2–3 (cf. Sen. *Marc.* 22.4); on standards, 1.91.

22. On Priscian, see note earlier in this section; on scholia, see Endt (1909), 329, 348–9, on 2.40.4, 2.53.3.

23. *Corpus Inscriptionum Latinarum* 8.10311.

24. Degrassi (1952), 16–17; Sumner (1970), 278 n. 124.

II. Velleius' *Historia Romana*

One work of Velleius has survived from antiquity, and it may well be the only one that he published. The original title that Velleius gave it eludes us; conventionally it is referred to as the *Historia Romana* ("Roman History"), but that designation seems to have been coined by his first editor, Beatus Rhenanus (see Note on the Text), without ancient authority. Nor does Velleius refer to it as a *historia* but merely as his *opus* ("work"; 2.48.6). In its earliest published form, and in all subsequent editions, the *opus* appears in two books, which almost certainly reflects its original arrangement, dictated by the amount of material that could be conveniently entered onto a single papyrus roll (it is probably safe to assume that both books would originally have been of similar length). Velleius himself refers to the first book as the *prior pars,* thus distinguishing it from the second or *posterior pars* (1.14.1). The second book is more or less intact, with some minor gaps. The first is very fragmentary indeed. The surviving text begins in midsentence with the founding of Metapontum by Epeus in the aftermath of the Trojan War. But it is safe to say that Velleius would *not* have begun his *opus* without preamble, and with such an obscure event. It is very likely that he would have started with a preface, a traditional way of beginning a history, as do Livy and Sallust. Such a preface most likely would have laid out Velleius' intentions and have contained a dedication to Marcus Vinicius. In two separate places Velleius speaks of his *promise* of brevity (2.89.6) and of his declared commitment to write summarily (2.55.1), undertakings that must presumably have been made in the preface. Whether or not the *opus* had a preface, the narrative proper would almost certainly have begun with the Trojan War.[25] This was a major turning point in myth and legend, intimately linked with the future history of Rome and with its imperial family, through the myth of Aeneas and his part in the creation of the Roman people and the establishment of the ancestral line of the Caesars.[26] Since the surviving fragment begins with accounts of the Greek heroes returning from Troy, it is likely that the gap at the beginning is a fairly small one. The first surviving eight chapters pass very summarily and selectively through four centuries, ending, in the last section of chapter 8, with Romulus and the foundation of Rome, which is traditionally placed in the eighth century BC. Between then and the mid-second century BC only one line of Velleius' narrative has survived, by the accident that the grammarian Priscian quoted it in a discussion of the genitive form "Miltiadis." This indicates that at some point

---

25. Kramer (2005, 144–6) argues that Velleius began with the foundation of the Assyrian empire.

26. Brozek (1962), 125; Starr (1981), 163.

Velleius dealt with Miltiades' son Cimon and the history of fifth-century BC Athens.[27] Apart from that single line there is a gap of nearly six centuries down to the 170s BC and the wars between Rome and Macedonia. Velleius then takes us in five chapters to the destruction of Corinth and Carthage in the 140s and completes Book 1 with digressions on the history of Roman colonization and Greek and Roman literary and intellectual history (1.14–18). Book 2 begins with the aftermath of the destruction of Carthage in 146 BC and proceeds without serious hiatus to the death of Livia in AD 29, the last specific event to be mentioned.

Velleius' range is clearly a vast one, from the Trojan War to the principate of Tiberius, and this enormous period is covered within the compass of two books. In order to bring this off, Velleius claims that he had to write with speed and to impose brevity on his text, and he characterizes the finished product as a *transcursus* ("rapid survey").[28] Paradoxically for a work that supposedly had to be composed quickly, and economically, the *opus* is written in a flowing, copious form of Latin. This stands in great contrast to the Latin style of Sallust (c. 86–35 BC), author of the *Conspiracy of Catiline* and the *Jugurthine War,* as well as of a lost *Histories* (dealing with the 70s and 60s BC and preserved only in fragments). Velleius knew Sallust's writings well and echoes them in certain phrases and expressions (he calls Sallust Rome's Thucydides at 2.36.2), but he forswore Sallust's abrupt and sparse style and his precious mannerisms.[29]

Heavily influenced by the rhetorical schools, Velleius writes in long, complex sentences and is very fond of the type of antithesis that we associate with the "silver age" Latin of Seneca and Tacitus. These antitheses can on occasion be turned to deft historical purpose, as in the observation on the somewhat venal Quintilius Varus' governance of Syria: "he entered a rich province poor and departed from a poor one rich" (2.117.2). Velleius' style can be awkward. Sometimes he does not write in proper periods, in the Ciceronian sense, but in series of clauses interrupted by parentheses. He is much given to interjections and will address Vinicius directly. But occasional awkwardness is a failing of most Roman historians, and in Velleius' case it certainly cannot be characterized as slapdash. His style is strikingly at variance with his declared intention to complete his work speedily.

---

27. Appendix B. We cannot, of course, rule out the possibility that the reference to Cimon occurs not in its proper chronological context but in one of Velleius' "digressions."

28. On speed, see 1.16.1, 2.41.1, 2.108.2, 2.124.1; brevity, 1.16.1, 2.29.2, 2.52.3, 2.55.1, 2.66.3, 2.86.1, 2.89.1, 2.96.3, 2.99.4, 2.103.4, 2.117.1 (by implication), 2.119.1; *transcursus,* 2.55.1, 2.86.1, 2.99.4.

29. See Woodman (1969).

If we take Velleius at his word, his *opus* was essentially a preliminary project, a prelude to a major work on history. This planned separate undertaking is distinguished as his "full-scale work" (*iustum opus/iustum volumen*).[30] It has been suggested that we should not take Velleius too seriously when he makes these claims.[31] Deprecation of one's current work as minor and trivial was something of a literary trope. But Velleius' language is often divorced from that of the conventional apologia. In suggesting that his major work will cover the early stages of the civil war between Caesar and Pompey, he describes his intentions in a matter-of-fact way that draws an analogy with other histories of the period and seems meant to be taken seriously (2.48.6). Velleius repeatedly asserts that the *iustum volumen* was intended to be his primary undertaking, which reinforces the impression that he should be taken at his word.

It is also to be noted that Velleius is quite specific about this projected serious history. From internal comments it can be seen that he planned to cover the preliminaries to the civil war between Pompey and Caesar (and might have begun with them, but we cannot be sure) and intended to include more detailed treatment of Tiberius' decision to retire to Rhodes in 6 BC, his adoption by Augustus in AD 4, his campaigns in Pannonia and Dalmatia, and the destruction of the Roman legions under the command of Varus in AD 9.[32] If this was indeed a real project, we have no evidence that it was ever completed. Nor can we assert with confidence that it was never written. Velleius' extant history survived by the accident that the one known existing manuscript containing it was discovered in the sixteenth century and fortunately was copied before it again disappeared. A similar fate, but with a less happy outcome, might well have befallen the putative *iustum volumen*.

It often happens that we have only a general notion of when an ancient author published a given work. In the case of Velleius' *opus* we are able to pinpoint the publication date fairly accurately and confidently. The very latest date by which the work must have been published is October 31, when Sejanus was brought down. There is no possibility that Velleius' admiring comments could have been published after then. We can almost certainly move the date a little earlier. Velleius frequently refers to Vinicius' consulship, which he entered on January 1, 30, and remained in for six months. There is no explicit reference to any event that occurred after or

---

30. On *opus,* see 1.16.1, 2.29.2, 2.38.1, 2.66.3, 2.86.1, 2.89.1, 2.96.3; *iustum opus/volumen,* 2.48.6, 2.89.1, 2.99.3, 2.103.4, 2.114.4, 2.119.1.

31. Peter (1911, 366), for instance, suggests that the putative major work might just be a rhetorical pose; discussed by Woodman (1975a, 287–8; 1977, 108–9).

32. 2.96.3, 2.99.3, 2.103.4, 2.114.4, 2.119.1.

during that consulship.[33] The latest events other than the consulship to be explicitly recorded by Velleius are the exiles of Germanicus' widow Agrippina the Elder and their son Nero, and the death of Livia, all of which belong to 29 (2.130.4–5). He uses the consulship as a way of dating events, which points quite clearly to the period of its tenure as the time when the *opus* was published. It could perhaps be argued that Velleius is referring to Vinicius' *impending* consulship, in which case publication could have taken place as early as the summer of 29, by which time Vinicius would have been elected. But the repeated references to the office make it far more likely that he would have delayed publication until the actual investiture the following January.[34] There were distinguished precedents for such a procedure. In his *Eclogues,* for example, Virgil honored Asinius Pollio on his assumption of the consulship in 40 BC.[35] Hence, there are good reasons for thinking that the *opus* was composed before the end of 29 and published at some point in the first half of 30.

While there is general agreement, at least within a year or so, about the date Velleius finished his *opus,* the question of when he *began* it is much more vexed. A number of scholars have argued that he can have started writing no sooner than July of 29, when Vinicius would have been elected.[36] This would have allowed at most only a year for composition, according to the generally accepted date of publication. Support for such a short time period is found in Velleius' frequent allusion to the need for haste and brevity to enable him to complete his project, which suits the idea of a very tight schedule. Also, throughout the work, beginning in the first fragment of Book 1, references to the consulship are interwoven into the text, suggesting that it was written after it was known that Vinicius would assume the office. Sumner cites the very first reference, to illustrate how the consulship is integral to the sense: "Next, the most famous games of all, the ones most effective in promoting physical and mental excellence, were inaugurated by Iphitus of Elis. He established these games, and their commercial activities, 823 years before you entered your consulship, Marcus Vinicius."[37] Woodman,

---

33. Sumner (1970, 286), however, following Lana (1952, 299), argues that Velleius' references to the invaluable contribution of the *novus homo* to the well-being of the state and to Tiberius' calling on Sejanus to "lighten the burdens of the princeps" (2.128.4) allude to Sejanus' consulship, which he assumed in January of 31 and to which he would presumably have been elected in summer of 30.

34. 1.8.1, 1.8.4, 1.12.6, 2.7.5, 2.49.1, 2.65.2.

35. Virg. *Ecl.* 4; Horace (*Od.* 1.4) may well have written his ode to Lucius Sestius Albinus to celebrate his consulship of 23 BC.

36. This was for long the standard view, laid out clearly by Sumner (1970, 284–5); Syme (1986, 437) inclines toward Sumner's conclusion; see also Dihle (1955), 640.

37. 1.8.1; Sumner (1970), 284 n. 145.

however, has observed that for him to have written the work between July 29 and January 30, Velleius would have had to write at a furious pace.[38] As noted above, his Latin style, characterized by long, convoluted sentences, is hardly consonant with what would almost have amounted to a kind of speed-writing. Woodman argues accordingly for a longer period of composition. He points out that while Vinicius' actual election would probably have occurred in mid-29, he might well have been earmarked as candidate some years before then, and Velleius might have known about the forthcoming honor from about the mid-20s.[39] Woodman further observes that statements about haste are conventional and need not be taken literally. *Festinatio* (haste) and *brevitas* (brevity), he notes, represent the ability to express oneself succinctly and are virtually interchangeable *topoi* of literary criticism, not literally a true commitment to speed.[40]

There is in fact no way of being certain when Velleius began his *opus*. It could very well have started out independently of Vinicius and have been adapted when Velleius decided to dedicate the work to the future consul. While it is undoubtedly the case that the references to Vinicius' consulship are integral to the text *as it stands,* there is nothing to preclude Velleius' having revised and reworded an earlier draft of his history to insert those references. There is internal evidence that the *opus* did in fact go through at least one draft revision. In the excursus on the history of Roman colonies that Velleius provides in Book 1, he refers to the founding of the colony at Carthage, which he says he has mentioned earlier: "as I said above" ("ut praediximus"). In fact, the other reference to the founding of Carthage does not appear until afterward, in Book 2. Given the presumed subject matter of the missing section of Book 1, it is hard to see how a reference to the Roman colony of Carthage could have appeared there. But in any case, Velleius' language more or less precludes such an earlier reference. What he claims to have mentioned previously was not only the founding of Carthage, but that it was "the first colony outside Italy" ("Carthagoque in Africa prima, ut praediximus, extra Italiam colonia condita est"; 1.15.4). He clearly has in mind the entry in Book 2, where he observes that Carthage was "the first colony founded outside Italy" ("prima autem extra Italiam colonia Carthago condita est"; 2.7.8). Thus the almost identical language in both places leads to the inescapable conclusion that the long digression on colony foundations

---

38. Woodman (1975), 276.

39. Woodman (1975), 280–2. Steffen (1954, 2) suggests that the history was completed just before 29 and that Velleius then added the necessary references. Jodry (1951, 271) says that he could have started after the termination of military service, in AD 14/5. Lana (1952, 299) says before 29.

40. Woodman (1975), 278–84; see also Starr (1981), 170.

must have been inserted in Book 1 as an afterthought, when the rest of the text was already complete. It is possible that Velleius was simply mistaken in thinking that he was placing the digression *after* rather than *before* the reference he had already made to Carthage, but it is equally possible that in an earlier draft he included the digression on the colonies in Book 2 and later decided to move it to the end of Book 1, where he felt it could serve as a useful bridging section.

It is the case that, despite the prominent position that Marcus Vinicius occupies throughout the narrative, there is no proof that it was his impending consulship that *initially* provided Velleius with the impetus to write his history. He might have been inspired by a desire to record his own service in Germany or the Balkans under Tiberius, or by the special family pride he felt on entering a senatorial career. We cannot preclude the possibility that Velleius had for a considerable time been collecting material for a major work, possibly well before the election was mooted. When the intended honor became known (whether in mid-29 or, as Woodman plausibly suggests, earlier in the 20s), Velleius could have felt impelled to produce some work to honor the occasion and pirated his already assembled material to put together the surviving volume.[41] In doing so, he adopted a highly apologetic tone, since he regarded his *opus* as something of a *parergon,* merely a prelude to his major project.

It is not easy to characterize Velleius' *opus* or to assign it precisely to any well-established genre. In many ways it defies categorization and is one of the most idiosyncratic of surviving ancient texts, described by Syme as a "most peculiar product."[42] Despite the traditional title of *Roman History,* Velleius' composition, taken as a whole, is not in fact "Roman History" in the strict sense of the expression. What Velleius set out to write was rather a "universal" history, perhaps not as universal as the term might promise, and essentially a history of the Greeks and Romans from the time of the Trojan War down to his own day.[43] His notice on the overthrow of the Assyrian empire shows that there was a place for other civilizations, but it would almost certainly have been a modest one.[44] The surviving chapters from near

---

41. Sumner (1970, 284 n. 143) and Woodman (1975) both leave open the question of whether Velleius' *iustum opus* was seriously and genuinely intended. Elefante (1997, 2) notes that a fragment of a work by Velleius on the war against the Suevi is recorded in a catalog of ancient manuscripts.

42. Syme (1986), 423.

43. On universal history, see Liddel and Fear (2010).

44. Appendix A.6.1; Kramer (2005, 153) points out that there are only five non-Greek/non-Roman events in the extant part of Book 1: the migration of the Tyrrhenians, the foundations of Cadiz and Utica by the Phoenicians, the foundation of Carthage, and the fall of the Assyrian empire, and that the first four all have a direct connection with the later history of Rome.

the opening of the *opus* contain nothing that is specifically Roman or that has a familiar Roman association. Even after we have reached the "Roman" period and Romulus has been introduced, Velleius does not apparently restrict himself to purely Roman matters (1.8.4). The fragment quoted by Priscian about Cimon, son of Miltiades, suggests that Velleius devotes space to the history of Athens even after he has entered the Roman period. This is suggested by the digression at the end of Book 1, where he asks why talent flourished in short time bursts and refers to the philosophers that followed Plato and Aristotle as "the men I mentioned slightly earlier" (1.16.4), further evidence that Greek topics had a place in the lost section of Book 1. Moreover, after Roman history has been introduced in Book 1, it does not seem to have received special treatment. Romulus' foundation of Rome receives less space than does Teucer's foundation of Salamis, and nothing is said about the story of the wolf, so central a motif in Roman legend, or about Remus.[45] The surviving text of Velleius' work may create a false impression. It is true that, after the destruction of Carthage and Corinth, Rome dominates the narrative. But that was inevitable, since now Rome was the foremost Mediterranean power.

It is also the case that as Velleius draws closer to his own day, and closer to the dominant role of Rome, the pace slows and the text becomes more detailed. The first book began with the Trojan War and covered about a thousand years of history. The second, from the destruction of Carthage to AD 30, covered less than two hundred years. Thus it is a matter of a few chapters to go from Troy to the Sabine women. There is then a major gap and the narrative resumes at the beginning of the Third Macedonian War in the middle of the first half of the second century. The narrative now slows down, but it is again only a matter of a few chapters to cover the quarter century to the destruction of Carthage and Corinth. Then from chapter 41, when Caesar entered the consulship, ninety chapters cover the final ninety years. The more extensive treatment becomes even more pronounced when Velleius deals with events that he himself has witnessed. Hence the ten years up to the death of Augustus, a period when Velleius served at the critical center of events, takes up roughly the same amount of text as the thirty-four years from the battle of Actium.[46] Somewhat similarly, halfway through his 142 books Livy had, by book 71, covered the period from Aeneas to 91 BC; books 72–142 take up the eighty-two years between then and 9 BC.[47] This phenomenon is not unique to ancient writing and is what one authority on the modern period has described as the "landscape principle": "things nearer

---

45. Starr (1981), 165.

46. 2.84–104, 2.104–23; see Sumner (1970), 270.

47. Starr (1981), 166.

xxviii   *Introduction*

to the observer loom larger, are perceived in closer detail, than the mistier general views of the distant horizons."[48] Hence the fact that Rome has the lion's share of the surviving narrative is essentially a reflection of an inevitable tendency of *universal* history, rather than a conscious political stance.[49]

In some respects, however, Velleius does possibly violate the conventions of universal history. A curious feature of the *opus* is the way he uses what are generally referred to as his "digressions," although in Velleius' case that is perhaps something of a misnomer. From time to time he will summarize in potted overviews important political and cultural phenomena. In Book 1 he indulges in a major excursus on colonization (1.14–15) and in Book 2, in a similar one on the development of Rome's empire (2.38–9). At the end of Book 1 there is a summary of Greek and Roman intellectual history (1.16–18), and in Book 2 there are two excursuses on writers of the first and second centuries BC (2.9, 2.36.2–3). These are not digressions in the traditional sense of passages where one wanders away from the primary theme of a narrative to expatiate at some length on a topic only tangential to the main subject matter. Velleius' "digressions" have no proper relevance to the historical context where they appear and can range over several hundred years; they are in essence compendiums inserted into what is in the first place a compendium. Velleius defends them, not implausibly, as a way of examining discrete topical themes as unitary wholes, to enable the reader to "get a concise overview of what I have noted in piecemeal fashion" (2.38.1). He is on less secure ground when he tries to insist that they are not intrusions but integral parts of his *opus*. His claim that the first two, on colonies and intellectual history, are transitional sections between Book 1 and Book 2 sounds like a forlorn attempt to rationalize their insertion into what is in reality an arbitrary point in the narrative. In introducing the excursus on the expansion of empire in Book 2, he ventures that "it [i.e., the digression] does not seem inappropriate to the schema I have proposed." The two digressions on writers, of the first and second centuries, in Book 2 are introduced without preamble. Some argue that there is an element of propaganda in these digressions and that they are intended to illustrate the expansion and ultimate destiny of Rome. But that can hardly have been intended in the sections on intellectual history in Book 1, where the material is divided fairly evenly between Greeks and Romans. It may be that we look in vain for a traditional or formal explanation and that the truth lies in Velleius' admission, made in connection with his study of intellectual history, that some things he feels impelled to pursue because they are his favorite hobbyhorses, even though he is generally obliged to trim down his material severely: "Even so,

---

48. Fulbrook (2001), xv.
49. Sumner (1970), 282.

I am unable to resist putting into writing something I have often pondered in my mind but have not completely reasoned out" (1.16.1).

More significantly, toward the end of his *opus,* when he engages in praise of the emperor Tiberius, Velleius in a very real sense abandons the genre of universal history. Woodman shows that many of the features of this eulogy of Tiberius are characteristic of the genre of panegyric. Thus Velleius begins by insisting that the achievements of Tiberius are so great that they are beyond his capacity to describe, a traditional conceit of the panegyrist (although one that does not prevent him from doing precisely what he says he cannot do). He then does what the traditional panegyrist also does: he elevates his subject by relating him to his predecessor and stresses the things that have been restored, such as peace and justice. Woodman shows that many of the achievements of Tiberius detailed by Velleius can be found in extant panegyrics, achievements such as electoral reforms, restoration of justice, generosity to individuals and communities, the setting of an example.[50] How conscious Velleius was of not adhering to any strict genre is difficult to say, but it may be no coincidence that he uses an imprecise word like *opus,* and not a more specific literary term, to describe his history.

Velleius did not write in a vacuum and would naturally have drawn on the great tradition of historical writing to provide his models. Clearly, any historical work undertaken in this period would have been written in the shadow of Livy's monumental work, the *Ab Urbe Condita* (From the Founding of Rome), which covered Roman history from the founding of the city down to 9 BC. The publication date of Livy's work is hotly disputed. The early books were apparently written by 25 BC, but the final publication might have postdated Augustus' death. In any case, the impact of this work would certainly still have been felt when Velleius wrote his own. Clearly, however, Velleius' aim was to produce a compendium, with an emphasis on brevity; just as clearly he has not taken Livy as his model. Woodman suggests that in fact the opposite might have been the case, and that Velleius was exploiting the reaction to very bulky works like Livy's.[51] The same reservation would apply to the Latin historical writers who preceded Livy. Their historical works survive only in fragments; most notable among those was Marcus Porcius Cato (234–149 BC), the first to write Italian history in Latin. His *Origines* is an account of the history of the towns of Italy, with particular emphasis on Rome, from the time of their foundation, whether legendary or history, down to his own day. We do know that Velleius used this work and that he had considerable respect for it (Appendix A.7.3–4).

---

50. 2.129–30; Woodman (1975), 290–93; see also Ramage (1982). Woodman notes that Mesk (1911, 85–7) was the first to realize that Velleius had written a panegyric in the formal sense.

51. Woodman (1975), 284.

But he did not accept its conclusions unquestioningly, nor could it have provided a very useful model, since Cato also treats his topic at length, in seven books. The same lengthy treatment was characteristic of other known early writers of history who came after Cato, and in fact the broad tendency seems generally to have been toward ever more extensive treatments: for example, Gaius Aelius Tubero (at least 14 books), Gaius Licinius Macer (16), Quintus Claudius Quadrigarius (23), Valerius Antias (75), Pompeius Trogus (44), and finally, of course, Livy (142).[52] By contrast Velleius produced a quick historical summary, which, until he came close to his own day, provided only the barest outlines of Greek and Roman political and cultural history.

The most likely models would have belonged to the generation of writers that immediately preceded Velleius. Some of these seem to have treated their material in small numbers of books.[53] Notable among these was Marcus Terentius Varro (116–27 BC). Two fragments of his *Annales* have survived, dealing with the reign of Servius Tullius and the execution of Marcus Manlius in 384 BC, but otherwise virtually nothing is known of this work. It probably dealt with the history of Rome from Aeneas down to Varro's own day. His four-volume *De Gente Populi Romani* reached the founding of Rome in the third book, the fourth book covering Roman history in compendious form. Like Velleius, he tried to coordinate Roman and non-Roman chronology. Cornelius Nepos (c. 100–c. 25 BC) wrote three books of what should probably be seen as a universal history. Catullus describes it as embracing *omne aevum* ("every age"), and its universality is further suggested by the fragments that have survived, which include entries on such non-Roman topics as Homer and Archilochus.[54] The *Liber Annalis* of Titus Pomponius Atticus (110–32 BC) seems to have begun with the arrival of Aeneas in Italy after the fall of Troy. It extended until at least 155 BC and the visit of the philosopher Carneades to Rome, but we do not know how much further. The work was admired by Cicero, who suggests that while its focus was on Rome it did cover other nations.[55] Atticus' discussion of the playwright Livius Andronicus suggests that literary topics were included. Moreover, Cicero stresses its universality, observing that it dealt with the history of other powerful nations and famous rulers. Like Velleius, Atticus was much committed to recording the dates of the events that he covered.[56] Pompeius

---

52. See most recently T. Cornell (2010), 102–15.
53. See especially Woodman (1975), 286 n. 4; Starr (1981), 167–9.
54. Cat. *Carm.* 1.6.
55. Cic. *Orat.* 120.
56. Cic. *Orat.* 34. 120; Nep. *Att.* 18.1; Starr (1981), 167–8.

Trogus was a contemporary of Livy.[57] He continued to write on a large scale but all the same might well have influenced Velleius. A native of Gallia Narbonensis, Trogus could claim a vast range of knowledge and wrote a work on plants and animals that is frequently cited by Pliny the Elder. His major historical work, the *Historicae Philippae,* is in effect a universal history of those parts of the world that came under the control of Alexander and his successors. It is now lost, but a series of summaries (*prologi*) of the individual books by an unknown hand was preserved in the manuscripts of an epitome made by Justin some two centuries later. In Trogus' case possible specific instances of Velleius' borrowing can be identified.[58]

If there are any shortcomings in Velleius' *opus,* it is he, not his predecessors, who, rightly, is held responsible for them. Generally speaking, critics have not been kind to him. One broad cause of censure is the perception that he is little more than a spokesman for the regime of Tiberius. At one point in his narrative, after enumerating a number of individuals he deems worthy of laudatory comments, he concludes by observing that "impartial frankness free of mendacity is no crime in the eyes of decent men" (2.116.5). The judgment of earlier commentators has been that he fell far short of his own ideal. The distinguished scholar Ronald Syme regarded Velleius "a government writer" with utter contempt: "His loyal fervour insists everywhere on rendering praise where praise is safe and profitable, with manifold convolutions of deceit and flattery." Syme judged him "mendacious," "fraudulent," and "obsequious." Even from the grave he continued the tirade, in a collection of essays on Strabo published posthumously, where he described Velleius as a "poisonous fountain," given to "omitting what he cannot distort."[59] Syme was not alone in taking this stand. Lana argued at some length in the 1950s that Velleius was not a historian but a mere propagandist of Tiberius, and in the same period Klingner, in a survey of the historians before Tacitus, concluded that Velleius could just be dismissed.[60] Moreover, such attitudes were not new. The influential German scholar W. S. Teuffel had many years earlier declared himself thoroughly offended by Velleius'

57. Trogus' latest securely datable reference is to the surrender of Phraates' sons and grandsons to Augustus as hostages in 10 BC (Just. *Epit.* 42.5.11); see Yardley and Heckel (1997), 5–6.

58. As an example, the phrase *paterna maiestas* ("father's greatness") at 1.10.3 may well be borrowed from Trogus, as cited in Justin's *Epitome* (10.1.6, 10.2.6). For other possible instances see Yardley (2003), 282.

59. Fraudulent, government writer: (1939), 393 n. 1, 488; mendacious: (1933), 147 n. 3; obsequious: (1956), 262; loyal fervour, unscrupulous: (1958), 367; poisonous fountain, distortions: (1995), 289, 323.

60. Lana (1952); Klingner (1958), 194: "wir . . . hier ausser Betracht lassen können."

ecstatic praise of Tiberius, but even before that, in the eighteenth century, Morgenstern was defending Velleius against the charge of flattery.[61]

That Velleius admired Tiberius and wrote effusively about him cannot be denied. But does this make him "a government writer"? If his aim in the *opus* is simply to propagandize the achievements of Tiberius, Velleius went about this task in a strange way. He started, probably, with the Trojan War and for much of Book 1 dealt largely with Greek history. By the end of the first book he had reached the destruction of Carthage and Corinth in the latter part of the second century BC. There is no mention of Tiberius in the surviving sections of that book, and it is unlikely that he appeared in the original complete text. Book 2 says nothing of Tiberius for thirty-nine chapters; then he is first alluded to, briefly and inevitably, in the history of Rome's imperial expansion (2.39.3) and is not mentioned again for another thirty-six chapters, when it is noted that Tiberius Claudius Nero, the commander of Velleius' grandfather, was the father of the future emperor (2.75.1, 2.75.3). And it is not until a further twenty chapters that Tiberius starts to receive extensive treatment (2.94.1). Thus, on the assumption that Book 1 in its original form was the same general length as Book 2, the *opus* does not begin to focus on Tiberius until it is around 85 percent complete. Much of that 85 percent is taken up with detailed excursuses on Greek literature or Roman colonies and the like, and, where it keeps to the narrative, it revels in digging up the arcane and the abstruse, in drawing attention to historical coincidences that are not particularly convincing, and in moralizing that can, at times, if not most of the time, be trite and banal. If Tiberius read Velleius' *opus*, he must have felt weary as he waited to discover when the propaganda would begin. It might be argued that Velleius' intention was to represent Tiberius' reign as the climax of history. But if such was the case, Velleius kept that intention well disguised. He makes no effort to foreshadow the reign, and even after Tiberius has entered the historical stage Velleius occasionally neglects the opportunity to draw attention to the emperor's qualities. As noted earlier, he records that the captured Roman standards were returned to Rome by the Parthian king Phraates, in 20 BC, but he refrains from mentioning that they were in fact handed over to Tiberius, who was present in the east to reestablish Tigranes on the throne of Armenia (2.91). It is also worth observing that for all his fulsome tone in places, Velleius cannot be accused of actually falsifying events. The achievements of Tiberius, which he extols in his narrative section, are to a considerable extent echoed in Tacitus' account of Tiberius' activities in the early part of his reign.[62]

---

61. Morgenstern (1798); Teuffel and Schwabe (1900), vol. 2, 17.

62. Tac. *Ann.* 4.6; Woodman (1975), 290–96.

Another human element should be acknowledged here. For Roman senators there was no clear distinction between a military and a civilian career, and the senator was expected to give service in whatever capacity was required.[63] The notion of the "professional" soldier was alien to the senatorial class. But this was not true of equestrians, and it could certainly be said of a number of equestrians who subsequently entered the senate that they had pursued a "military career." A striking example of this is a contemporary of Velleius, Aulus Caecina Severus, an equestrian who reached senatorial rank in 1 BC. He, in AD 41, could speak of his service in no fewer than forty campaigns.[64] Velleius could not match this figure, but it is fair to describe him as a career soldier, and he speaks with pride of his service in the field. The attitude of serving soldiers toward their commander, if that commander was as successful as Tiberius clearly was, whatever his limitations in the political sphere, has throughout history often been one of almost sentimental affection.[65] Velleius has a vivid description of the reaction of the troops when Tiberius returned to the field to deal with the serious situation in Germany, after his adoption in AD 4. He was a witness to this, a *spectator,* and the account of the touching reaction of the old campaigners to Tiberius' arrival has the ring of truth (2.104.3). The dividing line between a propagandist and a sincere admirer is not necessarily a sharp one. Admiration for one's subject, whether genuine or contrived, can, of course, get in the way of objective history. But the verdict of such critics as Teuffel, Lana, and Syme, that Velleius was an obsequious and mendacious propagandist, should be treated circumspectly.[66]

Nor should Velleius be dismissed as a historian. There are aspects of his writing that deserve some praise. From time to time he indicates the source of his information, and he does not follow it slavishly. He thinks highly of Hortensius' account of the Social War in his work, the *Annales,* and praises it for its clarity, using it as a source for the exploits of his ancestor Magius Minatus (2.16.3). He disagrees with Cato on the foundation date of Capua and Nola but expresses his disagreement respectfully (Appendix A.7.3–4). Sometimes he does cite his specific sources but indicates that he has used a

---

63. Campbell (1975), 27.

64. *L'Année Épigraphique* 1937.62; Tac. *Ann.* 3.33.1; cf. 2.112.4.

65. Even Tacitus (*Ann.* 1.4) concedes that Tiberius had a distinguished military record and Syme (1986, 436) observes that what Velleius reports on Tiberius in the field is convincing; see De Monte (1999), 122–3.

66. Sumner (1979), in a review of Woodman (1977), provides useful refutations of some of the detailed claims made by Syme; apart from in Woodman and Sumner, more balanced treatments are found in Hellegouarc'h (1964, 1980); Seager (1972), 267–9; Manuwald (1990), 20–21; Christ (2001).

number of authorities, as when he concludes that those who have recorded that Romulus had military support in the founding of Rome must be right (1.8.5). He even makes use of primary evidence. He confirms the dedication made by Sulla to Diana after his victory over Gaius Norbanus, by citing an inscription found within Diana's temple on Mount Tifata (2.25.4). By modern standards such references are infrequent, but ancient historians very rarely provide their sources, and Velleius' record is at least as good as most. He was also very conscious of the need for accuracy in his chronology, even if he might not always have attained it. Numerals are very prone to error when transmitted in manuscripts, and the corrupt nature of his text makes it impossible for us to test Velleius properly on this matter, since what might seem to be an error in his calculations could very well turn out to be an error in transmission instead. But we do know that it was certainly an issue that he took seriously. For instance, in observing that Scipio Aemilianus died at about the age of fifty-six (2.4.7), he explains that to confirm the age one can correlate it to his first consulship, which he held at the age of thirty-six. He notes that there are those who miscalculated Pompey's death in his fifty-eighth year by five years and states that he calculated the years from the consulship of Gaius Atilius and Quintus Servilius (2.53.4).

Velleius has much to recommend him. He was a witness to the transformation of the Roman Republic into an imperial system and is the only contemporary to provide, in the form of Book 2, a continuous narrative from the second century BC, when the republican system began to break down, to AD 30, by which time the imperial system was firmly and irrevocably in place. Does he have a philosophy of history? At times it seems that he simply pursues topics that he finds interesting, such as the quality of Opimian wine (2.7.5). Sometimes this interest is narrowly personal, such as the fascination with his own family history, which might be expressed directly or indirectly—his interest in Capua (1.7.2–4) almost certainly stems from the Campanian origins of his family. If there is a philosophy of history, it is that he sees it as a "seamless whole," in which the present is very much at one with the past.[67] Hence, while he does on occasion date events by the traditional methods of antiquity, from the founding of the city of Rome or the names of the consuls, he is also in the habit of recording how many years ago before the present time events took place, using the year of Vinicius' consulship, AD 30, or referring generally to the year of writing/publication.[68] His *opus* makes clear that for all that we may tend, under the influence of Tacitus' view of the period, to look upon the Augustan settlement as a

---

67. Gowing (2005), 34.
68. 1.8.1,1.8.4, 2.7.5, 2.49.1, 2.65.2; from year of writing, 1.15, 2.90.2, 2.90.4, 2.93.1, 2.100.2, 2.103.3; Starr (1980), 288.

dramatic turning point in history, from Velleius' perspective, events followed a natural course, and that Augustus' role was not so much to discard a venerable system of government as to expunge from it the corrupt and tainted elements. Augustus (to be followed in this by his successor Tiberius) did not transform the Roman constitution so much as he initiated a period of good government and internal order that allowed the Republic to get onto its feet again after decades of strife. To Velleius there was no inherent difference between the Rome before the Augustan settlement and the Rome after it. If there is a transition period it comes rather in the second half of the second century BC, with the destruction of Corinth and Carthage in 146, when, after a period of vigorous military achievements, Rome entered into a period of debilitating luxury.[69] The more conventional divide that modern historians see between Republic and empire, with the first settlement of Augustus in 27 BC as the symbolic beginning, does not really appear in Velleius. Augustus and Tiberius represent a form of continuity, since Roman history in the eyes of Velleius has been one of a succession of great men (the *opus* does focus on the personalities of history), such as Scipio, the destroyer of Carthage, a man of immortal fame (2.4.3), or Cato Uticensis, who was "the very embodiment of Virtue and in nature was in all respects closer to the gods than to human beings" (2.35.2). Even the term "princeps" is by no means an imperial innovation. The skeptical might argue that it *was* a tool to disguise Augustus' conversion of the Republic into a monarchy. But its republican pedigree is stressed by Velleius, who applies it to Gaius Gracchus, Marcus Antonius, Marius and Caesar, and has Crassus aspire to *principatum*.[70] This enthusiasm for the principate probably stems from Velleius' own experience, since the new dispensation opened up opportunities for orderly and legal advancement to men of his class as had hardly been known under the Republic.

There is little evidence that Velleius made any impact on historiography during the classical period. There are conscious or unconscious echoes that suggest that Tacitus was familiar with his work, and the same has been claimed, perhaps unconvincingly, of Seneca and Curtius Rufus, but it is not until Sulpicius Severus, in the early fifth century AD, that we find what seems to be a distinctive attempt to copy his style.[71] Priscian is the only author of antiquity to refer to him by name, the sole ancient source on Velleius

---

69. See Schultze (2010); Sallust may have been the first to attribute internal strife and moral degeneration to the destruction of Carthage, and Velleius may have been influenced by this precedent.

70. Syme (1939), 10, 311–12; (1996), 74. On Gracchus, see 2.6.2; Antonius, 2.22.3; Marius, 2.19.4; Caesar, 2.68.5; Crassus, 2.44.2 (cf. 2.30.6).

71. Klebs (1890), 285–312.

outside his own writings.[72] After the publication of the surviving portion of his work by Beatus Rhenanus, he did enjoy a certain vogue. Dr. Johnson included him among the Latin writers an educated person should read, and literary figures such as Chapman and Dryden cited him with respect. But the strictures of such luminaries as Teuffel and Syme had a chilling effect on his reception. Latterly, however, this dismissive attitude seems to have given way to a recognition that Velleius does have much to teach us and an important role to play in our understanding of late republican and early imperial history. A major contribution to this change in thinking was made in the 1970s, with the important reappraisal made by Graham Sumner and a series of important essays and commentaries by A. J. Woodman, who has done more than any other to draw our attention to the value of Velleius. This revival in his reputation is reflected in the non-English-speaking world, in such works as the translation and the major commentary by Maria Elefante and a series of monographs by German scholars.[73] A sign of his rehabilitation is the almost simultaneous but totally independent appearance of this edition of Velleius' history at the same time as the publication of a collection of scholarly papers emanating from a conference on Velleius held in Leicester, England, in 2008 (unfortunately not available to us). It would be nice to think that the synchronicity of these two events would have fascinated Velleius and that it would have given him considerable pride to think that almost two thousand years on he is still contributing to his family's lasting fame.

III. The Roman Political System

The Roman constitution evolved over an extended period of time, and the following account uses as its general point of reference the system as it functioned when Velleius began his career. It should be noted at the outset that with the exception of certain priesthoods there was no access for women to a public career, although they did engage in entrepreneurial activities and could be indirectly influential. The chief deliberative body in the Roman system was the senate. In the early Republic the senate seems to have consisted of three hundred men. The number was raised to as many as nine hundred by Julius Caesar, but in Velleius' days its numbers were set at approximately six hundred, made up essentially of those who had held the

---

72. Velleius is referred to twice in the scholia (Latin commentaries) on Lucan, but Werner (1998, 143–9) has shown that Lucan's scholia are Carolingian, not ancient.

73. Kuntze (1985); Schmitzer (2000); Kober (2000); also to be noted is the thesis of Merker (1968); echoes of Syme can still be detected, as in Eder (2005, 15), who calls Velleius a "court historian."

rank of quaestor or higher. One usually became a senator for life, but individual tenure was monitored by the censor, who maintained the list of citizens and could remove a member because of immoral behavior or if his assets fell below a certain amount. This amount was set under Augustus at one million sesterces (something more than a thousand times the annual pay of a legionary soldier). The senate usually met in the Curia in the Forum but could also meet from time to time in other locations.

Strictly speaking, the senate could not in this period enact legislation, and its decrees (*consulta*) were forwarded to the popular assemblies. If approved there they became laws (*leges*). By Velleius' time this ratification tended to be something of a formality. A significant and controversial element of senatorial power was the *consultum de re publica defendenda* (decree for the defense of the state), generally referred to as the *consultum ultimum* (ultimate decree), which granted consuls far-reaching but ill-defined powers to deal with emergencies. It was first employed during the Gracchan crisis in 121 BC and was used also on later occasions, most notably during Cicero's suppression of the Catilinarian conspiracy in 63 BC.

Distinct from the senate was a complicated system of popular assemblies of Roman citizens, which were called together for specific tasks. There were four main assemblies in Velleius' day: the centuriate assembly (*comitia centuriata*), which was organized in "centuries" based on wealth and met to elect senior officials and to pass legislation; the curiate assembly (*comitia curiata*), which was based originally on the thirty *curiae* or parishes and in the early Republic passed laws, elected consuls, and tried judicial cases (its powers were later much diminished); the tribal assembly (*comitia tributa*), which represented the thirty-five Roman "tribes," elected junior officials, and passed minor legislation; and the plebeian council (*concilium plebis*), which elected tribunes of the plebs and plebeian aediles and enacted *plebiscita,* which were valid throughout the whole state.

At around the age of fourteen the Roman male underwent the ceremony of manhood. He might at this point assume one of the twenty minor magistracies, the *vigintivirate,* reduced from the earlier twenty-six by Augustus. Then he could enter military service as a military tribune and be attached to a legion. In the Republic the tribunes were usually equestrian, but under Augustus some military tribunacies were reserved for young men from senatorial families. By the age of twenty-five, if he hoped to pursue a senatorial career, he could seek election to the quaestorship. Before the time of Sulla, quaestors were regularly elevated to the senate by the censors. Under Sulla, tenure of a quaestorship became a prerequisite for entry into the senate. There were initially two, but by Velleius' time twenty were elected each year. Their responsibilities were mainly financial. The next stage in the senator's career would be one of two offices. The aedileship involved responsibility for various types of municipal administration in Rome. Instead of the aedileship, one might pursue the office of *tribunus plebei* (plebeian tribune). From an early period Romans had been divided between lower-class plebeians and upper-class patricians. By Velleius' time this distinction, while still formally maintained, had lost most of its force, and a plebeian background was no longer a barrier to a career or social prominence. But a few relics survived. The office of plebeian tribune was reserved for plebeians. It was created originally for the protection of the plebeians, and the holder could convene the senate and popular assemblies, as well as initiate or veto legislation. Through his tribunician *sacrosanctitas* an assault on the tribune's person was deemed sacrilegious. The tribune became a major force in Roman politics throughout the Republic, as Velleius' narrative illustrates, but by his own day played a fairly insignificant role. It should be noted that Augustus exercised legal authority by assuming the authority of the plebeian tribunes (*tribunicia potestas*) without holding the office.

The quaestor could in fact, should he choose, proceed directly to the next office, the praetorship. There had originally been two praetors, who were the senior magistrates in the state. In 366 BC a third, the "urban" praetor (*praetor urbanus*), was added, with responsibility for administering justice in Rome, and it was probably after this time that the two senior praetors became officially "consuls." In the middle of the third century an additional official, the "foreign" praetor (*praetor peregrinus*), was appointed to deal with lawsuits involving foreigners. The need for the administrators of overseas provinces meant that their numbers were gradually increased. When Velleius attained this office twelve were elected each year.

From the praetorship an ambitious senator might pursue the highest state office, one of the two annual consulships. During the republican period the consuls commanded the Roman armies and after election would as often as not find themselves conducting campaigns outside of Italy. Under Augustus this office, which previously had been open only to men who had reached the age of forty-two, could be pursued much earlier by candidates with a distinguished family pedigree, probably by age thirty-two, while members of the imperial family held the office even earlier. If a consul left office before the end of his term he was replaced by a suffect consul, and to open up the opportunity to hold the highest office to a larger number of candidates, it became routine after 5 BC for consuls to resign before their term was completed. There was a certain prestige in being elected one of the first two consuls in the year (the *ordinarii*), and the year would in fact be named after them. Even in the imperial period the consulship still commanded great prestige. In practice the office was the monopoly of a limited number of powerful families, and a man who succeeded in holding it despite having no consuls in his family background was known as a new man (*novus homo*).

Priesthoods were on the whole seen as elements of a political rather than a spiritual career, and the function of the regular priest (*pontifex*) was mainly seen as advising the magistrates in the carrying out of their sacred duties. The number of priests grew with time. Initially there may have been three, but that number had increased to sixteen by the time of Julius Caesar. They were organized in a college (*collegium*), headed by the senior member, the *pontifex maximus*. Besides the regular priests the *collegium* included fifteen flamines (the three senior members had to be patricians), specialized priests responsible for specific gods, most notably Jupiter (*flamen dialis, or* Flamen of Jupiter), Mars, Quirinus, and later the deified emperors; the Vestal Virgins, usually six, normally serving for thirty years, charged with tending the sacred hearth of Vesta; and the *rex sacrorum*, a patrician responsible for certain sacral functions that may have derived from the early kings. He was appointed for life and thus henceforth excluded from other office.

Velleius refers to the office of city prefect (*praefectus urbi*). This ancient office, held by a senator of consular rank, had become almost defunct by the late Republic. Its powers were revived by Augustus. This *praefectus* maintained order in Rome and commanded the *cohortes urbanae* (urban cohorts), a type of city police; he exercised summary justice in minor criminal cases.

In the early Republic, during times of crisis, a dictator could be appointed by the senate. He held supreme authority for a maximum of six months. This office was much adapted in the late Republic; Sulla was appointed dictator for an indefinite term in 82 BC, and Julius Caesar held the office a number of times, the last in 44 BC, when he was appointed for life. It was abolished after Caesar's death.

A magistrate's area of responsibility was defined as his *provincia;* by Velleius' day this expression was generally used for Rome's external territories. Three areas, frequently alluded to by Velleius, can be confusing. After the expulsion of the Carthaginians in 206 BC, Rome controlled part of Spain that was organized into two provinces, a northeastern and a southeastern coastal strip, both of which expanded with time. The more northerly was called *Hispania Citerior* (Nearer Spain, from the perspective of someone entering from Gaul), and the more southerly *Hispania Ulterior* (Further Spain). Under Augustus a third province in the west, Lusitania, was added. Further Spain became Baetica, and Nearer Spain, much expanded to the west, became Tarraconensis. The province of Illyricum stretched east from the Dalmatian coast. Rome had first become involved in the area in 229 BC in the First Illyrian War. The province was divided, possibly in about AD 9 (the date is much disputed), into two provinces, Dalmatia and Pannonia. "Illyricum" continued to be used as a geographical expression and in the late empire was revived as the official name of an administrative district. Gaul, the area inhabited by the Galli (Celts) was originally divided by the Romans into two provinces, Transalpine ("Across the Alps") and Cisalpine ("On this side of the Alps") Gaul. In the late Republic, Cisalpine Gaul was incorporated into Italy and ceased to be a province and Transalpine Gaul became the province of Gallia Narbonsensis.

Provinces were governed by the praetors and consuls when their standard terms had expired. Such officials would hold *imperium* (power) by virtue of their previous offices and thus governed as propraetors or proconsuls. An important modification to the system occurred in 27 BC, when Augustus ceded control of the vast regions under his control to the senate, and they in turn bestowed on him a huge *provincia,* consisting essentially of Gaul, Syria, and Spain (the exact extent varied over time). This grant was for a term of ten years, with the possibility of renewal. The "imperial" provinces generally housed the Roman armies, and their governors and legionary commanders were appointed by Augustus (and his successors). One consequence of this arrangement was that the triumph, granted for major success on the battlefield and marked by a splendid procession through Rome, became the prerogative of Augustus' family. Successful commanders outside the imperial family could aspire only to the insignia of the honor, *ornamenta triumphalia.* The remaining provinces, generally now called "public" rather than the once customary "senatorial," were governed by senators with consular authority (*proconsules*) chosen by a strictly regulated system of lots. Public provinces did not generally house troops; a notable exception was Africa, which held a single legion commanded by the senatorial proconsul (until the time of Caligula).

Below the senatorial order stood the equestrians, whose order required a lower property qualification (400,000 sesterces) and whose members, unlike the senators, involved themselves openly in commercial undertakings. The name referred originally to cavalry service. A man could not be a senator and equestrian simultaneously, but he could be transferred from one order to the other to match the change in his fortunes and ambitions. Velleius is a good example of an equestrian who did well and aspired to higher things. In the imperial period equestrians played an increasingly important role in administration, with exclusive entry to most of the prefectures. These include the prefecture of the imperial/praetorian guard, the cavalry unit attached to a legion (an office held by Velleius), the corn supply (*annona*), the fire service (*vigiles*), and, most prestigious of all, Egypt. The post of city prefect, described above, was a notable exception among the prefectures, being restricted to consulars.

Throughout the period covered by Velleius' *opus,* innovations were introduced into the Roman system, but he sees the constitution as a single phenomenon that remained essentially the same through the early Republic and the early empire.

Bibliography

Translations and Editions of Velleius

Elefante, M. *Velleius Paterculus: Ad Vinicium consulem libri duo.* Bibliotheca Weidmanniana III. Hildesheim: George Olms, 1997 (text and commentary in Italian).

———. *I due libri al console Marco Vinicio. Velleio Patercolo.* Naples: Loffredo, 1999 (translation into Italian).

Giebel, M. C. *Velleius Paterculus: Historia Romana: Römische Geschichte. Lateinisch/ Deutsch.* Stuttgart: Reclam, 2004.

Hellegouarc'h, J. *Velleius Paterculus: Histoire Romaine.* Paris: Société d'Édition Les Belles Lettres, 1982.

Portalupi, F. *Velleio Paterculo: Storia Romana.* Turin: Giappichelli, 1967.

Rhenanus, Beatus P. *Vellei Paterculi Historiae Romanae Duo Volumina.* Basel: J. Froben, 1520.

Rockwood, F. E. *Velleius Paterculus: Book II. Chapters XLI–CXXXI.* Boston and New York: Leach, Shewell and Sandborn, 1893.

Shipley, F. W. *Velleius Paterculus: Compendium of Roman History.* Cambridge, MA: Harvard University Press, 1924, 2002.

Watson, J. S. *Sallust, Florus and Velleius Paterculus.* London: Bohn's Classical Library, 1852.

Watt, W. S. *Velleius Paterculus: Historiae ad M. Vinicium Consulem.* Stuttgart and Leipzig: Teubner, 1998.

Woodman, A. J. *Velleius Paterculus: The Caesarian and Augustan Narrative (2.41–93).* Cambridge: Cambridge University Press, 1977.

———. *Velleius Paterculus: The Tiberian Narrative (2.94–131).* Cambridge: Cambridge University Press, 1983.

Books and Articles

Brozek, M. "De Vellei Paterculi opusculo mutilato." *Eos* 52 (1962): 125–8.

Campbell, B. "Who Were the *Viri Militares*?" *Journal of Roman Studies* 65 (1975): 11–31.

Christ, K. "Velleius und Tiberius." *Historia* 50 (2001): 180–92.

Cornell, T. "Universal History and the Early Roman Historians." In Liddel and Fear, *Historiae Mundi,* 102–15.

Cowan, E. (ed.). *Velleius Paterculus: Making History.* Swansea: Classical Press of Wales, 2011.

Degrassi, A. *I Fasti Consolari dell'Impero Romano.* Rome: Edizione di Storia e Letteratura, 1952.

De Monte, J. "Velleius Paterculus and 'Triumphal' History." *Ancient History Bulletin* 13 (1999): 121–35.

Dihle, A. "C. Velleius Paterculus, römischer Historiker." *Real-Encyclopaedie der classischen Alterthumswissenschaft* 8A 1 (1955): 637–59.

Eder, W. "Augustus and the Power of Tradition." In *The Cambridge Companion to the Age of Augustus,* edited by K. Galinsky, 13–32. Cambridge: Cambridge University Press, 2005.

Endt, I. *Annotationes super Lucanum.* Leipzig: Teubner, 1909.

Ehrenberg, V., and A. H. M. Jones. *Documents Illustrating the Reigns of Augustus and Tiberius.* Oxford: Clarendon Press, 1952.

Fulbrook, M. *A Concise History of Germany.* Cambridge: Cambridge University Press, 2001.

Galinsky, K. *Augustan Culture.* Princeton, NJ: Princeton University Press, 1996.

Goar, R. J. "Horace, Velleius Paterculus and Tiberius Caesar." *Latomus* 35 (1976): 43–54.

Gowing, A. M. *Empire and Memory: The Representation of the Roman Republic in Imperial Culture.* Cambridge: Cambridge University Press, 2005.

Hanslik, R. "M. Vinicius." *Real-Encyclopaedie der classischen Alterthumswissenschaft* 9A (1961): 116–19.

Harrison, S. J. "Velleius on Tiberius." *Symbolae Osloenses* 80 (2005): 58–9.

Hellegouarc'h, J. "Les buts de l'oeuvre historique de Velleius Paterculus." *Latomus* 23 (1964): 669–84.

———. "La figure de Tibère chez Tacite et Velleius Paterculus." In *Mélanges de littérature et d'épigraphie latines, d'histoire ancienne et d'archéologie: hommage à la mémoire de Pierre Wuilleumier,* 167–83. Paris: Société d'Édition Les Belles Lettres, 1980.

———. "Etat présent des travaux sur l'Histoire Romain de Velléius Paterculus." *Aufstieg und Niedergang der römischen Welt* 32, no. 1 (1984): 404–36.

Jodry, C. "L'utilisation des documents militaires chez Velleius Paterculus." *Revue des Etudes Latines* 29 (1951): 265–84.

Klebs, E. "Entlehnungen aus Velleius." *Philologus* 49 (1890): 285–312.

Klingner, F. "Tacitus und die Geschichtsschreiber des 1. Jahrhunderts." *Museum Helveticum* 15 (1958): 194–206.

Kober, M. *Die politische Anfänge Octavians in der Darstellung des Velleius und dessen Verhältnis zur historiographischen Tradition.* Würzburg: Königshausen und Neumann, 2000.

Kramer, E. A. "Book One of Velleius' *History:* Scope, Levels of Treatment and Non-Roman Elements." *Historia* 54 (2005): 144–61.

Kuntze, C. *Zur Darstellung des Kaisers Tiberius.* Frankfurt: Lang, 1985.

Lana, I. *Velleio Paterculo o della propaganda.* Turin: Giappichelli, 1952.

Liddel, P., and A. Fear (eds.) *Historiae Mundi: Studies in Universal Historiography.* London: Duckworth, 2010.

Lobur, J. A. "*Festinatio* (Haste), *Brevitas* (Concision), and the Generation of Imperial Ideology in Velleius Paterculus." *Transactions and Proceedings of the American Philological Association* 137 (2007): 211–30.

Manuwald, B. "Herrscher und Historiker: Zur Darstellung des Kaisers Tiberius in der antiken Geschichtsschreibung." In *Der Herrscher,* edited by H. Hecker, 19–41. Düsseldorf: Droste, 1990.

Merker, M. *Das Tiberiusbild bei Velleius Paterculus.* Freiburg: Dissertation, 1968.

Mesk, J. "Zur Quellenanalyse des Plinianischen Panegyricus." *Wiener Studien* 33 (1911): 71–100.

Morgenstern, C. *De fide historica Vellei Paterculi, imprimis de adulatione ei obiecta.* Danzig: Gedani, 1798.

Newbold, R. E. "Need for Achievement in Velleius." *Ancient History Bulletin* 2 (1988): 94–8.

Peter, H. *Wahrheit und Kunst.* Leipzig: Teubner, 1911.

Ramage, E. S. "Velleius Paterculus 2.126.2–3 and the Panegyric Tradition." *Classical Antiquity* 1 (1982): 266–71.

Saddington, D. B. "An Augustan Officer in the Roman Army." In *Documenting the Roman Army: Essays in Honour of Margaret Roxan,* edited by J. Wilkes, 19–29. London: Institute of Classical Studies, 2003.

Sanchex-Manzano, M. A. "Textual Level: Velleius' Paterculus' Exemplary Style." In *Grecs et Romains aux prises avec l'histoire,* edited by G. Lachenaud and D. Longrée, 343–56. Rennes: Presses universitaires de Rennes, 2003.

Schmitzer, U. *Velleius und das Interesse an der Geschichte im Zeitalter des Tiberius.* Heidelberg: Winter, 2000.

Schultze, C. "Universal and Particular in Velleius Paterculus: Carthage versus Rome." In Liddel and Fear, *Historiae Mundi,* 116–30.

Seager, R. *Tiberius.* London: Methuen, 1972.

Starr, R. J. "Velleius' Literary Techniques in the Organization of his *History.*" *Transactions and Proceedings of the American Philological Association* 110 (1980): 287–301.

———. "The Scope and Genre of Velleius' *History.*" *Classical Quarterly* 31 (1981): 162–74.

Steffen, H. J. *Die Regierung des Tiberius in der Darstellung des Velleius Paterculus.* Kiel: Dissertation, 1954.

Sumner, G. V. "The Truth about Velleius Paterculus: Prolegomena." *Harvard Studies in Classical Philology* 74 (1970): 257–97.

———. *Classical Philology* 74 (1979): 64–8.

Syme, R. "M. Vinicius (Cos. 19 B.C.)." *Classical Quarterly* 27 (1933): 142–8.

———. *The Roman Revolution.* Oxford: Clarendon Press, 1939

———. "Seianus on the Aventine." *Hermes* 84 (1956): 257–66.

———. *Tacitus.* Oxford: Clarendon Press, 1958.

———. "Mendacity in Velleius." *American Journal of Philology* 99 (1978): 45–63.

————. *The Augustan Aristocracy.* Oxford: Clarendon Press, 1986.

————. *Anatolica.* Oxford: Clarendon Press, 1995.

Teuffel, W. S., and L. Schwabe. *History of Roman Literature.* Translated by G. C. Warr. London: George Bell and Sons, 1900.

Werner, S. *The Transmission and Scholia to Lucan's* Bellum Civile. Hamburg: Lit, 1998.

Woodman, A. J. "Actium in Velleius." *Latomus* 25 (1969a): 564–6.

————. "Sallustian Influence on Velleius Paterculus." In *Hommages à Marcel Renard,* 785–99. Brussels: Latomus, 1969b.

————. "Questions of Date, Genre and Style in Velleius: Some Literary Answers." *Classical Quarterly* 25 (1975a): 272–306.

————. "Velleius Paterculus." In *Empire and Aftermath: Silver Latin* II, edited by T. A. Dorey, 1–25. London: Routledge, 1975b.

Wright, A. "Velleius Paterculus and L. Munatius Plancus." *Classical Philology* 97 (2002): 178–84.

Yardley, J. C. *Justin and Pompeius Trogus: A Study of the Language of Justin's Epitome of Trogus.* Toronto: University of Toronto Press, 2003.

Yardley, J. C., and W. Heckel. *Justin: Epitome of the* Philippic History *of Pompeius Trogus.* Oxford: Clarendon Press, 1997.

Epigraphic Sources

Corpus Inscriptionum Latinarum is a major scholarly project initiated in Germany in 1853, aiming to record the Latin inscriptions from the whole of the Roman empire. It now consists of seventeen volumes in seventy separate parts. *Inscriptiones Latinae Selectae,* also a German project, was published between 1892 and 1916 and contains a thorough selection of the more significant inscriptions found in the larger *Corpus.* The inscriptions from Italy are published also in a separate series, *Inscriptiones Italiae,* begun in Italy in 1936 and now comprising thirteen volumes. The discovery of inscriptions is an ongoing process, and the French annual publication *L'Année Epigraphique* catalogues all the new inscriptions reported in the year prior to publication.

Note on the Text

The text of Velleius presents its editors with major challenges, and, to understand why that is the case, it is important to know the history of how the first printed edition came into existence. The *editio princeps* ("first edition") has its origins in a single manuscript, located in about 1515 in the monastery of Murbach, a Benedictine foundation in Alsace. Its discoverer was the Renaissance scholar Beatus Rhenanus, son of a prosperous Alsatian butcher. Beatus used the manuscript to produce an edition of Velleius, but he was frank about the difficulties involved, observing that the manuscript text was so horribly corrupt as to make it humanly impossible to recover the original. He was convinced that the scribe did not understand a word of what he was copying. Because of his dissatisfaction with this particular manuscript he delayed publication for three years in the hope of gaining access to a more reliable copy (such as was rumored to exist in Milan). He finally gave up and arranged with J. Froben of Basel to bring out the *editio princeps* in 1520. Beatus can hardly be censured for the shortcomings of the Murbach manuscript, but he did compound the difficulties by not working with the original manuscript but with a copy made by an unidentified colleague. This casual approach does not seem to have been untypical of Beatus, since in his preface he defends himself against critics who charged that his earlier edition of the *Apocolocyntosis* (a satirical work probably written by Seneca the Younger) was done sloppily. He himself acknowledged the unsatisfactory state of his friend's copy and instructed his secretary Albertus Burer to compare his proofs with the original manuscript and make a list of the emendations. This list was printed as an appendix to the *editio princeps,* and the manuscript was returned to Murbach.

In the meantime a copy was also made by Bonifacius Amerbach (either of the actual manuscript or of the copy made for Beatus). Bonifacius was a young man of twenty-one, working for his late father's publishing house; he would go on to be a highly prominent humanist scholar and friend of Erasmus. His copy, dated 1516 and identified as *Vellei Paterculi ad Marcum Vinicium libri duo* (Two Books of Velleius Paterculus to Marcus Vinicius), did not in fact come to light until the 1830s. It was a useful discovery, since the original Murbach manuscript is now lost, as also is the copy of that manuscript made by Beatus' unnamed colleague. It should be noted, however, that Amerbach did not copy the complete text. The fragment of "Greek" material, for instance (our Appendix A), does not appear there. The original text of the Murbach manuscript has to be reconstructed by reconciling Amerbach's copy with Beatus' text, supplemented by Burer's list of emendations. It is a complex process, fraught with difficulties, and at best the outcome can be only the partial reconstruction of a manuscript that was hopelessly corrupt in the first place. This means that Velleius' text is one of the most problematic of any surviving classical author. For this translation we have used the edition of W. S. Watt in the Teubner series. A list of the very few variations from Watt's text is found as Appendix C.

Note on the Translation

In the process of compiling the translation we have, naturally, considered the translations of others (see Bibliography). The most accessible English versions are F. W. Shipley's in the Loeb series and that of the ill-starred Victorian schoolmaster the Reverend J. Selby Watson, who died in Parkhurst Prison on the Isle of Wight serving a life sentence for uxoricide after his death penalty was commuted. (His many translations, written to supplement his meager teacher's salary, include Sallust, Florus, and Justin.) The most useful we found to be the French version of Joseph Hellegouarc'h in the Budé series, to which we are much indebted. There is also a very useful, but not very accessible, Italian translation by Maria Elefante, and one in German by Giebel, which is equally difficult to find in English-speaking countries.

The most useful guide to Velleius, at least for chapters 41–131 of Book 2, is indubitably the rich two-volume commentary of A. J. Woodman, and where Woodman has offered translations in his notes we have for the most part accepted his interpretation if not his wording (though we have occasionally done that as well).

The Roman World in AD 30

THE ROMAN HISTORY

BOOK 1

[Although the continuous narrative of what has survived of Velleius' history does not begin until the mid-second century BC, at 1.9.1, a fragment of eight chapters on Greek history and legend is preserved from the early part of his original text (see Appendix A). The very end of the fragment consists of a small, tantalizing section on Romulus, the legendary founder of the city of Rome.]

8.4 In the sixth Olympiad, twenty-two years after the Olympic Games were first established, Romulus, son of Mars, avenged the wrongs inflicted on his grandfather and founded the city of Rome, on the Palatine, on the day of the festival of Parilia.[1] From that date to your consulships 781 years have passed, which means it happened 437 years after the taking of Troy.[2] [5] Romulus accomplished this with the help of the legions of his grandfather Latinus.[3] In fact, I would happily agree with those who have put this on record, since, otherwise, Romulus could hardly have secured a new city with a band of shepherds unused to war (even though he did augment their numbers by opening a place of refuge between two groves) when the Veians were so close, and other Etruscans and the Sabines, as well.[4] [6] He chose a hundred men, to whom he gave the name "fathers" [*patres*], and used them as a sort of state advisory council. It is from this that the term "patricians" is derived.[5]

---

1. The Olympic Games were by tradition founded in 776 and held in successive cycles of four years. Thus, for the beginning of Rome Velleius seems to be accepting the so-called Varronian date made popular by Marcus Terentius Varro, which placed the founding in 754/3. At 1.8.1 Velleius seems to date the games to 793, but one must be very cautious about the figures transmitted in the first edition.

2. Velleius elsewhere dates events by the consulship of Marcus Vinicius. In this case he addresses both Vinicius and his colleague in office, Cassius Longinus. Velleius' figure of 781 years before their consulships of AD 30, if his number has been transmitted correctly, would give 751 BC for Rome's founding, the so-called Catonian date, provided by Marcus Porcius Cato (see 1.13.1). The traditional date of the fall of Troy varied, but the most widely accepted was 1183. Velleius here seems to be dating it to 1188 (assuming, as ever, no corruption in the text).

3. Latinus is the legendary ruler of the Latins. In the familiar version of the legend he was the father of Lavinia, who married Aeneas, many generations before the time of Romulus.

4. We do not know Velleius' source here, but he clearly aligns himself with a tradition that does not accept the notion of a peaceful, pastoral origin for Rome.

5. From an early period Romans had been divided between lower-class plebeians and upper-class

1

[At this point there is a further gap in the text, of some six centuries. Only a single line survives from this intermission (see Appendix B). Velleius' continuous text resumes in the midst of his account of the war between Rome and Perses of Macedon. Perses succeeded his father Philip as king of Macedon in 179 BC and pursued an expansionist policy that brought him into conflict with the Romans, over whom he enjoyed a number of successes in 171 and 170, before being decisively defeated in 168. The text resumes in midsentence, and the first part of the sentence has been restored (restorations in italics) to reflect the general sense suggested by the surviving words.]

9.1 <*The Romans demanded punishment for Perses' actions* that was more severe than the enemy had feared.> Over a two-year period, Perses had kept up the fight against the consuls with such mixed fortunes that as often as not he had the upper hand, and he was able to bring a large part of Greece into an alliance with him.[6] [2] In fact, even the people of Rhodes, hitherto supremely loyal to Rome, on that occasion faltered in their allegiance and, with an eye on how things were developing, seemed to have inclined rather toward the side of the Macedonian king. In that war King Eumenes of Pergamum remained neutral, neither following his brother's lead nor conforming to his own pattern of behavior.[7] [3] The Roman senate and people then elected to the consulship Lucius Aemilius Paulus, who had celebrated triumphs both as a praetor and as consul, a man deserving all the praise that can be given for a courage as great as it can conceivably be. He was the son of the Paulus who, at Cannae, for all his reluctance to enter a battle so disastrous for the Republic, had still bravely accepted death in it. [4] He routed Perses in a great battle in Macedonia at the city called Pydna, put him to flight, and took his camp. After destroying Perses' forces and leaving him with no hope, he compelled the man to flee from Macedonia. Perses left the country and sought refuge on the island of Samothrace, where he entrusted his person, as a suppliant, to the sacrosanctity of the temple. There the praetor Gnaeus Octavius, who was in command of the fleet, came to him and

patricians. By Velleius' time this distinction, while still formally maintained, had lost most of its force, and a plebeian background was no longer a barrier to a career or social distinction.

6. Because the previous sentence is almost totally lost, the meaning of this section of the text is not clear. Velleius seems to be suggesting that Perses (which is how Velleius spells his name, though it is more familiarly Perseus) did much better in his campaign than the Romans had thought possible, and for this reason they exacted a heavier penalty from him when he was finally defeated.

7. The Rhodians' loyalty to Rome was tested because of the damage to their commerce. Eumenes II of Pergamum had been instrumental in persuading Rome to act against Macedonia, but all the same he made covert overtures to Perses; his brother Attalus II, who succeeded him in 159 BC, was a steadfast ally of Rome.

convinced him, by reason rather than force, to entrust himself to the Romans' sense of honor. [5] So it was that Paulus led along in his triumph the greatest and most famous of kings.[8]

That year also saw the famous triumphs of the praetor Octavius, commander of the fleet, and of Anicius, who had Gentius, king of the Illyrians, taken along before his chariot.[9] [6] Just how constantly jealousy accompanies superior fortune, and clings to those who are at the pinnacle of success, can be deduced also from this, that despite the fact that there were no objections to the triumphs of Anicius and Octavius, there were some trying to block that of Paulus.[10] But because of the prestige of King Perses, or the impressiveness of the statues, or the amount of money on display, Paulus' triumph far outstripped those of his predecessors, to the point that he brought 200 million sesterces to the treasury and surpassed in magnificence all triumphs previously held.

10. Antiochus Epiphanes (the man who started the work on the temple of Olympian Zeus in Athens) was then king of Syria, and at about this time he was laying siege to Ptolemy, who was still a boy, in Alexandria. Marcus Popilius Laenas was sent to him as an ambassador to order him to abandon his operations. [2] Popilius delivered his message, and the king said he would think the matter over, at which point the ambassador drew a line around him with his staff and told him to give his answer before he stepped out of the circle traced in the sand. Roman determination in this way put an end to the king's plans and the order was obeyed.[11]

---

8. Perses suffered an overwhelming defeat at Pydna on June 21, 168 BC, at the hands of Lucius Aemilius Paulus (Macedonicus), leading to the end of the Macedonian kingdom. Twenty thousand Macedonians died in battle and eleven thousand were taken prisoner, compared to one hundred Roman casualties (Livy 44.42.7–8). Perses was paraded in the subsequent triumph. Lucius had been praetor in 191 and conducted an ultimately successful campaign in Spain ending in 189, for which Velleius indicates that he was awarded a triumph (otherwise unknown). He held the consulship in 182 and was given command against the Ligurians, for which we do know he was awarded a triumph. Lucius' father, of the same name, held the consulship in 216 and died that year at the battle of Cannae, when his impetuous colleague Gaius Terentius Varro reputedly ignored his pleas for caution and brought the Romans to a disastrous defeat.

9. Velleius reports three triumphs in 167 BC. Gnaeus Octavius commanded the Roman fleet as praetor in 168. He built the Porticus Octavia (see 2.1.2). Gentius, king of the Illyrians, had conducted pirate raids against the Roman allies. He had supported Perses on the strength of a bribe of three hundred talents, which was never paid. He was defeated by Lucius Anicius Gallus.

10. Lucius Aemilius Paulus' triumph faced opposition because of the resentment felt by some of his soldiers over his strict discipline, particularly the restriction on the booty they could collect after Pydna (Livy 44.36–42).

11. Antiochus Epiphanes came to the throne of Syria in 175 BC after the assassination of his

[3] The winner of the great victory, Lucius Paulus, had four sons, and of these he had given the two eldest in adoption, one to Publius Scipio, who was the son of Publius Scipio Africanus but a man who retained none of his father's greatness (apart from an illustrious name and dynamic speaking ability), and the other to Fabius Maximus. The two younger ones, who were still in the *toga praetexta* at the time when he won his victory, he kept at home.[12] [4] Following ancestral custom Paulus presented a list of his achievements at a popular assembly outside the city the day before his triumph, and there he made a prayer to the immortal gods to the effect that, if any of them envied his record and his fortune, that god should inflict his wrath on Paulus himself rather than on the Republic. [5] These words, as though issuing from an oracle, robbed him of a large part of his progeny: a few days before his triumph he lost one of the children that he still had at home, and he lost the other even fewer days after it.

[6] The censorship of Fulvius Flaccus and Postumius Albinus, dated to about this time, was marked by its severity. Indeed, Gnaeus Fulvius was removed from the senate by these censors despite being brother of the censor Fulvius and in fact a co-inheritor of their father's estate.[13]

11. After the defeat and capture of Perses (who died four years later at Alba where he was kept under open arrest), PseudoPhilippus seized Macedonia by armed force and assumed the royal insignia, but shortly afterward he paid the penalty for his brazenness. (He was called PseudoPhilippus because of the story he concocted about his origins—he claimed that he was a Philip and of royal stock when he was, in fact, of very low birth.)[14] [2] The praetor

---

brother Seleucus IV. He had spent fourteen years as a hostage in Rome. In 170 he launched a preemptive strike against Ptolemy VI Philometor, king of Egypt 181–145, to thwart a threat against Coele-Syria, but in deference to Rome he desisted from total conquest. Velleius alludes here to a second invasion of Egypt in 168, famously blocked by the intercession of Gaius Popilius Laenas (consul 172 and 158) before Antiochus could reach Alexandria.

Construction of the great temple of Olympian Zeus at Athens, some five hundred yards southeast of the Acropolis, began in the sixth century, but the work was not completed. The project was revived by Antiochus on a grand scale but only partially finished at his death. It was not completed until the reign of Hadrian, who dedicated it in AD 132.

12. The sons of Lucius Aemilius Paulus were adopted into distinguished families. Publius Cornelius Scipio Aemilianus Africanus Minor Numantinus, consul in 147 and 138 BC and patron of the historian Polybius, eventually crushed Carthage in 146. He was adopted by the son of Publius Cornelius Scipio Africanus Maior (see 2.1.1). Quintus Fabius Maximus Aemilianus (2.5.3) was adopted into the *gens Fabia*.

13. According to Livy (41.27.1–2), the censors of 174, Quintus Fulvius Flaccus and Aulus Postumius Albinus Luscus, excluded nine senators. Fulvius' brother is called Gnaeus by Velleius, Lucius by others.

14. Perses died as prisoner of the Romans at Alba Fucens, in the Abruzzi area of central Italy,

Quintus Metellus, who was given the cognomen Macedonicus for his bravery, defeated him and his people in a brilliant victory, and he also routed the Achaeans, who had started an insurrection, in a brutal engagement.[15] [3] This is the Metellus Macedonicus who was responsible for the construction of the porticoes that surrounded the two temples that were erected without an inscription and which are now enclosed by the colonnades of the Porticus Octaviae. It was he, too, who brought from Macedonia the set of equestrian statues that look toward the facade of the temples and which represent today the greatest decorative feature of that area.[16] [4] They say that the background to this set is as follows: Alexander the Great prevailed upon Lysippus, an outstanding artist of works of this kind, to produce statues of those cavalrymen in his squadron who had fallen at the River Granicus, bringing out their physical likeness, and to add a statue of himself among them.[17]

[5] It was also this Metellus who was the very first to construct a temple of marble amid these monuments and was thus the originator of such grandeur—or extravagance. [6] One would have difficulty finding a man of any nation, age, or rank whose happiness could be compared with the fortunes that Metellus enjoyed. There were the outstanding triumphs and highest honors accorded to him, and there was his uniquely high standing within the state, his extended life span, and his acrimonious (but honorable)

---

in 165 BC, as a result of either self-imposed starvation or weakness from being deprived of sleep.

Andriscus, the ambitious son of a dyer from Adramyttium on the Mysian coast, claimed falsely to be Perses' son Philip, hence his nickname PseudoPhilippus (False Philip). He turned first to Demetrius Soter, ruler of Syria, for help, but Demetrius handed him over to the Romans. Undaunted, he escaped, raised an army in Thrace, and invaded Macedonia, defeating a Roman army under Publius Juventius (who died in the battle) in 149. He then established himself as King Philip VI, conquering Thessaly and dangerously concluding a treaty with Carthage.

15. Andriscus was defeated by the Romans under Quintus Caecilius Metellus (Macedonicus) at the second battle of Pydna, in 148 BC. Macedonia then became a Roman province. Metellus was called to deal with the Achaeans, who had rebelled over Roman attempts to intervene in their dispute with Sparta. He defeated them at the battle of Scarpheia in 146 but was obliged to hand over command to Lucius Mummius (1.12.1).

16. Metellus engaged in a major building program and built the portico that surrounds the temple of Juno Regina and Jupiter Stator near the Circus Flaminius. The portico of Metellus, whose name was not recorded there, according to Velleius, was refurbished by Augustus and named the Porticus Octaviae in honor of his sister, Octavia. For the quite distinct Porticus Octavia, see 2.1.2.

17. Lysippus, born in Sicyon in about 390 BC, was considered one of the great sculptors of his age and was uniquely commissioned by Alexander the Great to sculpt his statue. The Granicus, in northwest Turkey, was the scene of one of Alexander's great victories over the Persian king Darius in 334.

conflicts with his enemies on behalf of the state.[18] And, in addition to these blessings, he brought up four sons, saw all of them reach adulthood, and left them all surviving him and laden with honors.[19] [7] On his death the four sons carried his bier before the Rostra, one of them a former consul and former censor, the second a former consul, the third then serving as consul, and the fourth a candidate for the consulship, a post that he subsequently attained. This could clearly be described as passing happily from life rather than dying.

[In 146 BC Rome destroys two major powers: its old enemy Carthage and the Greek city of Corinth, a leader in the war between Rome and the Achaean League.]

12. Most of Achaea, as I have noted, had already been reduced by the bravery and arms of the aforementioned Metellus Macedonicus, but at that point the whole country was aroused to military action; and it was the Corinthians who were the principal instigators of the war through serious indignities they inflicted even on the Romans. The man earmarked for conduct of operations was the consul Lucius Mummius.[20]

[2] In the same period the senate made the decision to destroy Carthage, and this was more because of the Romans' readiness to believe anything that was said about the Carthaginians than because the reports they received merited acceptance. [3] So it came about that, at this same time, Publius Scipio Aemilianus, though he was only a candidate for the aedileship, was elected consul.[21] Scipio was a man whose fine qualities bore a great resemblance to

18. Metellus often found himself at loggerheads with Publius Cornelius Scipio Aemilianus Africanus Minor Numantinus, the destroyer of Carthage in 146 BC, though he maintained his respect for him.

19. Metellus died in 115 BC, the paradigm of the successful Roman, who had combined an illustrious civil and military career with producing four successful sons. Quintus Caecilius Metellus Balearicus was consul in 123 and censor in 120, Lucius Caecilius Metellus Diadematus was consul in 117, Marcus Caecilius Metellus was consul in 115, and Gaius Caecilius Metellus Caprarius was consul in 113 and censor in 102.

20. Lucius Mummius was the first of his family to achieve the consulship (his father had attained the praetorship in 177 BC) and hence was a "new man" (*novus homo*). Lucius served in Spain, for which he was granted a triumph in 152. Consul in 146, he assumed command in Macedonia and was also assigned the war against the Achaean League. Corinth was the main target, nominally because of its ill treatment of Roman ambassadors but probably mainly because of its dominant commercial position. The city was utterly destroyed and the site had minimal occupation until it was refounded as a Roman colony under Julius Caesar.

21. Publius Cornelius Scipio, the destroyer of Carthage, was one of Rome's most celebrated generals. He was also a great literary patron. In addition to the Greek historian Polybius and

those of his grandfather Publius Africanus and his father Lucius Paulus (he was, as I have noted, Paulus' son but was adopted by Scipio, son of Scipio Africanus), and he was the most eminent man of his generation in all accomplishments in both the military and the civilian sphere, as well as in raw intellect and literary studies. Throughout his life no deed, word, or thought of his was undeserving of praise.

[4] Scipio had earlier been awarded a mural crown in Spain and a siege crown in Africa; and in Spain he had killed an enemy soldier of immense size after actually issuing a challenge to him, although Scipio himself was a man of unremarkable physique.[22] By now the war with Carthage had been in progress for two years under the former consuls, but Scipio prosecuted it with greater intensity. [5] He totally destroyed this city, which was hated by the Roman nation from resentment over its power rather than for any harm it had done them at that time, and Scipio made a monument to his own ruthlessness of what had been a monument to his grandfather's clemency. After standing for 666 years, Carthage was destroyed in the consulship of Gnaeus Cornelius Lentulus and Lucius Mummius, that is, 177 years ago. [6] Such was the end of the Roman empire's rival, with whom our ancestors began fighting in the consulship of Claudius and Fulvius, that is, 296 years before you embarked on your consulship, Marcus Vinicius.[23] That means that for 115 years there existed, between those two peoples, either war or preparations for war or uneasy peace. [7] Even when it had conquered the world, Rome felt it had no hope of security if there remained anywhere the renown of a still-existing Carthage. So far does the hatred that arises from power struggles last beyond the fear they generate, not even being set aside

---

the Stoic philosopher Panaetius, his circle included the playwright Terence and the poet and satirist Lucilius. Born the son of Lucius Aemilius Paulus (1.9) in 185/4, he was adopted by Publius Scipio (and consequently was the adopted grandson of Publius Cornelius Scipio Africanus, who had defeated the Carthaginians at the battle of Zama in 202 but had spared Carthage afterward). He served with his biological father at the battle of Pydna in 168. He volunteered for service in Spain in 151 as military tribune under Lucius Licinius Lucullus, after Rome had suffered a series of disasters there, and he achieved great distinction.

22. The mural crown (*corona muralis*) was a gold crown designed to resemble a circular battlement and was intended for the soldier who had played a key role in storming walls. Scipio was awarded it at Intercatia (in the modern province of Zamora). The siege crown (*corona obsidionalis*) was granted to a commander who lifted the siege of a city; it was woven from grasses in the area of the besieged town. He was elected consul for 147, five years earlier than allowed by strict interpretation of the rules (he was only thirty-eight), and the province of Africa was assigned to him personally rather than selected by lot (sortition).

23. Velleius traces events from the beginning of the First Punic War in 264 BC, specifically placing it in the consulship of Appius Claudius Caudex and Marcus Fulvius Flaccus. The figure of 296 may have been transcribed wrongly, CCXCVI (296) for CCXCIV (294), since an interval of 296 years would place the beginning of hostilities two years earlier, in 266.

when an enemy is defeated, and that hatred does not cease <. . .> until the
object of it ceases to exist.

13. Three years before Carthage was destroyed, in the consulship of Lucius
Censorinus and Manius Manilius, Marcus Cato died, the man who had
been the perpetual advocate of its annihilation.[24]
In the same year that Carthage fell, <Aulus> Mummius razed Corinth to
the ground, 952 years after its foundation by Aletes' son Hippotes.[25] [2] The
two generals were each honored with a name taken from the people conquered by them, one being styled "Africanus" and the other "Achaicus," and
prior to Mummius no "new man" had laid claim to a cognomen earned by
military achievement.[26]
[3] The commanders had different characters and different interests.
Scipio was so refined a promoter and admirer of the liberal arts, and of all
branches of learning, that he kept at his side, at home and on campaign,
Polybius and Panaetius, two preeminent intellectuals.[27] Nobody showed
greater taste than this Scipio in interspersing his periods of active service
with leisure time, and in his constant commitment to the arts of war or
peace. Always engaged in military action or intellectual pursuits, he received
his physical exercise from the dangers of battle, and his mental exercise from
his studies.
[4] Mummius was such a boor that when, after the capture of Corinth,
he was arranging a contract for shipping to Italy some pictures and statues

24. Marcus Porcius Cato (234–149 BC), known as "the Elder" and "the Censor," was celebrated for his rigid personal behavior and his application of strict discipline to matters of state.
He served with some distinction in the Second Punic War and reached the consulship in 197,
as a "new man" (see note 20). In his later years he vigorously urged the Romans to undertake
the Third Punic War and is famous for supposedly ending every speech in the senate with the
statement that, in his judgment, Carthage must be destroyed ("ceterum censeo Carthaginem
esse delendam"). He was the author of a number of works, including the *Origines*, a history of
the cities of Italy, which Velleius consulted (see Appendix A.7.3).

25. The A (for Aulus) before Mummius' name cannot be correct, since the reference must be
to Lucius Mummius, destroyer of Corinth (see previous chapter). This could represent an error
of a copyist of the manuscript, or Velleius might have made a mistake. The traditional founder
of Corinth was in fact Sisyphus, son of Aeolus. Aletes later took the city by supposedly persuading the daughter of Creon, king of Corinth, to open the gates with a promise of marriage.
He refounded the city, in 1098 BC by Velleius' calculation (see Appendix A.3).

26. On "new man," see note 20.

27. Polybius (c. 200–c. 118 BC), the Greek historian, met Scipio in Rome, where Polybius
was being held captive, and he became a key member of the Scipionic Circle. He is a crucial
source for the history of Rome's rise as the dominant power in the Mediterranean. Panaetius of
Rhodes (c. 185–109), a famous Stoic philosopher, moved to Rome in the 140s. His emphasis
on the practical aspects of moral issues had much appeal for Romans.

that were masterpieces from the hands of the greatest artists, he ordered the contractors to be advised that, if they lost them, they were to provide new ones![28] [5] However, I do not think you would have any doubt, Vinicius, that our state would have been better off with a boor's appreciation of things Corinthian rather than that our appreciation of them should have reached the lengths it has now; and that the lack of culture of those days would have contributed more to public decorum than our "culture" does now.[29]

[Digressions on the Roman colonies and on the richest periods in the development of Greek and Roman literature. These passages form a transition between the end of Book 1 and the beginning of Book 2.]

14. In any subject, synthesis provides a format that is attractive to the eye and remains in the mind more easily than a chronological division of material. I have therefore decided to separate the first and second sections of this book with some information in summary form, knowledge of which will not prove superfluous, and to insert at this point a record, with dates, of the colonies founded on senatorial authority after the capture of Rome by the Gauls. For in the case of the military colonies, their rationale and founders are perfectly clear from their actual names. I think it will not be inappropriate if I weave into this record the extension of citizenship during this same period, and the expansion of the Roman nationality by the sharing of its privileges.[30]

[2] Seven years after the Gauls captured Rome, a colony was established at Sutrium, and a year later one at Setia. After an interval of nine years Nepe was colonized and after a further thirty-two years the people of Aricinum

---

28. Pliny (*NH* 35.24) reports that Mummius put up for sale a painting of Bacchus by Aristides which Attalus bought for 600,000 denarii. This alerted Mummius to its potential value, and he annulled the sale despite the protests of Attalus.

29. Vinicius is addressed frequently throughout Velleius' work, but this instance is unusual. Elsewhere the references seem essentially conventional or intended to date events with reference to Vinicius' consulship. Here Vinicius is brought into a discussion of the issues.

30. Velleius appears to have added this lengthy excursus on founding colonies (settlements intended to provide land for Romans and spread Roman civilization), as well, presumably, as the subsequent one on literature, after his opus was complete. He refers at 1.15.4 to a previous mention of the colony of Carthage as being the first outside of Italy, although the first reference in fact comes later (2.7.8), and it is difficult to see how the reference could have been made in the missing books. He draws a distinction between the citizen colonies in Roman territories and the *coloniae Latinae,* founded in non-Roman territories and holding not the full rights of Roman citizenship but more limited "Latin" rights, but does not observe that distinction in the catalog that follows.

were granted Roman citizenship.[31] [3] Three hundred and fifty years ago, during the consulship of Spurius Postumius and Veturius Calvinus, the Campanians and some of the Samnites were awarded citizenship without right of suffrage, and a colony was established at Cales that same year.[32] After a further lapse of three years the people of Fundi and Formiae were granted citizenship, in the very same year that Alexandria was founded. [4] In the consulship that followed, the people of Acerra were awarded citizenship by the censors Spurius Postumius and Philo Publilius.[33] Three years later the colony at Tarracina was established; subsequently, after a further four years, one was established at Luceria, and another three years after that at Suessa Aurunca and Saticula, to be followed by yet another at Interamna after two more years.[34] [5] There followed ten years with no such foundation, and then Sora and Alba were colonized, and Carseoli two years later.[35]

[6] In Quintus Fabius' fifth consulship, and Decius Mus' fourth—that was the year that saw the start of Pyrrhus' reign—colonists were sent out to Sinuessa and Minturnae, and four years later to Venusia. After an interval of two years, in the consulship of Manius Curius and Rufinus Cornelius, the Sabines were granted citizenship without the right of suffrage—that

---

31. Sutrium, to the north of Rome, thus became a Latin colony in 383 BC (according to the Varronian chronology, which dated the Gallic invasion of Rome to 390). Setia, in the Pomptine Marsh, followed in 382. Velleius places the date of the colony in the Etruscan town of Nepe in 373, although Livy (6.21.4) dates it ten years earlier. Livy (8.14.3) dates Aricia, at the foot of Mount Albanus, to 338, Velleius to 341.

32. There is some confusion over the foundation of Cales on the Latin Way (Via Latina). Livy (8.16.14) places it in 338 BC. Velleius dates it in the consulships of Postumius and Veturius, 334 or 321. Velleius provides a figure reported in the text of 350 years before AD 30, which gives 321/0 BC. The problem is compounded by the later reference to Spurius Postumius and Philo Publilius, censors in 332. Laurent emended the reading of the text to 360.

33. Fundi and Formiae, in Latium, were founded in 338 BC according to Livy (8.14.10), but 332 or 331 (Alexandria was founded in the winter between the two years) according to Velleius (we do not know whether the three-year gap is calculated by inclusive counting). A colony at the Oscan city of Acerra is placed in the following year but is said to belong to the censorship of Postumius and Publilius, in 332, the year given by Livy (8.17.12).

34. Tarracina, known also by its Volscian name, Anxur, became a Roman colony in 329 BC (Livy 8.21.11). Luceria, in Apulia, was founded in 326 by Velleius' reckoning but is otherwise dated to 314 (Livy 9.26.3; Diodorus 19.72.8). Suessa Aurunca in Campania and Saticula in Samnium were in fact founded in 313, not 311 (Livy 9.28.7). There may be confusion between the formal authorization of a colony and its practical creation. Similarly, Interamna on the Liris River in Latium was founded in 312.

35. Sora, on the Liris, the border between Campania and Latium, and Alba Fucens were founded in 303 BC (Livy 10.1.1). Livy (10.3.2) gives a date of 302 for Carseoli, but a date of 298 is extrapolated from another passage of Livy (10.13.1).

happened some 320 years ago.³⁶ [7] In the case of Cosa and Paestum, colonists were sent out about three hundred years ago, in the consulship of Fabius Dorso and Claudius Canina, and after a further period of five years, in the consulship of Sempronius Sophus and Appius the son of Caecus, colonists were also sent to Ariminum and Beneventum, and the Sabines were granted the right of suffrage.³⁷

[8] At the start of the First Punic War, Firmum and Castrum were colonized, as was Aesernia a year later and <Aefulum> and Alsium seventeen years after that. Fregenae was then colonized after a further two-year period, and Brundisium the following year, in the consulship of Torquatus and Sempronius. Three years later it was the turn of Spoletium, in the year that saw the commencement of the Floralia. Two years later Valentia was colonized and, just before Hannibal's arrival in Italy, so were Cremona and Placentia.³⁸

15. After that, both during the time that Hannibal remained in Italy and during the years immediately following his departure, the Romans had no time for founding colonies.³⁹ During the war they needed to muster soldiers, not discharge them; and after it they needed to restore their strength, not dissipate it. [2] In the consulship of Gnaeus Manlius Vulso and Fulvius Nobilior, however, that is, some 217 years ago, a colony was established at Bononia. Four years later two more were established, at Pisaurum and Potentia, and after a further three-year interval at Aquileia and Gravisca, and then at Luna four years after that.⁴⁰

---

36. Quintus and Decius were consuls in 295 BC, the year in which King Pyrrhus became sole ruler of Epirus. Sinuessa and Minternae became colonies in 296 according to Livy (10.21.8). Venusia, the home of the poet Horace, was founded in 291. The Sabines obtained citizenship without the right of suffrage (*civitas sine suffragio*) in 290; they obtained the right to vote in 268.
37. Fabius and Claudius Canina held the consulship in 273 BC. By Velleius' chronology, since the founding of Paestum and Cosa occurred three hundred years earlier, this would seem to date the composition of this part of his history to AD 27. Sempronius and Appius Claudius were consuls in 268.
38. Firmum and Castrum were founded in Picenum in 264 BC. Aesernia in Samnium became a colony in 263 (cf. Liv. *Per.* 16). Aefulum in Latium is dated to 247, Alsium in Etruria to 247 or 246. Fregenae, to the northwest of Ostia, is dated to 245. Brundisium is dated by the consular year to 244, and Spoletium accordingly to 241. The Floralia or *Ludi Florales* (Festival of Flora) were instituted in that year, when the temple of Flora was dedicated near the Circus Maximus. Valentia on the right bank of the Po was founded in 239, and Cremona and Placentia, on the left and right banks of the Po, respectively, in 218.
39. Hannibal was engaged in Italy between the fall of 218 and the fall of 203 BC.
40. Livy (37.57.7) places the founding of the colony at Bononia (Bologna) in 189 BC, the

[3] In the same time period (though the chronology is debated by some), colonists were sent to Puteoli, Salernum, and Buxentum, and also to Auximum in Picenum; this was about 187 years ago, three years before the censor Cassius started to build a theater from the Lupercal, facing the Palatium (the state's exceptional asceticism and the consul Caepio opposed its construction, something I would count as being one of the clearest indications of our national spirit).[41] [4] In the consulship of Cassius Longinus and Sextius Calvinus—it was Sextius who decisively defeated the Sallues at the waters that are named, after him, Aquae Sextiae (Sextian Waters)—Fabrateria was colonized, that is, about 154 years ago.[42] A year later Scolacium Minervia and Tarentum Neptunia were founded, along with Carthage in Africa, the first colony outside Italy, as I said above.[43] [5] The dating of Dertona is controversial, but Narbo Martius in Gaul was colonized in the consulship of Porcius and Marcius, that is, around <153> years ago. Eighteen years later, in the consulship of Marius (his sixth) and Valerius Flaccus, came Eporedia in the lands of the Bagienni. I would not find it easy to mention any colony, apart from a military colony, established after this time.[44]

---

year of the consulships mentioned. Velleius' calculation would give a founding date of 187. Pisaurum and Potentia in Picenum were founded in 184 (Livy 39.44.10). Aquileia near Trieste and Gravisca in Etruria became colonies in 181. The foundation date of Luna (in Etruria), 177, is confirmed by Livy (41.13.4). Note, however, that the original texts of both Livy and Velleius give the name as Luca (modern Lucca) and have been emended in each case.

41. The decision to found the colonies at Puteoli and Salernum in Campania and Buxentum in Lucania occurred in 197 BC (Livy 34.42.6), but their actual founding dates from 194 (Livy 34.45.2). Velleius' figure of 187 years before Vinicius' consulship (in AD 30) would produce a date of 157 BC for the founding of Auximum. Livy, however, implies that the colony was already in existence by 174 (41.21.12, 41.27.10, 42.20.6). Livy's date receives some confirmation from the consulship of Caepio, presumably Gnaeus Servilius Caepio, in 169.

The Lupercal is the cave located below the southwest corner of the Palatine Hill. According to legend it was there that the she-wolf suckled the infants Romulus and Remus. This reference is to the first stone theater in Rome, commissioned in 154 by the censors Cassius Longinus and Valerius Messalinus. Livy (*Per.* 48.25) reports that, three years later on the motion of Publius Cornelius Nasica, the theater was pulled down as being harmful to public morals (cf. Val. Max. 2.4.2). Velleius' description is not precise; the theater probably faced the valley of the Circus Maximus and was located beneath the temple of the Magna Mater.

42. Gaius Sextius Calvinus inflicted the defeat on the Sallues (more commonly "Salluvii") in 122 BC, for which he was awarded a triumph. The consulship of Calvinus and Longinus fell in 124; hence the transmitted figure of CLVII (157) must be incorrect and is generally emended to CLIIII (154). Fabrateria Nova in Bruttium was founded on the river Liris by Gaius Gracchus after the destruction of its predecessor in 125.

43. Scolacium in Bruttium was founded in 122 BC, as was Tarentum. They acquired their epithets through the prominent local cults of Minerva and Neptune. A colony (*Colonia Iunonia*) was founded at Carthage in 122. It is in fact first mentioned by Velleius later, at 2.7.8.

44. The colony at Dertona in Liguria is not dated by Velleius. His dating of Narbo Martius in

16. This section of my work has exceeded the limit, one might say, of what I proposed to do, and I also realize that in my precipitous haste (which, like a wheel or a cascading, swirling stream, never permits me to stop) I have almost a greater duty to pass over items of vital importance than to include superfluous details. Even so, I am unable to resist putting into writing something I have often pondered in my mind but have not completely reasoned out. [2] What can be more astonishing than this, that the most outstanding minds in each area of expertise have been clustered together for the same intellectual endeavor and have fallen within a very restricted time span? And that, as animals of various species that have been corralled on the same piece of land, or put in some other enclosure, still break away from those different from themselves and all gather together in a body, just so intellects that are capable of achieving distinction in each form of endeavor have segregated themselves from the rest of the herd, linked together by the closeness of their dates and similarity of their achievements? [3] One era, which lasted not many years, threw tragedy into relief, thanks to Aeschylus, Sophocles, and Euripides, men of divine inspiration; one era did the same for the early, old comedy, in the days of Cratinus, Aristophanes, and Eupolis; and another did it for the new comedy, which Menander, along with Philemon and Diphilus (who, as contemporaries of Menander, could be said to share his times but not his achievement), invented within the span of a very few years, but nevertheless left behind inimitable works.[45] [4] Then, too, there were all the philosophers, whose genius originated with the words of Socrates, the men I mentioned slightly earlier. How long was their heyday after the death of Plato and Aristotle?[46] [5] What fame attached to orators before Isocrates, or after the period of his students and their pupils?[47] Indeed, they were so tightly packed into a brief period of time that not one of those worth remembering could not have been seen in person by the others.

Gaul by the consulships of Cato and Marcius would place its founding in 118 BC. The figure of CLIII (153) is clearly an error. Eporedia at the foot of the Alps in southwest Cisalpine Gaul was founded in 100, the year of the consulship of Marius (see 2.11) and Flaccus.

45. Aeschylus (possibly 525/4–456/5 BC), Sophocles (496–406), and Euripides (probably 480–c. 406) are considered the three greatest of the Athenian tragedians. Cratinus (519–422), Eupolis (446–411), and Aristophanes (c. 450–c. 385) similarly dominated Athenian Old Comedy. The towering figure of New Comedy, the form that provided the model for the Roman comedians, was Menander (c. 342–292), although, perhaps to maintain the triptych pattern, Velleius mentions also Philemon (360s to mid-260s) and Diphilus (350s–290s).

46. Socrates (469–399 BC), who left no written works, had an immense influence on later generations. Velleius further maintains the pattern by mentioning only two other philosophers, the principal successors of Socrates: Plato (c. 429–c. 347) and Aristotle (384–322). The men Velleius has mentioned "slightly earlier" presumably appeared in a lost portion of the work.

47. Surprisingly, Velleius limits his survey of Attic orators to one figure, Isocrates (436–338 BC),

17. And this was not something more characteristic of Greece than it was of Rome. Unless you go back to uncouth, primitive compositions that merit praise only as the pioneering examples of the genre, Roman tragedy centers on and around Accius; and the pleasant witticisms of Latin humor sparkled essentially in the same period thanks to Caecilius, Terence, and Afranius.[48] [2] Historians, too, were the product of a circumscribed time period of fewer than eighty years (that is, putting Livy into the age of his predecessors, but omitting Cato and some antiquated and little-known authors), and the rich age of poetry extended neither far into the past nor close to the present.[49] [3] Then there is oratory, effectiveness in public speaking, and the perfect beauty of rhetorical prose. With Cato again excepted (and with due respect to Publius Crassus, Scipio, Laelius, the Gracchi, Fannius, and Servius Galba), these all burst out in completed form in the days of their chief proponent, Tullius Cicero, making it impossible for one to take pleasure from his predecessors, apart from very few, and at the same time to admire anyone who was not either seen by Cicero or who did not himself see Cicero.[50] [4] Anyone studying closely the salient features of various ages will find the very same thing to have happened in the case of grammarians, sculptors, painters, and engravers, namely, that greatness in each activity is confined within very narrow temporal limits.

---

even though that man was a contemporary of a number of distinguished orators, including Demosthenes (384–322) and Aeschines (c. 397–c. 322). It has been suggested that he was drawing an implicit parallel with the domination of Roman oratory by Cicero.

48. It is striking that Velleius begins his survey of Roman literature with Accius (170–c. 86 BC), the last of the great Roman tragedians, thus presumably characterizing the works of some of the luminaries of early Latin literature, such as Livius Andronicus, Naevius, and, most strikingly, Ennius, as "uncouth, primitive compositions." It is also noteworthy that he makes no mention of Plautus, although along with Plautus' only rival as a comic playwright, Terence (c. 190–159), he lists Caecilius Statius (died about 168) and Lucius Afranius (active 160–120). Plautus (c. 250–184) may have been considered too early to be their contemporaries, although the omission perhaps reflects a prejudice that we find earlier in Horace (*AP* 270–2). Also, Quintilian (*Inst.* 1.8.11) later omits Plautus from the list of playwrights most often quoted.

49. Velleius seems to be taking the nearly eighty years of the entire life span of Livy (59 BC–AD 17), as the period embracing the great Roman historians of the Augustan and pre-Augustan period. He excludes the old-fashioned figures, in keeping with the theme of this section, except that he must give credit to Cato (234–149 BC), whose *Origines,* begun in 168 and still incomplete at the time of his death, was the first Roman history written in Latin.

50. Velleius provides only a partial list of orators worthy to be included: Publius Licinius Crassus (died 130 BC), the ally of the Gracchi, Publius Cornelius Scipio Aemilianus (185/4–129; see 1.12.3), Gaius Laelius (c. 185–c. 115), Tiberius and Gaius Sempronius Gracchus (160s–133 and 154–121), Gaius Fannius (consul 122), and Servius Sulpicius Galba (died 129).

[5] I often look for explanations for such a similarity of talent <appearing in an age> and clustering around the same pursuit, and achieving the same success in it, but I never find any that I can confidently feel are correct. Some explanations, however, are quite plausible, the following in particular. [6] Competition nourishes genius, and envy in some cases, and admiration in others, sparks imitation; and any endeavor conducted with the utmost application swiftly reaches the highest level. Staying at that level of perfection, however, is difficult, and it is only natural for what cannot go forward to go back. [7] At the start we burn with desire to overtake those whom we perceive as being ahead of us; but, when we have lost all hope of being able to pass them or even reach their level, our enthusiasm declines along with our hope. It stops chasing after what it cannot catch and, leaving the field of endeavor as being one dominated by another, it seeks a new one. Abandoning the area in which we cannot be outstanding, we search for something in which we can shine; and the natural result is that such frequent and volatile changes represent a very great impediment to the perfection of any oeuvre.

18. Moving from the role played by specific periods to that played by specific cities, we again find reason for amazement. In terms of outstanding oratory, one city in Attica outdid all of Greece in the number of men and works that it produced, to the extent of making one think that while that nation's bodies were also dispersed among the other cities, its minds were to be found within the walls of Athens alone. [2] And there is nothing that could surprise me more than this, that no orator from Argos, Thebes, or Sparta was thought to have a commanding presence while he lived, or to be worthy of remembrance after his death. [3] These cities <and those in Italy> were unproductive of cultural pursuits, apart from Thebes, to which only the voice of Pindar added luster (for the Spartans are wrong in claiming Alcman as their own).[51]

---

51. Pindar of Thebes (c. 518–c. 438 BC) was widely regarded in antiquity as the greatest of the lyric poets. Alcman was active in Sparta in the seventh century, but in antiquity there was a controversy over his birthplace, some claiming that he was from Sparta, others that he originated from Sardis in Lydia, Asia Minor.

BOOK 2

[A major campaign in Spain follows the destruction of Carthage and Corinth. In Rome, political life is convulsed by the two brothers, Tiberius and Gaius Gracchus, between 133 and 121 BC.]

1. The earlier Scipio had opened up the road to Rome's power, the later one to its indulgent lifestyle. When it was rid of its fear of Carthage, and its rival for power was removed, its abandonment of virtue and shift into vice did not occur gradually but at breakneck speed. The old ways were abandoned, new ones introduced. The state turned from vigilance to indolence, from arms to pleasures, from activity to idleness.[1] [2] It was then that Scipio Nasica built his porticoes on the Capitol, and Metellus those that I mentioned earlier, and then, too, that Gnaeus Octavius built by far the most beautiful example in the Circus; and personal extravagance followed in the train of public munificence.[2]

[3] There followed a wretched and humiliating war in Spain with the guerrilla leader Viriathus, a war fought with shifting fortunes that more often than not went against the Romans. But when Viriathus was killed—thanks more to duplicity than courage on the part of Servilius Caepio—a war of greater severity flared up in Numantia.[3] [4] This city never put under

---

1. Publius Cornelius Scipio Africanus Maior was born in 236 BC and played a leading role in the Second Punic War. He is credited with rallying the Roman troops after the disaster at Cannae in 216, and in 209 he captured Carthago Nova in Spain. He effectively brought the war to an end with his victory over Hannibal at Zama in 202; his son Publius was undistinguished (see 1.10.3), but his grandson by adoption, Publius Cornelius Scipio Aemilianus Africanus Minor Numantinus (1.12.3–5), biological son of Lucius Aemilius Paulus Macedonicus (1.9.3), was responsible for the destruction of Carthage in 146. The notion of decadence following the removal of Rome's archenemy was something of a literary trope, much favored earlier by Sallust.

2. Publius Cornelius Scipio Nasica Corculum was consul in 162 and 155 BC; the porticoes mentioned here were constructed during his term as censor, in 159; on Metellus' buildings, see 1.11.3; the Porticus Octavia stood on the Campus Martius between the theater of Pompey and the Circus Flaminius. It was built by Gnaeus Octavius to commemorate his victory over the Illyrians during the Third Macedonian War. Damaged in a fire, it was restored by Octavian in 33. It is distinct from the Porticus Octaviae, named after Augustus' sister Octavia (1.11.3).

3. Viriathus led the Lusitanians in revolt between 147 and 139 BC and won over many other Spanish peoples. Using guerrilla tactics he defeated a series of Roman commanders; Quintus Servilius Caepio, consul 140, contrived Viriathus' assassination in 139 and brought the conflict

arms more than ten thousand of its own men, but because of its native belligerence or the incompetence of our commanders or the indulgence of Fortune, it forced various generals, including the renowned Pompey—he was the first consul from the Pompeii family—to accept disgraceful peace treaties, and the consul Mancinus Hostilius to assent to terms no less shabby and repugnant. [5] Pompey's personal influence, however, saved him from punishment, while Mancinus' feelings of shame <through not refusing . . .> led to his being surrendered to the enemy by the fetial priests, naked and with his hands tied behind his back. The Numantines refused to take him, however, replicating the act of the enemy at Caudium earlier; one man's blood was insufficient compensation for the state's collective breach of faith, they said.[4]

2. The surrender of Mancinus gave rise to dissension on a frightful scale within the state. Tiberius Gracchus, son of the famous and eminent Tiberius Gracchus and grandson of Publius Africanus (being born of Africanus' daughter), had been Mancinus' quaestor and had been responsible for the signing of the treaty.[5] He then wavered between outrage over the annulment

---

to an end the following year. Numantia, a settlement in northern Spain on the river Duero had been a center of Celtiberian resistance to Rome since the early second century. The Numantine War broke out first in 154; it was settled in 151 but flared up again in 143 and was finally brought to an end by Scipio Aemilianus in 133, after a protracted siege.

4. Quintus Pompeius, consul in 141 BC, was given command of the Numantine War, and facing disaster in 140 he entered into a bogus treaty with the Numantines, which he himself was obliged to repudiate and which the senate refused to ratify. Gaius Hostilius Mancinus was consul in 137; in the following year he suffered a shameful defeat marked by personal cowardice, leading to a treaty negotiated by his quaestor Tiberius Sempronius Gracchus, which the senate also repudiated. The senate handed Mancinus over to the Numantines with full ritual, presided over by the fetial priests, an ancient order concerned particularly with treaties and declarations of war. The Numantines refused to accept him. Similarly, when the Romans suffered a disastrous defeat by the Samnites at the Caudine Forks in 321, the senate repudiated the treaty of surrender and turned over its negotiators to the Samnites, who declined to receive them (Livy 9.5–11).

5. Tiberius Sempronius Gracchus (160s–133 BC) was the famous grandson of Publius Cornelius Scipio Africanus Maior and the cousin and brother-in-law of Publius Cornelius Scipio Aemilianus Africanus Minor Numantinus. He was the son of Cornelia and a distinguished consular father of the same name, Tiberius Sempronius Gracchus, who was awarded two triumphs for his achievements in Spain and Sardinia and produced two celebrated sons, Tiberius and Gaius. The younger Tiberius served at Carthage under his cousin Scipio and was quaestor in Spain in 137. On the motion of this Scipio the senate repudiated the treaty Tiberius had negotiated on behalf of Mancinus (see 2.1). Tiberius felt that his integrity had been impugned and threw in his lot with Scipio's opponents. In 133, as tribune, he proposed a law that reaffirmed the limit of 500 *iugera* (about 330 acres) of public land per person and appointed a commission to identify surplus land and redistribute it. It was presented to the plebeian assembly (*concilium plebis*) without senate approval and, accordingly, persistently vetoed by fellow tribune Marcus Octavius, whom Tiberius arranged to be removed from office.

of something he had negotiated and fear of exposing himself to a similar judgment or penalty. He was a man with an otherwise irreproachable record, who had an outstanding intellect and perfectly honorable goals—[2] in short, a man endowed with the greatest virtues that the human condition can acquire when it is perfected both by nature and hard work. When he became plebeian tribune, however, in the consulship of Publius Mucius Scaevola and Lucius Calpurnius, that is, 162 years ago, he abandoned the aristocratic party. He promised citizenship to the whole of Italy [3] and at the same time promulgated agrarian legislation at a point when everybody hungered for <stability>.⁶ He thus precipitated general upheaval and brought the Republic into imminent and serious danger. When his colleague Octavius made a stand for the public good, Gracchus forced him out of office and created a board of three, made up of himself, his father-in-law the ex-consul Appius, and his brother Gaius (who was still a very young man), to oversee the distribution of the land and foundation of colonies.⁷

3. It was at this point that Publius Scipio Nasica wrapped the hem of his toga around his left arm and, standing on the top steps in the upper part of the Capitol, urged all who wanted the state to be saved to follow him.⁸ Nasica was grandson of the Scipio who had been deemed by the senate to be the best man in Rome; he was the son of the Scipio who, as censor, had seen to the construction of the porticoes on the Capitol; and he was the great-grandson of Gnaeus Scipio, the famous uncle of Publius Africanus.

---

6. Velleius' claim that Tiberius intended to extend the citizenship to the Italians is thought by some to be an error, caused by confusion with a similar measure of his brother Gaius (see 2.6.2).

7. Velleius' natural conservatism and a family link, undefined, between Marcus Octavius and Octavian/Augustus explain the historian's reference to the "public good." Tiberius Gracchus was married to Claudia Pulchra, daughter of Appius Claudius Pulcher. Appius was consul in 143 BC, censor in 136, then *princeps senatus*, the senator who came first in the order of precedence. A committed *popularis* and an inveterate opponent of Scipio Aemilianus, he may have exercised an important ideological influence on the Gracchi.

8. Publius Cornelius Scipio Nasica Serapio was (a) the great-grandson of Gnaeus Cornelius Scipio Calvus (consul 222 BC), killed in battle in Spain during the Second Punic War after inflicting considerable defeats on the Carthaginians there, (b) the grandson of Publius Cornelius Scipio Nasica, consul in 191, who had been granted the designation *vir bonorum optimus* (best of the good men) and the privilege of receiving the statue of the Magna Mater when it was brought to Rome during the Second Punic War in 204, and (c) the son of Publius Cornelius Scipio Nasica Corculum (2.1.2). Scipio Serapio succeeded his father as *pontifex maximus*, perhaps in 141 (but possibly later), and was consul in 138. Plutarch attributes a less noble motive than does Velleius for his opposition to Tiberius Gracchus, that he had personally been affected by the new agrarian laws (*Ti. Gr.* 13.3, hinted at in Cic. *Sest.* 103). At least in part to protect Scipio from the vengeance of the Gracchi, the senate sent him on a mission to Asia to organize its annexation as a province, where he died.

He was at the time just a private citizen and wearing the toga, and although he was a cousin of Tiberius Gracchus, he set his country above family ties and thought that what was not for the good of the state was not in his personal interest, either (for which qualities he was the first man ever to be elected *pontifex maximus* in his absence). [2] Then the nobility, the senate, the majority (and the best) of the equestrian order, and those of the plebs not infected with these pernicious ideas charged at Gracchus as he stood in an open area with large numbers of his supporters trying to incite a crowd that was drawn from almost all of Italy. When Gracchus fled and was running down the road from the Capitol, he was struck by a broken piece of a bench, and he ended with a premature death a life in which he could have enjoyed the greatest distinction.

[3] This marked the beginning of civil bloodletting, and assassination without fear of punishment, in the city of Rome. From now on right was overwhelmed by might, and power took precedence. Differences between citizens, which had usually been remedied by compromise in earlier days, were now settled by the sword, and wars were started not for cause but on the basis of their profitability. Nor is this surprising. [4] Precedents once set do not end where they began. No matter how narrow the path on which they embark, they open up a way of deviating from it with the greatest latitude, and once one has wandered off the right path, it is a headlong drop that lies ahead. And nobody thinks that what another has found profitable is discreditable for himself.

4. Meanwhile, as this was taking place in Italy, King Attalus died and left Asia to the Roman people in his will (just as at a later date Bithynia was left to them by Nicomedes), but Aristonicus, falsely claiming to be born of royal stock, seized the country by force. Aristonicus was defeated by Marcus Perpenna and was led along in a triumphal procession, but by Manius Aquilius, not Perpenna; and he paid with his life the penalty for having at the start of the war executed Crassus Mucianus, the expert jurist and proconsul of Asia, as he was leaving his province.[9]

---

9. The childless Attalus III of Pergamum (c. 170–133 BC) bequeathed his kingdom to Rome, just as the pro-Roman Nicomedes IV Philopator later bequeathed his kingdom of Bithynia to the Romans on his death in 75/4. The Romans were dilatory in establishing their right, and Aristonicus claimed to be the illegitimate son of Eumenes II, father of Attalus III, and seized the throne under the name of Eumenes III. In the first attempt to remove him, the consul of 131, the noted orator and jurist Publius Licinius Crassus Mucianus, father-in-law of Gaius Gracchus, was defeated by Aristonicus at Leukai and reportedly killed, having refused to reveal his identity in order to avoid the humiliation of imprisonment. Aristonicus was defeated in 130 by Marcus Perpenna, who died before he could return to Rome. Manius Aquilus, consul in 129, succeeded Perpenna in Asia and completed the war, then took a leading role in organizing Asia as a province. He paraded Aristonicus through Rome during his triumph and had him strangled.

[2] Publius Scipio Africanus Aemilianus, the man who had destroyed Carthage, was elected to his second consulship and sent to Spain following a large number of serious defeats at Numantia. In Spain his record of good fortune and bravery matched that which he had earned in Africa, and within a year and three months of his arrival he surrounded Numantia with siege works, destroyed it, and razed it to the ground. [3] Before Scipio no one in the world had immortalized his name as a more famous destroyer of cities, for by his destruction of Carthage and Numantia he delivered us from fear in the first case and humiliation in the second.[10]

[4] When the tribune Carbo asked him for his thoughts on the murder of Tiberius Gracchus, Scipio replied that the killing was justified if Gracchus' aim had been to seize control of the state.[11] And when the entire assembly remonstrated, he said: "I was not frightened at so often hearing the shouts of the enemy in arms, so how can I be concerned by your shouts, when you have Italy only as a stepmother?"

[5] Scipio returned to Rome and shortly afterward, in the consulship of Manius Aquilius and Gaius Sempronius (that is, 160 years ago), the man who had served two consulships, celebrated two triumphs, and twice eradicated dire threats to the Republic was one morning found dead in his bed. There were also a number of marks of strangulation found on his neck.[12] [6] For all his greatness, there was no inquest held on his death, and the funeral of the man whose efforts had enabled Rome to raise its head above the entire world was conducted with *his* head veiled. Whether he died of natural causes, as most claim, or as the result of a conspiracy, as some have recorded, he at all events lived a most meritorious life, one surpassed in glory by none up to that time, with the exception of his grandfather. [7] He died at about the age of fifty-six. Anyone questioning that should remember his first consulship, to which he was elected in his thirty-sixth year—then he will doubt no more.

10. The resistance of Numantia in Spain (2.1.3) was broken by Publius Cornelius Scipio Aemilianus Africanus Minor Numantinus in 133 BC after an eight-month blockade. Scipio celebrated a triumph in 132 and assumed the honorific Numantinus.

11. Gaius Papirius Carbo was initially an ally of Gaius Gracchus and as tribune in 131 BC proposed a law that tribunes could be candidates for repeated terms of the same office. He later went over to the *optimates* and as consul in 120 defended Lucius Opimius. He was impeached for involvement in the death of Gaius and either committed suicide or went into exile.

12. When challenged by the plebeian tribune of 131 BC, Carbo, a supporter of Tiberius Gracchus and later (in 120) consul, Scipio expressed his approval of Tiberius' murder. On Scipio's own death in 129, which was probably natural, a number of prominent individuals, including his wife Sempronia (sister of the Gracchi), Cornelia (their mother), and Gaius Gracchus himself, were suspected of having brought it about.

5. Prior to the destruction of Numantia a brilliant campaign had been conducted in Spain by Decimus Brutus, who had penetrated so far as to reach all the Spanish tribes. He took into his power huge numbers of people and cities, and visited places that had barely been heard about, thus earning the cognomen Gallaecus.[13]

[2] A few years before Brutus' campaign, the famous Quintus Macedonicus was also operating among the Spanish tribes, and his command was characterized by extreme severity.[14] When he was attacking a Spanish city called Contrebia, five legionary cohorts were driven back down a steep incline, and Macedonicus ordered them to climb up again. [3] They all proceeded to draft their wills as they prepared for action, assuming that they were marching to certain death, but there was no deterring Macedonicus from his resolve, and he welcomed back as victors the men he had sent to their deaths. Such was the effect of shame mixed with fear, and hope that came from despair. Macedonicus' fame in Spain rested on the courage and severity of this act, but the fame of Fabius Aemilianus, son of Paulus, rested on his exemplary discipline.[15]

6. Ten years passed and then the lunacy that had overtaken Tiberius Gracchus also overtook his brother Gaius.[16] Gaius resembled his brother in all his good points as well as this aberration, but he was also far superior to him in intellect and speaking ability. [2] The man could have reached the

---

13. Decimus Junius Brutus Gallaecus was consul in 138 BC and conquered much of what is now modern Galicia (hence his cognomen) and northern Portugal in 137.

14. After his successes in Macedonia (see 1.11, 1.12.1) Quintus Caecilius Metellus Macedonicus became consul in 143 BC and was sent to Spain where he defeated a rebellion of the Celtiberi but reputedly handed over his army in very bad condition to his successor, his opponent Quintus Pompeius (2.1.4–5).

15. Quintus Fabius Maximus Aemilianus was the biological son of Lucius Aemilius Paulus Macedonicus, victor over the Macedonians at the first battle of Pydna in 168 BC (see 1.9.3–4), whose harsh discipline Fabius is said to have emulated. Fabius was adopted into the *gens Fabia* in 181. After serving with his biological father in Macedonia he campaigned in Spain as consul in 145 and in 144 defeated Viriathus on two occasions but failed to capture him and bring the war to an end. He served at Numantia in 144–143 and died shortly afterward.

16. Gaius Gracchus (c. 154–121 BC) served under Scipio Aemilianus at Numantia. As a member of his brother's land commission he supported the progressive agenda of his friend Fulvius Flaccus in 126; then, after service in Sardinia, he entered the tribunate in 123 and was reelected in 122. Velleius' suggestion that Gaius sought "absolute power" refers to his scheme to alternate that office with Fulvius Flaccus, consul in 125. His program, far more ambitious than his brother's, included a proposal to offer citizenship to Latins and Latin status to Italian allies (also attributed by Velleius to Tiberius; see 2.2.2). It was defeated, and he was not reelected for 121. The *lex Licinia* of 367, among other things, restricted the exploitation of unassigned public land.

highest level in politics with complete equanimity, but, whether to avenge his brother's death or to prepare his bid for absolute power, he followed his brother's example and entered the tribunate. His agenda, however, was far more ambitious and radical than his brother's. He favored granting citizenship to all Italians (he wanted to extend it almost to the Alps), [3] redistributing the lands, not allowing any citizen to own more than 500 *iugera* (a provision once made by the *lex Licinia*), creating new harbor taxes, filling the provinces with new colonies, and transferring judicial authority from the senate to the equites; and he was also for grain-distributions to the common people. He left nothing unaltered, nothing peaceful, nothing tranquil—nothing, in short, in the same condition as before. Indeed, he even secured a continuation of his tribunate for a second term.

[4] The consul Lucius Opimius (who had razed Fregellae during his praetorship) took up arms against him and murdered him, along with Fulvius Flaccus, an ex-consul who had also celebrated a triumph.[17] Gaius Gracchus had named Flaccus, who had the same misguided aims as he did, as triumvir to replace his brother Tiberius and had enlisted him as his partner in his bid for absolute power. [5] The one unconscionable act of which Opimius was guilty was putting a price (which he undertook to pay in gold) on the head, I shall not say of Gracchus, but of a Roman citizen. [6] Flaccus was killed on the Aventine, together with his elder son, as he spurred on his armed followers to fight. Gracchus fled and, when he was about to be caught by the men Opimius had sent after him, he stretched his neck out to his slave Euporus, who, having promptly lent this assistance to his master, just as promptly killed himself. That day also witnessed singular loyalty to Gracchus on the part of the Roman equestrian Pomponius. He held back Gracchus' enemies on a bridge, like Cocles, and then ran himself through with his sword.[18] [7] In an act of astonishing callousness, the body of Gaius was thrown into the Tiber by his victors, as that of Tiberius had been earlier.

7. Such were the lives and deaths of the sons of Tiberius Gracchus, the grandchildren of Publius Scipio Africanus, men who had put their fine intellects to poor use; and their mother Cornelia, daughter of Africanus, was

---

17. Lucius Opimius had, as praetor in 125 BC, crushed Fregellae, which had joined in the revolt following the rejection of Flaccus' proposal as consul to extend citizenship to all Italians. He was elected consul in 121 and given the task of dealing with Gaius and Flaccus. The latter's son Quintus acted as an intermediary between his father and Opimius. He was taken prisoner by Opimius and put to death.

18. Marcus Pomponius' gesture occurred at the Pons Sublicius. Velleius compares him with the legendary Publius Horatius Cocles, who defended that bridge against the Etruscan army under Lars Porsenna.

still alive.[19] Had their ambitions been limited to the honors befitting a citizen, the Republic would have conferred on them in peace whatever they longed to gain through fomenting disorder.

[2] This atrocity was compounded by a novel crime. Fulvius Flaccus' son, a young man of superlative good looks, not yet past his eighteenth year, had played no part in his father's transgressions, but when his father sent him as a representative to discuss terms he was put to death by Opimius. When an Etruscan soothsayer, who was a friend of his, saw the young man being hauled off to prison in tears, he said to him: "Why not do this instead?" and immediately smashed his own head against the stone doorpost of the prison, dashed out his brains, and breathed his last.

[3] There followed merciless judicial investigations of friends and clients of the Gracchi. Opimius, however, otherwise a man of upright and respectable character, was later on judged guilty in a criminal suit, and he found no sympathy among his fellow citizens because of the memory of his ruthlessness.[20] [4] The same odium deservedly overtook Rupilius and Popilius, who as consuls had been extremely savage in their persecution of the friends of Tiberius Gracchus, <. . .> when they later faced criminal courts. (Let me interject here something that has little to do with the history of this important affair.[21] [5] This is the Opimius from whose consulship comes the name of the celebrated Opimian wine.[22] That none exists today can be gathered from the number of years that have elapsed, since it is 151 years from his consulship to yours, Marcus Vinicius.) [6] What Opimius did in seeking retribution for private differences won little approval, and that retribution was seen as an act of personal vengeance rather than as punishment exacted by the state.

---

19. After her husband's death Cornelia, the daughter of Scipio Africanus, devoted her energies to the education and upbringing of her sons Tiberius and Gaius. She was a woman of considerable sophistication, whose writings were admired by Cicero (*Brut.* 104, 211), Tacitus (*Dial.* 28), and Quintilian (*Inst.* 1.1.6).

20. Lucius Opimius was prosecuted for his actions in suppressing the Gracchi and his acquittal confirmed the constitutionality of the *consultum ultimum*. He later headed a commission that divided Numidia between its royal claimants and was censured for bribery by Jugurtha. He went into exile in Dyrrhachium where he died about 100 BC.

21. Publius Popilius Laenas was consul in 132 BC. He inflicted severe punishment on Tiberius Gracchus' supporters and was forced into exile by legislation of Gaius Gracchus. Popilius was joined in his action by his fellow consul Publius Rupilius, who then went to Sicily to suppress a slave revolt. There is no other reference to a court action against Rupilius.

22. The vintage of Opimius' consular year (121 BC) was noted as being very fine; Pliny the Elder contradicts Velleius since he asserts that Opimian wine was still available in his own day, more than two hundred years after Opimius' time. Pliny observes that it had a honey taste but was bitter (*NH* 14.55).

[7] Among the most pernicious laws of Gracchus I would count the founding of colonies outside Italy. This is something our ancestors had assiduously avoided since they saw that Carthage was so much more powerful than Tyre, Massilia more powerful than Phocaea, Syracuse than Corinth, Cyzicus and Byzantium than Miletus—that is, cities much more powerful than their homelands. That is why they would call Roman citizens back to Italy from the provinces for the census. [8] Now the first colony founded outside Italy was Carthage; and shortly afterward, in the consulship of Porcius and Marcius, Narbo Martius was established as a colony.[23]

[Activities of a number of Roman individuals in the late second century BC. The flowering of talent in the political, but also in the literary, field around that time.]

8. Next, the severity of the judiciary must be put on record. The ex-consul Gaius Cato, grandson of Marcus Cato and son of Africanus' sister, was found guilty of extortion in Macedonia, though the damages against him were assessed at a mere 4,000 sesterces.[24] Such was the extent to which men of those times considered intent in wrongdoing rather than its magnitude, and they weighed up actions in light of motive and the nature of the crime, not its size. [2] It was at about this same time that the two Metellus brothers celebrated triumphs on the same day.[25] An instance of such congruity that is no less famous, and which remains unparalleled, was the sons of Fulvius Flaccus (the man who had captured Capua) being colleagues in the consulship (though one of the sons had been presented for adoption and had passed into the household of Acidinus Manlius). In the case of the shared censorship of the Metelli, they were cousins, not brothers (a congruence that had occurred only among the Scipios).[26]

---

23. Colonia Iunonia was founded as a colony at Carthage by Gaius Gracchus in 122 BC (see 1.15.4); it failed, but Augustus revived the project. On Narbo Martius, see 1.15.4.

24. Gaius Porcius Cato was consul in 114 BC. His province was Macedonia, where he fought a disastrous campaign and was convicted of extortion. He went to live in exile in Tarraco in Spain. He was the son of Aemilia, sister of Publius Cornelius Scipio Aemilianus.

25. Marcus Caecilius Metellus (consul 115 BC) celebrated a triumph in July 111 for suppressing an insurrection in Sardinia. On the same day his brother Gaius Caecilius Metellus (consul 113) celebrated one for his campaigns against the Parthians. Sallust (*Jug.* 63.6) commented that the Metelli passed the consulship down to one another.

26. Quintus Fulvius Flaccus was consul in 237, 224, 212, and 209 BC. He was notorious for his brutal treatment of Capua, where in 211 he executed the leading citizens because the city had sided with the Carthaginians. His sons Quintus Fulvius Flaccus and Lucius Manlius Acidinus were consuls in 179; his grandson was Flaccus, the supporter of Gaius Gracchus. Gaius Caecilius Metellus Caprarius, son of Quintus Caecilius Metellus Macedonicus (consul 143),

[3] At that time the Cimbri and the Teutoni—soon to become notorious for many defeats inflicted on us, and many they suffered themselves—crossed the Rhine. Dated to about this time, too, is the renowned triumph over the Scordisci celebrated by the Minucius who built the porticoes that are still highly regarded today.[27]

9. In the same time period Scipio Aemilianus and Laelius distinguished themselves as orators, as did Servius Galba, the two Gracchi, Gaius Fannius, and Carbo Papirius.[28] Nor must we omit Metellus Numidicus and Scaurus, and above all Lucius Crassus and Marcus Antonius.[29] [2] Following them, both chronologically and in terms of talent, were Gaius Caesar Strabo and Publius Sulpicius, for Quintus Mucius owed his fame more to his jurisprudence than actual speaking ability.[30]

[3] Other famous talents of the same period were Afranius, in Roman comedy, and Pacuvius and Accius in tragedy.[31] (Accius rose to prominence

---

and Quintus Caecilius Metellus Numidicus, son of Macedonicus' brother, were censors in 114. The brothers Publius and Lucius Cornelius Scipio were both censors in 340.

27. Velleius' chronology is very broad at this point. The Cimbri and Teutoni began to invade in 113 BC and were defeated in a series of battles in 102–101. The Scordisci, a people of Moesia and Pannonia, had crushed an army commanded by Marcus Porcius Cato in 114 but were finally defeated by Marcus Minucius Rufus (consul 110) in 106. The Porticus Minucia was located to the south of the Campus Martius, between the Circus Flaminius and the Tiber.

28. This review of Roman literature covers the period from the sack of Carthage (146 BC) to the death of Marius and speaks to the range and vigor of letters during that period. The list of orators differs somewhat from that already provided at 1.17.3, in that it lacks Cato and Licinius Crassus but includes Papirius Carbo, supporter of Tiberius Gracchus and an orator of some distinction.

Scipio Aemilianus and Laelius are linked also by Cicero (*Brut.* 82), who considers Laelius the more distinguished. Servius Galba, consul in 144, was noted for the emotional effect of his oratory. Cicero (*Brut.* 99.101) distinguishes two men called Fannius (perhaps in reality the same person): Gaius, the consul of 122, who opposed Gaius Gracchus' legislation in a famous speech, and Marcus, a Stoic follower of Panaetius. On Gaius Papirius Carbo, see 2.4.4.

29. On Metellus Numidicus, see 2.11; Cicero (*Brut.* 135) couples him with Marcus Aurelius Scaurus, consul of 108 BC, praising their good taste. Lucius Licinius Crassus was used as a model by Cicero, who admired him immensely. Marcus Antonius, consul in 99, was, with Crassus, the leading orator of his age.

30. Gaius Julius Caesar Strabo, tribune in 88 BC, was decapitated on Sulla's orders. Cicero (*Brut.* 203) describes him as a *tragicus orator* (theatrical orator). Publius Sulpicius Rufus was an orator of great distinction who pursued a tumultuous career as supporter, then opponent, of Sulla (see 2.18.5). Quintus Mucius Scaevola was an outstanding lawyer (2.26.2) who wrote the first proper treatise on civil law and whose reorganization of the province of Asia was a model for other provinces.

31. Lucius Afranius was born about 150 BC. His comedies on domestic life in Italy were immensely popular and still performed in the imperial period. Horace (*Ep.* 2.1.57) compares him with

to the point of being compared with the Greek masters, and he secured a great place for his own work among these very authors, with the qualification, however, that there seems to have been more polish in them, and more vitality in him.) [4] Fame also attended the name of Lucilius, who had served as a cavalryman in the Numantine War under Publius Africanus.[32] At that time, too, Jugurtha and Marius, who were still young men and also both serving under Africanus, received in a shared campaign the training they would later put to use in opposing campaigns.[33]

[5] At that point the historian Sisenna was still a young man; his work on the civil war and the Sullan War was published by him many years later when he was quite old.[34] [6] Coelius was earlier than Sisenna, but Rutilius, Claudius Quadrigarius, and Valerius Antias were Sisenna's contemporaries. Of course, we should not forget that this was also the period of Pomponius, who was celebrated for his ideas but had a rough style and is to be credited for his invention of a new literary genre.[35]

Menander. Pacuvius, born about 220, was the nephew of Ennius and wrote only tragedies, which were marked by bold and inventive language. Cicero (*Tusc.* 2.48) considered him Rome's greatest tragic poet. He is often linked with his friend Lucius Accius, born about 170, who wrote in a variety of genres but gained most fame for his tragedies and was imitated by Virgil (Macr. *Sat.* 6.1).

32. Lucilius died in old age in 102/1 BC. He made a major contribution to the evolution of the satire and was a powerful influence on authors such as Horace.

33. Gaius Marius was one of the towering military figures of the late Republic. Born near Arpinum about 157 BC to an equestrian family, he served with Scipio at Numantia. In 109 he served with Metellus against Jugurtha in Numidia and took his place as commander there after winning the consulship for 107.

Jugurtha was the grandson of the Numidian king Masinissa but stood outside the line of succession until he was adopted by King Micipsa on the recommendation of Scipio Aemilianus, with whom he served at Numantia. Campaigning against his rival Adherbal, Jugurtha attacked the city of Cirta in 112, putting a number of Romans to death. This drew him into war with Rome, which eventually came under the command of Marius. Jugurtha was at the end handed over to the Romans and died after Marius' triumph in 104.

34. Lucius Cornelius Sisenna was born about 120 BC and would have been a teenager when the Jugurthine War ended (105). His historical works were admired by Sallust (*Jug.* 95.2).

35. Lucius Coelius (or Caelius) Antipater was a lawyer, orator, and historian who introduced the historical monograph to Rome. He wrote seven books on the Second Punic War and was highly regarded by Cicero and Livy. Publius Rutilius Rufus served with Metellus in Numidia and was active in the reorganization of the Roman armies during his consulship in 105 BC. He assisted Scaevola in the reorganization of Asia. On his return he was convicted unfairly of extortion and went into exile in Smyrna. The notoriety of the trial influenced Drusus' desire to reform the courts (see 2.13.2). Rutilius, a pupil of Panaetius, wrote a history of his own era, used by Sallust. Claudius Quadrigarius wrote a history of Rome from its sack by the Gauls down to his own time, in a simple, archaic style. He was considered one of the leading annalists before Livy, along with Valerius Antias, who similarly wrote a major history of Rome from its

10. Let us continue by touching on the strictness of the censors Cassius Longinus and Caepio who, 154 years ago, ordered the augur Aemilius Lepidus to appear before them for having rented a house for 6,000 sesterces.[36] Anyone renting for that amount these days is barely recognized as a senator. So true is it that people swiftly pass from rectitude to vice and from vice to depravity.

[2] The same period of time saw a famous victory won by Domitius over the Arverni and another by Fabius over the Allobroges. In honor of his victory Fabius, the grandson of Paulus, was given the cognomen Allobrogicus. A singular piece of good fortune, and a very famous one, must be related in connection with the family of the Domitii, particularly in view of its small numbers. Before the present Gnaeus Domitius, a young man of celebrated candor, there were seven boys born as only children to their respective parents. All of them reached the consulship and priesthood, and nearly all attained the distinction of a triumph.[37]

[The war in Africa against Jugurtha and the rise of Marius, who goes on to score successes against the invading Germanic tribes in 102 and 101 BC.]

11. There followed the war against Jugurtha, fought under the direction of Quintus Metellus, a man second to none of his generation.[38] His legate was Gaius Marius, whom we mentioned above. Marius, who was of equestrian stock, was an uncouth and rough character but had a virtuous lifestyle. His

---

origins down to the 70s. He wrote in a vigorous rhetorical style, with much coloring of battles and speeches from his own imagination. Lucius Pomponius, a Cisalpine Gaul who flourished in the early first century, was a major exponent of broad farces known as *fabulae Atellanae,* enlivened by stock characters and coarse scenes. He did not invent them but might be said to have given them a formal literary character.

36. Gnaeus Servilius Caepio and Lucius Cassius Longinus were censors in 125 BC. Marcus Aemilius Lepidus had been consul in 136. The augur was a member of one of the four priestly colleges with expertise in divination based on the characteristics and behavior of birds.

37. Gnaeus Domitius Ahenobarbus (consul 122 BC), ancestor of the emperor Nero, defeated the Arverni near Avignon (see 2.39.1). Quintus Fabius Maximus defeated the Allobroges in 121, in a battle in which a hundred thousand Gauls died.

The Domitii were noted for their eccentricity and ruthlessness, as well as their occasional mediocrity, but they produced a succession of consuls. Velleius is, as often, casual with his statistics. Of the seven consular Domitii, five were only sons. The "present Domitius" is Gnaeus Domitius Ahenobarbus (consul AD 32), a man of little achievement and described by Suetonius as detestable in every respect (*Nero* 5.1). His only claim to fame was as father of Nero.

38. Quintus Caecilius Metellus was elected consul in 109 BC and charged with bringing the war with Jugurtha to an end. He clashed with Marius, one of his legates, who intrigued against him and was elected consul in 107 and appointed by a special law to replace him, despite Metellus' successes (see 2.9.4). On his return to Rome Metellus was prosecuted but acquitted. He celebrated his triumph in 106.

fine qualities in war, however, were matched by bad ones in time of peace; he had an inordinate thirst for glory, his ambition was insatiable, he lacked self-control, and he was always restless. [2] He used tax collectors and other businessmen in Africa to spread negative reports about the slow progress being made by Metellus, who was now drawing out the war into its third year, and about Metellus' arrogance (an innate feature of the nobility, he said) and his desire to prolong his military commands. The upshot was that, having applied for a leave of absence, Marius came to Rome, was elected consul, and had the supreme command of the war, which had almost been finished off by Metellus (who had twice defeated Jugurtha in pitched battle), assigned to him. Nevertheless, Metellus had a triumph that was a brilliant affair, and he was also awarded the cognomen Numidicus in recognition of his bravery.

[3] As I did with the Domitian family a short while ago, I must also call attention to the distinction of the Caecilian family. Within the space of some twelve years in this epoch, Metelli were either consuls or censors, or celebrated triumphs, on more than twelve occasions, making it clear that, as happens with cities and empires, the fortunes of families also prosper at one moment, decline at another, and at another die out altogether.[39]

12. Gaius Marius even at that point had Lucius Sulla attached to him as his quaestor, as though the Fates were giving him an early warning, and it was by sending Sulla on a mission to King Bocchus that Marius succeeded in capturing King Jugurtha.[40] This was about 134 years ago. Now consul-designate for the second time, Marius returned to Rome and, at the beginning of his second consulship, on January 1 [of the year 104], he had the king led along in his triumph. [2] An immense force of German tribes, called the Cimbri and the Teutoni, were streaming abroad at this time, as I noted above. In Gaul they defeated and put to flight the consuls Caepio and Manlius, as they had done Carbo and Silanus earlier, and robbed them of their armies;

---

39. As often, Velleius' figures are a little imprecise: there were twelve Metellan consulships, censorships, or triumphs between 123 and 109 BC (Quintus Metellus' consulship), that is, in a space of fifteen, not twelve, years.

40. Lucius Cornelius Sulla (c. 138–78 BC), who came from a patrician family, later rose to prominence as leader of the *optimates* in opposition to Marius. He supposedly led a dissolute youth but later served meritoriously in the war against Jugurtha, as Marius' quaestor, and in the campaigns against the Germanic tribes and in the Social War, where he particularly distinguished himself (see 2.17).

Bocchus was king of Mauretania, linked by marriage to Jugurtha, who was possibly his son-in-law. His unenthusiastic support of Jugurtha was secured by the offer of part of Numidia. After defeats by the Romans he made overtures to them and was obliged to give a strong pledge of his seriousness, which he did by betraying Jugurtha and surrendering him to Marius' lieutenant Sulla.

they also butchered the former consul Aurelius Scaurus and other very famous men.[41] The Roman people then thought there was no other commander better qualified to drive back so powerful an enemy than Marius.
[3] There followed his multiple consulships. The third of these was taken up
with preparations for the war, and that was the year in which the plebeian
tribune Gnaeus Domitius carried a law authorizing the people to take
charge of electing the priests (prior to that, it was the priestly college that
made these appointments).[42] [4] In the fourth, Marius came to grips with
the Teutoni on the other side of the Alps in the area of Aquae Sextiae, where
he slaughtered more than 150,000 of the enemy on the first and second
days of the battle and the Teutoni tribe was wiped out. [5] In his fifth, the
consul himself, along with the proconsul Quintus Lutatius Catulus, fought
out a very successful engagement on the so-called Raudian Plains, in which
more than a hundred thousand men were either killed or captured.[43] By this
victory Marius seems to have earned the right not to have the Republic feel
any qualms about his lineage, and also to have compensated for his bad
qualities with his good ones. [6] He was granted his sixth consulship as a
reward for his meritorious service. But this consulship, too, should not be
cheated of its glory. This was the time when Servilius Glaucia and Saturninus Apuleius were tearing the Republic apart with back-to-back terms in
office and disrupting elections by armed violence and bloodshed. Marius
used the armed force available to a consul to suppress their violent excesses,
and he had these vicious individuals put to death in the Curia Hostilia.[44]

41. Marius held his second consulship in 104 BC. Rome had suffered a series of defeats before
this period. Quintus Servilius Caepio and Gnaeus Manilius Maximus were crushed in separate
battles on October 6, 105. Gnaeus Papirius Carbo (consul 113) was defeated at Noreia in Noricum. Marcus Junius Silanus suffered his loss in the vicinity of Lugdunum (Lyon) in the year of
his consulate, 109. Marcus Aurelius Scaurus (consul 108) was captured by the Cimbri when trying to prevent them from crossing the Alps and was executed by them for his arrogant attitude.

42. Gnaeus Domitius Ahenobarbus was tribune in 104 BC (Marius would have been elected
to his third consulship in that year but actually held it in 103). Previously, priests had been
replaced by co-option. Domitius carried a law that transferred their election to the people in
the *comitia tributa.* The law was repealed by Sulla, revived by Caesar, and possibly repealed
again by Mark Antony.

43. Marius defeated the Teutoni in a great victory at Aquae Sextiae (Aix-en-Provence) in
Transalpine Gaul in 102 BC and the Cimbri in 101 at Vercellae, aided by Quintus Lutatius
Catulus and Sulla. The Raudian Plains stretched along the left bank of the Po.

44. Marius held his sixth consulship in 100 BC. Lucius Apuleius Saturninus was initially seen
as his ally and as tribune provided land for Marius' veterans. Saturninus tried to secure the
consulship for his accomplice Gaius Servilius Glaucia, who was technically ineligible because
he held the praetorship and should have waited at least two years before seeking the next office.
They murdered his rival Gaius Memmius, a friend of Marius. The senate declared Saturninus
and Glaucia public enemies and authorized Marius to deal with them. He defeated them in a

[The tribune Livius Drusus fails to secure an accommodation with the Italians and is murdered in 91 BC. The bitterly fought Social War.]

13. A few years passed and then Marcus Livius Drusus entered the tribunate.[45] He was a man of the highest birth, extremely eloquent and virtuous, but his abilities and intellect were, in all that he did, superior to the success he achieved. [2] He dearly wished to restore to the senate its former eminence and transfer the legal process to that order from the equites. That authority the equites had acquired through the legislation of the Gracchi, who had inflicted severe damage on large numbers of very distinguished and perfectly innocent men. Notable among them was Publius Rutilius, one of the finest not only of his own generation but of any period.[46] They had tried him under the extortion law and, to the great anguish of the community, had found him guilty. However, in those very exertions that he underwent on behalf of the senate, Drusus found the senate standing against him. It did not understand that any proposals he made that were of benefit to the plebs were intended as a seductive inducement for the masses to let through more important reforms in return for trivial gains. [3] Eventually, Drusus' luck was such that the senate approved the villainous proposals of his colleagues over his own well-conceived measures. It rejected the prestige with which he was attempting to vest it and submitted quite calmly to the insults hurled at it by the others, eyeing Drusus' truly great distinction with envy while tolerating the inflated reputation of his colleagues.

14. Since his well-intentioned plans were faring badly, Drusus' thoughts turned to granting citizens' rights to Italy. He was at work on this when, after coming home from the Forum, surrounded by the great, unruly crowd that always accompanied him, he was stabbed in the courtyard of his house with

---

pitched battle on December 10, 100, after which they were put to death, though it is not certain that this was on Marius' orders.

The Curia Hostilia, built by tradition on the site of an Etruscan temple, was the assembly place of the senate from the time of King Tullius Hostilius in the seventh century BC. It was demolished under Sulla to make way for larger premises.

45. Marcus Livius Drusus was almost certainly the grandfather, by adoption, of Livia. Velleius does not allude to this relationship, which is often stated by modern sources as a fact, though there is no direct evidence to support it. It is noticeable, however, that Velleius says nothing of his negative attributes, such as the arrogance and cruelty reported in other sources, which may reflect Velleius' respect for this family connection. A man of considerable wealth, Livius Drusus entered the tribunate in 91 BC and championed a number of causes, including agrarian reform, the enfranchisement of Italians south of the Po, and a plan to raise three hundred equestrians to the senate and assign the law courts to them.

46. On Publius Rutilius Rufus, see 2.9.6.

a small knife, which was left stuck in his side, and he died within a few hours.[47] [2] As he breathed his last, he looked at the crowd standing grief-stricken around him and uttered words that well reflected his inner thoughts. "My friends and relatives," he said, "will the Republic ever see a citizen like me?" Such was the end of this illustrious young man. One piece of evidence illustrating his character must certainly not be omitted. [3] He was building his house on the Palatine on the spot where now stands the house that once belonged to Cicero, and subsequently to Censorinus (these days it belongs to Statilius Sisenna), and his architect undertook to build it in such a way that he would be out of public view and free of onlookers, with no one able to peer down into the building. "No," said Drusus. "Use whatever talent you have to construct my house in such a way that anything I do can be observed by everybody."[48]

15. Drusus' death brought to a head the long-festering Italian War, and in the consulship of Lucius Caesar and Publius Rutilius, 120 years ago, Italy as a whole took up arms against Rome. The lamentable affair started with the people of Asculum—they had killed the praetor Servilius and his legate Fonteius—and the cause was then taken up by the Marsi, after which it had permeated all regions of Italy.[49] [2] The fortune that overtook the Italians was grim, and their cause absolutely legitimate: they were seeking membership in a state whose empire they had been defending with their weapons. Through all the years and all the wars, they thought, they had been providing twice as many infantry and cavalry as the Romans, and yet they were not granted the right of citizenship in a state that, thanks to them, had reached heights from which it could disdain as outsiders and foreigners men who were of the same race and blood as they.

[3] That war wiped out more than three hundred thousand of Italy's young men. The most famous Roman commanders in the conflict were Gnaeus Pompeius, father of Gnaeus Pompey the Great; Gaius Marius, of whom we

---

47. Drusus died in early October of 91 BC. There were rumors that his death was suicide (Sen. *Brev. Vit.* 6.2), but most ancient authors opt for murder: Cic. *Mil.* 16; Liv. *Per.* 71; Suet. *Tib.* 3.2; App. *BC* 1.164; Florus 2.6.4; *Vir. Ill.* 66.3.

48. Despite the pressure of time under which he was supposedly operating, Velleius revels in providing inconsequential information: Lucius Marcius Censorinus was consul in 39 BC and had been one of only two senators to come to Caesar's aid during the assassination; he was later a supporter of Antony. Titus Statilius Sisenna was consul in 16. On Cicero, see 2.34.3. The tribune was to leave his door open at all times to those seeking his protection (Plut. *Quaest. Rom.* 81), but Drusus may also have been wanting higher visibility.

49. The conflict is variously called the "Italian War" or the "Social War" in the sources. Velleius used the former; modern authorities prefer the latter. The Social War lasted from 90 to 87 BC, the main battles occurring in 90–89. Rome was victorious in the end but achieved victory by the extension of citizenship. Asculum was a city in Picenum where assassinations occurred in 91.

spoke earlier; Lucius Sulla, who had held the praetorship the previous year; and Quintus Metellus, son of Numidicus, who had acquired the cognomen Pius, which was well deserved.[50] [4] Metellus' father had been exiled from the state by the plebeian tribune Lucius Saturninus because he alone had refused to swear obedience to Saturninus' legislation, and Metellus, through his own filial piety, and with the authority of the senate and full agreement of the Roman people, brought about his recall. And Metellus Numidicus was no more celebrated for his triumphs and public offices than he was for what occasioned his exile, the exile itself, and the manner of his return.

16. The most famous of the Italian commanders were Silo Popaedius, Herius Asinius, Insteius Cato, Gaius Pontidius, Telesinus Pontius, Marius Egnatius, and Papius Mutilus.[51] [2] And I shall not from modesty cheat my own family's bloodline of any honor it merits, as long as my claims are well founded; for a lot of respect is owed to the memory of my ancestor Minatus Magius of Aeculanum, who was the grandson of Decius Magius and a leading citizen of Capua, a man of great fame and reliability. In this war the loyalty he showed toward the Romans was such that, along with Titus Didius, he captured Herculaneum with a legion he had personally raised among the Hirpini, and alongside Lucius Sulla he laid siege to Pompeii and captured Compsa. [3] While others have recorded his valiant exploits, of particular note is the very clear account of Quintus Hortensius in his *Annals*.[52]

---

50. The war involved a number of distinguished Romans. Sulla and Marius are already familiar in Velleius' text. Gnaeus Pompeius, the father of Pompey the Great, fought in the Social War as legatus and in 89 BC as consul, when he captured Asculum and celebrated a discreet triumph at the end of that year.

   Quintus Caecilius Metellus Pius served with distinction in the Social War, most notably defeating one of the northern leaders, Quintus Poppaedius Silo (2.16.1); on his father, Quintus Caecilius Metellus Numidicus, see 2.11. The father, as censor, had tried to remove Saturninus (2.12.6) from office on grounds of immorality but was unable to persuade his colleague to support him. Saturninus introduced a law that obliged senators to swear allegiance to Marius. Marius in fact limited the obligation of senators to swearing allegiance to the agrarian law that awarded land to his veterans. Numidicus did not, however, accept the compromise and refused to swear even this limited allegiance; he was accordingly obliged to go into exile.

51. Two main groups opposed the Romans. The Marsi fought under a close friend of Drusus, Quintus Poppaedius Silo, who succeeded in defeating two Roman armies in 90 and 89 BC and in causing the deaths of their commanders then was defeated and killed in 88 by Metellus Pius. The Samnites were led by Gaius Papius Mutilus, who was defeated by the consul Lucius Caesar (2.15.1) in 90 and by Sulla in 89. Mutilus survived the war but committed suicide after being proscribed by Sulla. Velleius indulges his encyclopedic tendencies by listing the commanders of the minor tribes also. The Marrucini were led by Herius Asinius, the Telesini by Pontius Telesinus (2.27) and Martius Egnatius. Insteius Cato, whose name was in fact Publius Vettius Scato (Cic. *Phil.* 12.27), commanded the Peligni. Gaius Pontidius perhaps commanded the Vesitini.

52. Quintus Hortensius Hortalus (114–50 BC) was a distinguished orator who garnered

The Romans repaid Magius in full for this loyal service by making him a personal grant of citizenship and by electing his two sons praetors at a time when the number elected was still only six.[53]

[4] The Italian War's shifting fortunes and violent nature were such that, within a two-year period, two Roman consuls were killed by the enemy— Rutilius first, and then Porcius Cato—and the armies of the Roman people were routed in numerous locations, everyone now assuming the military cloak and remaining long in such attire.[54] The Italians had chosen Corfinium as their capital city and had named it Italica. Then the strength of the Romans was reconstituted by the gradual admission to citizenship of those who had either not taken up arms or had laid them down early on, while Pompeius, Sulla, and Marius also helped restore the faltering and sinking fortunes of the Roman Republic.

[Sulla's rise to prominence and his march on Rome (88 BC).]

17. Apart from some remnants of fighting around Nola, the Italian War was now mostly finished. It was a war that saw the Romans preferring to grant citizenship to a number of defeated and crushed peoples even though they had exhausted themselves, rather than give it to all of them when the Italians' power was unimpaired.[55] Now Quintus Pompeius and Lucius Cornelius Sulla entered the consulship.[56] Sulla was a man whose record cannot be highly enough praised up to the time he finally established his victory, nor amply reviled for the period following it. [2] He was born into a noble family, sixth in descent from Cornelius Rufinus, who had been among the most famous commanders in the war with Pyrrhus, but the family's distinction had faded and for a long time Sulla's conduct suggested that he had no intention of canvassing for the consulship.[57] [3] Then, following his

---

much praise for his powers as a speaker, rivaling Cicero. He wrote erotic poems and a treatise on oratory, as well as a historical work, the *Annales.*

53. The number of praetors was raised from four to six in 198 BC, then to eight, by Sulla, in 81.

54. Publius Rutilius Rufus, consul in 90 BC and commander of the Roman forces facing the Marsi, was killed in combat near Alba Fucens by Insteius Cato (Vettius Scato) in that year. Lucius Porcius Cato (consul 89) was killed in the same region by Popaedius Silo. The military cloak (*sagum*) was a simple rectangle of cloth, Gallic in origin, of coarse wool waterproofed with lanolin. It was the traditional garb of military service.

55. In 89 BC, under the *lex Iulia* and *lex Plautia Papiria,* full citizenship was granted to those Italians south of the Rubicon who requested it within sixty days.

56. Sulla (2.12.1), born probably in 138 BC, was elected consul in 89 and entered office in 88. During the Social War he inflicted a major defeat on the Campanian commander Aulus Cluentius but was then confronted by the siege of Nola, which lasted until 80.

57. Cornelius Rufinus was consul in 290 BC and in 277 was instrumental in the capture of

praetorship, having made a name for himself in the Italian War, and earlier as a legate under Marius in Gaul, where he had routed the most outstanding enemy leaders, he gained confidence as a result of his success. He stood for the consulship and was elected on the votes of almost all the citizens (though he did not gain that office until he was in his forty-ninth year).

18. Mithridates, king of Pontus, is not a person to be passed over in silence or taken lightly.[58] Dynamic in warfare and possessed of outstanding courage, he was a great man and, though sometimes great through luck, he was always great in spirit; in planning he was a general but in action a soldier, and for the Romans he had the hatred of a Hannibal. He had seized Asia and executed all Roman citizens within it, [2] having sent letters around the various communities and, with lavish promises of rewards, issued instructions for all the Romans to be put to death on the same day and at the same hour. [3] At that time nobody matched in courage the people of Rhodes in facing Mithridates and in loyalty to Rome, a loyalty highlighted by the treachery of the Mytileneans, who delivered Manius Aquilius and others to Mithridates in chains (though these later had their freedom restored by Pompey, as a personal favor to Theophanes).[59] Then, when Mithridates appeared to pose a terrifying threat to Italy, the province of Asia came by sortition to Sulla.

[4] Sulla left the city but was held up in the area of Nola.[60] This city was obstinately continuing its armed resistance—as if it regretted the consummate loyalty that it, more than all other cities, had displayed in the [Second] Punic War—and was under siege from a Roman army. [5] Meanwhile, the plebeian tribune Publius Sulpicius underwent a sudden personality change.[61]

Croton, an ally of the Samnites, during the war against Pyrrhus. Sulla was sixth in descent by inclusive reckoning (fifth in our terms).

58. Mithridates VI, king of Pontus, traced his descent from Darius I, king of Persia. He reigned at first with his brother, whom he murdered along with their mother, and as sole ruler extended his power in the Black Sea area, engaging in a series of wars with the Romans. In the first (89–85 BC) he conquered Bithynia and much of Asia, initially with the defection of Mytilene, which handed over to him Manius Aquilius (consul 101 with Marius), who had been sent to Asia to manage affairs. On a specific date in 88 Mithridates had most of the Roman and Italian residents of Asia put to death, supposedly 80,000 (or 150,000 in Plut. *Sull.* 24.4), during the so-called Asiatic Vespers. He was unable to take Rhodes but was generally welcomed in Greece.

59. Theophanes of Mytilene had subsequently become a supporter of the Romans and was a close confidant of Pompey the Great, mentioned here, and a historian of his war against Mithridates. It was he who advised Pompey to go to Egypt after the defeat at Pharsalus.

60. On Nola, see 2.17.

61. Publius Sulpicius Rufus was legate of Gnaeus Pompeius in the Social War and an orator of some distinction (see 2.9.2). Made tribune of the plebs in 88 BC with the aid of Sulla, he

An eloquent and dynamic man, well known for his wealth, his personal influence, his range of friendships, and his quick intelligence and strength of character, he had previously earned a very high standing with the people since his aims were irreproachable. Now, as if he were annoyed by his own virtues, and as if all his good measures were meeting with failure, [6] he turned evil and impetuously threw his support behind Gaius Marius, who, after his seventieth year, was still hungry for every command and every province. Sulpicius then placed before the people a bill by which Sulla's command would be annulled and the Mithridatic War assigned to Gaius Marius; and he also proposed other pernicious and venomous laws that were anathema to a free state. Indeed, he even had his henchmen in his faction put to death the consul Quintus Pompeius' son, who was also Sulla's son-in-law.[62]

19. Sulla then raised an army, returned to the city, and took it by force of arms. After that he drove out the twelve men behind the loathsome revolutionary measures, including Marius, Marius' son, and Publius Sulpicius, and passed legislation making them exiles.[63] Some horsemen even overtook Sulpicius in the Laurentian marshlands and assassinated him. The man's head was raised aloft and put on display before the Rostra, a forewarning of the proscriptions to come. [2] After six consulships, and now beyond his seventieth year, Marius was dragged naked and mud-covered from a reed bed in the area of the Marica marsh, where only his eyes and nose protruded above the water (he had hidden there while on the run from a posse of Sulla's horsemen). A strap was put around his neck and, on the orders of the duumvir, he was taken to the prison at Minturnae.

[3] A public slave, of German nationality, was sent to him armed with a sword, in order to kill him. It so happened that the slave had been taken

---

proved duplicitous and threw his support behind Marius, attempting to secure for him the command of the Mithridatic War in return for help with his debts. He made use of a series of bills dealing with the return of exiles, the expulsion of indebted senators, and the place of the newly enfranchised Italians in elections. Riots followed, but Sulpicius' bill was successful. He fled when Sulla marched on Rome; he was executed and his law abrogated.

62. Quintus Pompeius Rufus, a partisan of Sulla, was one of the orators heard by Cicero in his youth. He was praetor in 91 BC and consul in 88 with Sulla, and his son Quintus married Sulla's daughter Cornelia.

63. Sulla returned to Rome, supported by six legions (though his officers, with the exception of his relative Lucius Licinius Lucullus, deserted him), and occupied the city. He exhibited considerable brutality. Marius, who was born in 157 BC and thus in fact not quite seventy in 88, hid in the marshes near Minturnae, a town in Latium on the northwest bank of the Liris, then escaped to Ischia (Aenaria) in the Bay of Naples and then to Africa. His son was born about 110 and fled at the same time as his father and joined him in Africa, to return with him later. He received the consulship in 82 but was defeated in battle in that year by Sulla and died in the siege of Praeneste.

prisoner by Marius when the latter was commander in the war with the
Cimbri, and when he recognized him he let out a loud cry of indignation
over what had become of the great man, threw down the sword, and ran
from the prison. [4] The citizens, taught by an enemy to have compassion
for someone who had just recently been their leader, then furnished Marius
with traveling money, gave him some clothing, and put him on board a
ship. Marius caught up with his son close to the island of Aenaria and then
steered a course for Africa. There he endured an impoverished life in a hovel
amid the ruins of Carthage where, as he looked on Carthage and Carthage
gazed on him, each was able to provide solace for the other.

*[During Sulla's campaign against Mithridates, Cornelius Cinna and Marius
take control of Rome (87 BC).]*

20. This year, for the first time, the hands of a Roman soldier were stained
with the blood of a Roman consul when Sulla's colleague Quintus Pompeius was killed by the army of the proconsul Gnaeus Pompeius in a mutiny
that its commander had himself fomented.[64]

[2] Cinna had no more self-discipline than Marius and Sulpicius.[65] The
citizenship had been granted to Italy on the understanding that the new
citizens would be concentrated in eight tribes so that their voting strength and
numbers would not diminish the influence of the older citizens, and that
those receiving the benefit would not have greater power than those bestow-
ing it. Cinna instead promised to distribute them among all the tribes, and
with that in view had brought into the city huge crowds from all over Italy.

[3] He was, however, driven out by the combined influence of his colleague and the *optimates,* and when he was heading for Campania he was,
by senatorial authority, relieved of his consulship and replaced by the Flamen of Jupiter, Lucius Cornelius Merula. Such an insult was worthy of the

---

64. Quintus Pompeius Rufus (2.18) was sent to take over the army of a distant relative, Gnaeus Pompeius Strabo (2.15.3). He was killed by Strabo's troops.

65. Lucius Cornelius Cinna, of a patrician family, campaigned successfully in the Social War.
Despite Sulla's opposition he became consul in 87 BC, along with Gnaeus Octavius; on the
departure of Sulla for the east, Cinna set about reviving the measures of Sulpicius (2.18) to
manipulate the newly enfranchised Italians within the voting system. This led to violent opposition and he was illegally deposed by his colleague Octavius and replaced by Lucius Cornelius Merula, who, as Flamen of Jupiter, was technically not allowed a political career. He allied
himself with Marius, collected an army of legionaries and Italians, and succeeded in taking
Rome. This led to savage reprisals against Sulla's supporters, which Cinna tried unsuccessfully
to prevent. Merula committed suicide (see 2.22). Cinna held successive consulships from 87
to 84 when he was killed in a mutiny. His daughter Cornelia married Julius Caesar and bore
him Julia, who married Pompey.

individual but did not set a worthy precedent. [4] Cinna then first of all bribed centurions and tribunes, but subsequently even the rank and file, with promises of reward and was thus welcomed by the army that was in the environs of Nola. When the force swore loyalty to him in its entirety, he made war on his native land still wearing the consul's insignia, and he did so relying on the huge numbers of new citizens, from whom he had managed to raise by conscription more than three hundred cohorts, a complement equivalent to thirty legions. [5] What his party needed was prestige, and to bolster that he recalled from exile Gaius Marius and his son, and the others who had been driven out with them.

21. As I explained above, the Republic had availed itself of the exceptional services of Gnaeus Pompeius, father of Pompey the Great, in the war against the Marsi, especially in the area of Picenum, where he had captured Asculum. (It was near Asculum that 75,000 Roman citizens and more than 60,000 Italians had clashed in a single day, although troops were spread out in many other areas as well.) While Cinna made war on his native land, [2] Pompeius lost hope of another term in the consulship and now adopted an equivocal, neutral posture toward both sides.[66] It appeared that all his actions were in the furtherance of his own interests and that he was watching out for favorable opportunities as he turned this way and that with his army, wherever some prospect of power seemed to glitter more brightly.

[3] Finally, however, he came to grips with Cinna in a momentous and savage battle. It was started and brought to completion close to the walls of the city of Rome and under its eyes, and how disastrous the outcome was for the fighters and spectators alike can scarcely be expressed in words. [4] After it, both armies, as though insufficiently exhausted by the war, were racked by a plague, and Gnaeus Pompeius died. The joy over his death, it was thought, almost compensated for the loss of the citizens carried off by the sword or disease, and the people of Rome directed onto the dead man's corpse the anger they had owed him in his lifetime.

[5] Whether there were two or three Pompeii families, the first consul of that name was Quintus Pompeius (who had Gnaeus Servilius as his colleague), some 172 years ago.[67]

[6] Cinna and Marius took possession of the city after a number of battles that saw much blood spilled on both sides. Cinna, however, entered first, and he drafted a bill for Marius' recall.

---

66. On Pompeius Strabo's role in the Social War, see 2.15.3. He was asked to defend Rome against Cinna but initially played an ambiguous role and negotiated with Cinna over the possibility of a joint consulship. When he died in the plague, his body was dragged through the streets.

67. The three Pompeian families were the Bithynici, the Rufi, and the Strabones, to which Pompeius Magnus belonged. Quintus Pompeius was consul in 141 BC.

22. Soon Gaius Marius arrived in the city, in a return that spelled catastrophe for his fellow citizens. Nothing would have been more savage than that victory had not Sulla's soon followed it. Nor was it just on the lowly that the unrestrained sword wreaked its havoc; the most eminent and distinguished men of the body politic had various kinds of punishment inflicted on them, too.[68] [2] These included the consul Octavius, a man of the meekest disposition, who was executed on Cinna's orders. Merula, however, who had resigned his consulship just before Cinna's arrival, severed his veins. While his blood flowed over the altar, Merula prayed to the gods to whom he had, as Flamen of Jupiter, often prayed for the safety of the Republic, calling on them to curse Cinna and his party, and then he surrendered his soul, one that had done so well by the Republic. [3] Marcus Antonius, a leading statesman and orator, was, on orders from Marius and Cinna, run through by the swords of some soldiers whom he had held back for a time by his eloquence. [4] Then there was Quintus Catulus, a man renowned for his various fine attributes, and particularly for his glorious record, which he had in common with Marius, in the war against the Cimbri. When he was being hunted down for execution, he shut himself in a room that had just been finished off with a coating of chalk and sand. He then applied fire to the surface of the coating to bring out the strong fumes and, by breathing in the deadly vapors and holding his breath, brought on himself the death his enemies wanted, but not in a manner of their choosing.

[5] Everything was going to rack and ruin in the Republic, and yet there was still no one to be found who would dare make a gift of any Roman citizen's property or had the effrontery to claim it for himself. Later on, this point was also reached, where greed offered a motive for brutality and the extent of a person's "guilt" was established by the extent of his fortune: a man of means became a guilty party and was himself always the reward for the danger that he had to face. Nothing that brought gain appeared immoral.

[Sulla's campaign against Mithridates after the death of Marius in 86 BC, and his return to Italy and second seizure of Rome (83–82).]

23. Cinna then embarked on his second consulship and Marius on his seventh, bringing discredit upon his previous six. He died at the start of it,

---

68. The victims of Cinna included Gnaeus Octavius, a supporter of Sulla and Cinna's fellow consul of 87 BC, when he had Cinna deposed (see 2.20). After the death of Pompeius Strabo the senate surrendered the city and Octavius died, wearing his consular robes. The distinguished orator Marcus Antonius (2.9) had initially been a friend of Marius but later turned against him and paid the price for it after Marius' recall. Quintus Lutatius Catulus had served with distinction with Marius during the German invasions (2.12.2) and had shared in his triumph but later became a major opponent. He was prosecuted by Marius' nephew after Marius' return and committed suicide. He was a highly cultured individual and a patron of literary figures.

struck down by a disease, a man vicious toward his enemies in war and toward his fellow citizens in peace, and one who could not stand inactivity.[69] [2] He was replaced by Valerius Flaccus, who had proposed a disgraceful law under which he stipulated that creditors be repaid only a quarter of an outstanding debt—an act for which well-deserved punishment overtook him within two years.[70] [3] While Cinna held power in Italy, most of the nobility sought refuge with Sulla in Achaea, and later in Asia.

Sulla meanwhile fought with Mithridates' commanders in the area of Athens, in Boeotia and in Macedonia, recovering Athens and also killing two hundred thousand men and taking just as many captives on the conclusion of his strenuous efforts around the port of Piraeus' multiple fortifications. [4] Anyone blaming the Athenians for this period of rebellion, during which Athens was besieged by Sulla, clearly has no knowledge of the historical truth. So steadfast was Athenian loyalty to Rome that, on all occasions and in all circumstances, the Romans would refer to any action that was taken with transparent loyalty as being carried out "with Athenian loyalty." [5] At that time, however, these people, oppressed by Mithridates' military power, were in a wretched plight, held in subjection by their enemies and being besieged by their friends; their hearts lay beyond their fortifications, but, bowing to necessity, their bodies remained within the walls.

[6] Sulla then crossed over to Asia where he found Mithridates totally compliant and submissive. Exacting a financial indemnity from him and confiscating a number of his ships, he forced him to leave Asia and all the other provinces that he had seized by force of arms. He also recovered prisoners of war, punished deserters and other miscreants, and ordered Mithridates to remain content with the territory of his forefathers, that is, with Pontus.[71]

24. Before Sulla's arrival, a cavalry commander, Gaius Flavius Fimbria, had put to death a former consul, Valerius Flaccus.[72] He had then taken over

69. Marius died on January 17, 86 BC.

70. Valerius Flaccus, having served as governor of Asia after his praetorship, became suffect consul on the death of Marius and enacted a law that canceled three-quarters of all debts. He was given command of the war against Mithridates (see 2.24 for his death).

71. After Cinna became consul, Sulla set out for Greece, where Athens had sided with Mithridates. Athens surrendered to Sulla on March 1, 86 BC, and after a bitter siege, Piraeus surrendered on March 15. Velleius telescopes Sulla's later campaign, which took up 86 and early 85 and involved two major victories in Boeotia. Peace was concluded with Mithridates in August of 85.

72. Gaius Flavius Fimbria was the son of the consul of the same name of 104 BC. He supported Cinna and went to Asia in 86 as legate of Lucius Valerius Flaccus, but fell out with him and stirred up a mutiny in which Flaccus was killed. He took over Flaccus' army and scored many successes against Mithridates, shutting him off at Pitane. He could have captured him

Flaccus' army and been proclaimed imperator, after which he was successful in defeating Mithridates in a ferocious battle. Just before Sulla's arrival, however, he committed suicide. Detestable though his ventures had been, he was a young man who had at least carried them out courageously. [2] That same year the plebeian tribune Publius Laenas had Sextus Lucilius, a plebeian tribune the previous year, hurled from the Tarpeian Rock, and when his colleagues, against whom he had brought charges, sought refuge with Sulla out of fear, he had them forbidden water and fire.[73] [3] Sulla now became the very first Roman to whom envoys came from the Parthians, and among them were some magi who, on the basis of various marks on his body, made the oracular prediction that his life and posthumous reputation would be those of a god.[74] So, when he had settled affairs overseas, he returned to Italy and at Brundisium disembarked no more than 30,000 men under arms to face an enemy in excess of 200,000. [4] I would consider hardly anything in Sulla's career more splendid than this, that during the three-year period that Marius' and Cinna's supporters had Italy in their grip, he neither concealed his intention to make war on them nor abandoned the war that he had on his hands.[75] He thought that the enemy needed to be crushed before revenge should be taken on a fellow citizen, and that only when the threat from abroad had been fought off, and when he had defeated the external foe, should he surmount the domestic problem.

[5] Before Lucius Sulla's arrival, Cinna was killed by his troops during a mutiny, though he deserved rather a death of his victors' choosing than one that came from his soldiers' wrath.[76] It can be truly said of him that he dared to do things that no decent man would dare to do, but also that he achieved

---

had Lucullus (2.33) cooperated with his fleet. Fimbria treated the communities who had proved disloyal with considerable severity. After Sulla had made peace with Mithridates, he directed his troops against Fimbria.

73. This murder is dated to January 1, 86 BC. Livy (*Per.* 80.9) and Plutarch (*Mar.* 45.1) name Marius as the perpetrator and give the victim's name as Sextus Licinius. Publius Laenas is not mentioned in any other source. The denial of fire and water was the formal designation for a form of exile.

74. Plutarch reports that the embassy was headed by Orobazus and that a Chaldean in his retinue was able to predict Sulla's greatness from his physiognomy (*Sull.* 5). The magi (whose name seems to be of Old Persian origin) were members of a hereditary priestly class though not strictly priests in the conventional sense. They were experts in divination and the interpretation of dreams. By Velleius' day the term was often loosely applied to astrologers and soothsayers.

75. Cinna's continuous tenure of the consulship 87–84 BC was in violation of the *lex Villia Annalis* of 180, which laid down intervals between the senior magistracies.

76. Cinna had sailed to the Illyrian coast probably with the intention of facing Sulla, but his fleet was dispersed in a storm and he returned to Ancona. He was killed by his troops when he was about to renew the attempt.

what could be achieved by none but the most courageous, and that while he was reckless in his plans he was a man in carrying them through. Carbo remained sole consul throughout the year, with no colleague for him elected in Cinna's place.[77]

25. One might have thought Sulla had come to Italy not to prosecute a war but to establish peace, so tranquil was his progress with the army through Calabria and Apulia and into Campania. He made a special effort to spare crops, agricultural land, people, and cities, and tried to terminate hostilities on fair terms and with equitable provisions; but peace could not be pleasing to men whose circumstances were dire and their avarice boundless.

[2] Meanwhile, Sulla's forces were growing every day as all the best and most clear-thinking men flocked to his cause. Then, by a lucky stroke, he defeated the consuls Scipio and Norbanus near Capua.[78] Norbanus was overcome in battle, but Scipio was deserted by his army and handed over to Sulla, by whom he was set free unharmed. [3] So unlike were Sulla the warrior and Sulla the victor: while winning his victories he was more lenient <than the most reasonable man>, but after a victory he was more ruthless than any on record. As I noted above, he set the consul free, unharmed, after taking his weapons, as he did in the case of Quintus Sertorius—and what a war that man would soon ignite!—and many others who came into his power.[79] I suppose his aim was to provide a clear example of a dual and contradictory character in the same person!

[4] After his victory on Mount Tifata <where . . .> he had encountered Gaius Norbanus, Sulla gave his thanks to Diana, to whose divine power that region was sacred, dedicating to the goddess the waters famous for their

---

77. Gnaeus Papirius Carbo had fought in the Social War, and in 87 BC he supported Cinna, who regarded him highly enough to make him colleague in his consulships of 85 and 84. He gave up the consulship at the end of the year but resumed it in 82, with Marius as colleague, and campaigned unsuccessfully against Sulla, Quintus Metellus, and Pompey. He fled to Africa, where he was captured by Pompey and executed.

78. Of the two consuls of 83 BC, Gaius Norbanus, an old supporter of Marius, was defeated near Casilinum and took refuge in Capua, which Sulla allowed him to leave. He was defeated again in the following year in Gaul and fled to Rhodes, where he committed suicide while the Rhodians debated handing him over to Sulla. The other consul, Lucius Cornelius Scipio Asiaticus, was taken prisoner in his camp and allowed to leave. He appeared in the proscription list the following year and fled to Massilia (Marseille).

79. Quintus Sertorius was a distinguished commander who fought with Marius against the Cimbri and later campaigned in Spain and in the Social War, where he lost an eye. He continued the struggle against Sulla longer than any of his other opponents, first in Spain and then in Mauretania. Returning to Spain he raised a force and pursued a guerrilla campaign. He became the dominant figure in Spain and made links with Mithridates and the Cilician pirates. He went on to suffer a number of failures and was eventually murdered by a subordinate, Marcus Perpenna (2.30).

health-giving and healing properties, and all the adjacent lands.[80] An inscription affixed to a doorpost of the temple as well as a bronze tablet within the shrine even today bear witness to this religious act of gratitude.

26. The consuls next entering office were Carbo (for the third time) and Gaius Marius, then twenty-six, the son of the man who had been consul seven times.[81] Marius was blessed with his father's enterprise, though not his <longevity>, and in his many courageous exploits he never as consul let down the family name. Defeated in battle by Sulla at Sacriportus, he withdrew with his troops to Praeneste, whose natural defenses he had earlier strengthened with a garrison.

[2] To ensure that it nowhere went short of national afflictions, the state that had always striven to lead in virtues now strove to lead in criminality, and those who thought themselves the best of people were the worst offenders. While the fighting went on at Sacriportus, the praetor Damasippus had the following men cut down in the Curia Hostilia, purportedly as supporters of Sulla's party: Domitius <. . . >; even Scaevola, *pontifex maximus* and a renowned authority on religious and secular law; the former praetor Gaius Carbo, brother of a consul; and the former aedile Antistius.[82] [3] I pray that the renown of the noble deed of Antistius' wife Calpurnia, daughter of Bestia, not fade away—when her husband was murdered, as I just noted, she ran herself through with a sword. How she added luster to this man's glory and fame! Now he enjoys distinction thanks to a woman's courage, though his own is not inconspicuous.[83]

---

80. Mount Tifata is some three miles north of Capua. The famous temple of Diana Tifata was located on its southwest slope.

81. On Marius' death in 86 BC the leadership of his faction was assumed by his son, who shared his father's name, Gaius Marius, but, despite Velleius' encomium, seems to have lacked his leadership qualities. Although still young (born between 110 and 108), he was elected consul in 82. His colleague was Gaius Papirius Carbo (2.24), who used his name to rouse support against Sulla. Marius was defeated by Sulla at the battle of Sacriportus and withdrew to Praeneste with his surviving troops. As the siege drew to its close, he committed suicide.

82. Lucius Junius Brutus Damasippus was praetor in 82 BC. Lucius Domitius was the brother of Gnaeus Domitius (2.12). On Quintus Mucius Scaevola, see 2.9. Gaius Papirius Carbo Arvina, brother of Gnaeus Papirius Carbo (2.24), was an opponent of the reforms of Marcus Livius Drusus and was praetor, probably in 83, as a supporter of Cinna. Publius Antistius was tribune of the plebs in 88 and aedile in 86. Plutarch (*Pomp.* 4.2–3) claims that the daughter of the "praetor" Antistius was secretly betrothed to Pompey the Great.

83. Velleius is our only source on the noble death of Calpurnia. Her conduct stands in contrast to that of her father, Lucius Calpurnius Bestia, who as consul in command against Jugurtha took bribes from him and was later condemned by the commission set up to investigate misconduct in the war (Sall. *Jug.* 29.1).

27. The Samnite chieftain Pontius Telesinus, a man of great spirit and out-standing fortitude in war, had a deep-seated hatred of the Roman race and had brought together some forty thousand courageous young warriors who were resolutely determined to remain under arms.[84] On November 1 in the consulship of Carbo and Marius (111 years ago), he put up such a fight with Sulla at the Colline Gate that he brought both Sulla and the Republic into the most dire peril. [2] The state faced no greater danger when it sighted Hanni-bal's camp within the third milestone than it did on that day. Darting about the ranks of his army, Telesinus kept exclaiming that the Romans' final day had come, and loudly urged his men to destroy the city root and branch—there would be no end to the wolves devouring Italy's liberty, he added, unless the wood where they habitually sought refuge were cut down. [3] It was only after the first hour of the night that the Roman forces recovered their breath and those of the enemy withdrew. The following day Telesinus was found half dead, wearing the expression of a victor rather than a dying man. Sulla or-dered his head cut off and carried on display around Praeneste.

[4] Finally despairing of his situation, the young Marius then attempted to break out of the town using the tunnels—an amazing piece of engineering—that led out to different areas of the countryside. However, after emerging through an aperture from under the ground, he was killed by men posted there expressly for that purpose. [5] There are some who claim that he died by his own hand, and some that he died alongside Telesinus' younger brother, who joined him in the escape attempt after enduring the siege with him, the two running onto each other's swords. Whatever the manner of his death, his memory is not dimmed even today by the towering image of his father. Sulla's opinion of the young man is clear; it was only after Marius' death that he adopted the name Felix, one that he would have been most justified in taking up if the end of his life had coincided with the end of his victories. [6] The commanding officer in the siege of Marius at Praeneste had been Afella Lucretius, who had earlier been a supporter of the party of Marius but had gone over to Sulla.[85]

---

84. Pontius Telesinus came from Telesia in Samnium. He was a general in the Social War (see 2.16). In 82 BC he commanded the Samnites and Lucani with Marcus Lamponius and at-tempted unsuccessfully to relieve the beleaguered Marius in Praeneste. When that failed, he turned against Rome. He advanced to within almost a mile of the Colline Gate but Sulla ar-rived in time to defeat him. The battle of the Colline Gate, in November of 82, marked the final battle by which Sulla took control of Italy and the last major battle to be fought by the Samnites. The Samnite prisoners were executed afterward on the Via Publica.

85. Quintus Lucretius Afella (or Ofella) was initially a supporter of Marius but switched al-legiance to Sulla and took Praeneste. He sent Sulla Marius' head. Lucretius was killed on Sulla's instructions during his bid for the consulate of 81 BC.

Sulla paid enduring honor to the good fortune of the day that saw the defeat of the army of the Samnites and Telesinus by instituting games in the Circus to commemorate it in perpetuity. These are still celebrated under his name as "The Victory of Sulla."[86]

28. A short time before Sulla's battle at Sacriportus, four supporters of his cause had routed enemy armies in superb engagements: the two Servilii at Clusium, Metellus Pius at Faventia, and Marcus Lucullus in the environs of Fidentia.[87]

[2] It looked as if the woes of civil war were at an end when they were multiplied by Sulla's ruthlessness. He was made dictator, a position that had fallen into disuse for 120 years.[88] (The last person to hold it did so the year after Hannibal's departure from Italy, which makes it clear that, while the Roman people favored employing a dictator in times of dread, they also feared such power in peacetime.) That office his predecessors had used in the past to safeguard the Republic in times of the most dire peril, but Sulla used it to unleash an orgy of cruelty. [3] It was he who initially established the precedent of proscription—and I wish he had been the last to use it! The result was that in a society where abusive language called for court proceedings <. . .> a fee was established officially for the murder of a Roman citizen, with that man gaining the most who had killed the most. It meant that the prize for killing an enemy was no more generous than that for killing a citizen, and each man became the reward for his own death. [4] Nor was the savagery restricted to those who had taken up arms against Sulla; it was directed against many innocent people, too. An added affliction was the sale of the goods belonging to the proscribed, with children being debarred from inheriting their parents' wealth and denied the right to stand for office. And so at the same time—the most appalling thing of all—sons of senators were shouldered with the burdens of their rank but also lost its privileges.

---

86. The games instituted by Sulla were celebrated from October 27 to November 1.

87. There is no further information on the two Servilii, although one was presumably Publius Servilius Vatia, an adherent of Sulla elected consul in 79 BC. Metellus inflicted a major defeat on Carbo, who was trying to prevent him from reaching Ariminium. The Lucullus mentioned here is the brother of the famous Lucius Licinius Lucullus (2.33). Born Marcus Licinius Lucullus, he was later adopted by a Marcus Terentius Varro (not the writer); he defeated Quintus, the subordinate of Carbo, between Placentia and Fidentia.

88. On the deaths of Marius and Carbo, Lucius Valerius Flaccus was commissioned to preside over the election of suffect consuls, and proposed, in December of 82 BC, the law by which Sulla become dictator. Quintus Fabius Maximus Cunctator had been appointed dictator in the full sense in 216, during the military crisis of the Second Punic War, but in citing a gap of 120 years Velleius seems to have in mind Gaius Servilius Geminus, who was appointed dictator in 202 for the purpose of presiding over the elections, the most common reason for such appointments.

[Pompey's rise to prominence. His success against Sertorius in Spain and his special command against the pirates (67 BC).]

29. Gnaeus Pompey was the son of that Gnaeus Pompeius whose superb record in the Marsian War during his consulship I touched on above.[89] Just before Lucius Sulla's arrival in Italy, this man, at the age of twenty-three (that is, 113 years ago), relied on his private resources and his own enterprise to launch a daring project, which he splendidly brought to fruition. To champion his fatherland and restore its dignity, he brought together at Firmum an army drawn from the territory of Picenum that was filled entirely with his father's clients. [2] The man's greatness would require many volumes, but the scope of my work limits me to a few words on him.

He was, through his mother Lucilia, the descendant of a senatorial family.[90] He possessed strikingly good looks, not those that characterize the bloom of youth but the kind that came from an enduring dignity and matched his distinction and good fortune—looks that remained with him till his final day. [3] He was a man of outstanding integrity and exceptional moral probity but mediocre oratorical ability. He had a fervent craving for power that could be conferred on him as a mark of distinction, but not power needing to be taken by force; he was a very skillful military commander and in civilian life the most level-headed citizen, except when he feared he might have an equal. In friendships he was steadfast; he could be moved by appeals when wronged; he was extremely loyal when reconciliation was effected; and he very readily accepted apologies. He never, or only rarely, employed his power to excess and was almost completely free of character flaws, [4] unless indignation over seeing anyone equal to him in prestige is to be counted among the greatest of flaws in a free state that is mistress of the world, a state in which one would be right to regard all citizens as one's equals.

[5] From the time of adopting the *toga virilis* Pompey had received his military training under a very shrewd leader, his father, and had cultivated

---

89. Gnaeus Pompeius Magnus, Pompey the Great, was one of the dominating personalities of the late Republic. The *gens Pompeia,* from the region of Picenum between the Apennines and the Adriatic Sea, gained stature from the early second century. Born in 106 BC, Pompey served with his father (see 2.15.3, 2.21.1) at Asculum in 89 and in 83 used a private army of his father's veterans and family clients to fight for Sulla. Although he had held no office, he campaigned in Sicily as propraetor, where he killed Papirius Carbo, and in Africa, where he defeated Gnaeus Domitius and King Iarbas. Sulla grudgingly allowed him a triumph for this last victory in 81, though he was only twenty-five and had not held a regular magistracy. In 77 he was sent as proconsul to Spain to assist Metellus Pius against Sertorius, despite not having been consul.

90. Pompey's mother was the daughter of Manius Lucilius, brother of the famous satirist Gaius Lucilius (2.9.4).

a fine natural talent, which was able to grasp all that was best, through a superb grounding in the practicalities of the military arts. <...> The result was that while Metellus received higher praise from Sertorius, it was Pompey who aroused greater fear in him.

30. At that time one of the proscribed men, the ex-praetor Marcus Perpenna, who was distinguished more for his family background than for his character, murdered Sertorius during a dinner at Osca.[91] By this foul crime he secured certain victory for the Romans, annihilation for his own party, and a most ignominious death for himself. [2] Metellus and Pompey triumphed over the Spanish provinces.[92] Even at the time of this triumph Pompey was still a Roman equestrian, but he nevertheless rode the chariot into the city the day before taking up his consulship. [3] Who could not feel surprise that this man, who rose to the top by so many extraordinary commands, should have been aggrieved over the Roman senate and people officially recognizing Gaius Caesar's candidacy, <in absentia>, for a second consulship?[93] It is such a common human inclination to forgive oneself anything but overlook no failing in others, and to base resentment over things not on the facts but on other people's motives and personality. [4] In this consulship of his, Pompey restored the power of the tribunate, in which Sulla had left remaining only a trace of its former authority.

[5] While the war with Sertorius was going on in Spain, sixty-four runaway slaves, led by Spartacus, escaped from a gladiatorial school in Capua.[94]

91. Marcus Perpenna (or Perperna) Veiento supported Marius. Praetor in 82 BC, he was sent to Sicily but abandoned it to Pompey. He became involved in the rebellion of Marcus Aemilius Lepidus, who in 77 tried unsuccessfully to march on Rome (an event not mentioned by Velleius). On Lepidus' death he took the remnants of his army to Spain, joining with those of Sertorius. After Sertorius' assassination, Perpenna took command of his army but was defeated by Pompey. He sought to ingratiate himself with Pompey by turning over papers of Sertorius that implicated a number of leading Romans in an attempt to subvert the constitution established by Sulla. Pompey ordered the papers destroyed and Perpenna executed.

92. Pompey celebrated his second triumph for his Spanish campaign on December 29, 71 BC (Metellus Pius a few days before), and assumed the consulship in 70, even though he had not yet entered into a senatorial career and his status was still technically equestrian. Pompey, along with Crassus, restored to the tribunes the full right of veto even over the actions of superior magistrates (*intercessio*), restricted by Sulla, and removed the bar against their later running for other offices.

93. Apart from the extraordinary consulship in 70 BC, Pompey later received other extraordinary appointments, such as the command against the pirates, granted by the *lex Gabinia* of 67 (see 2.31), and the assignments of the provinces of Bithynia and Cilicia, as well as the command against Mithridates and Tigranes, with extraordinary authority over the armies in the east, granted by the *lex Manilia* of 66 (see 2.33.1). On Julius Caesar's second consulship, see 2.46.

94. Spartacus, a Thracian by birth, led a slave revolt in 73 BC that originated in the gladiatorial

They took swords from the town and headed first for Mount Vesuvius; and soon, as their numbers swelled each day, they brought upon Italy all manner of serious problems. [6] So great did their numbers become that in the last battle that they fought <40,800> men faced the Roman army. The distinction of finishing off this business lay with Marcus Crassus, soon <to be leading man of all in the Republic>.[95]

31. The charisma of Gnaeus Pompey had attracted the attention of the whole world, and he was in every sphere considered to be greater than an ordinary citizen. While he was consul he had very admirably sworn that he would not, on leaving that office, take up any of the provinces, and he had kept the promise. [2] Two years later, however, pirates were terrorizing the world, fighting a war rather than conducting raids, and using fleets of ships rather than making secretive forays, and they had even sacked a number of Italian cities. At this point the tribune Aulus Gabinius proposed a bill authorizing Gnaeus Pompey to be sent out to crush the pirates and to be granted authority in all the provinces, on a par with that of the proconsular governors, as far as the fiftieth milestone from the sea.[96] [3] By that decree an attempt was being made to put power over virtually the entire world in the hands of one man, although this same authority had actually been decreed seven years earlier in the case of Marcus Antonius, when he was praetor.[97] [4] But it sometimes happens that personality appears to set a bad precedent, increasing or diminishing antipathy toward the individual. In

---

school of Gnaeus Lentulus Baliatus. The number of slaves who broke out varies in the ancient sources between 30 and 78 (Liv. *Per.* 95.2 gives 74). They inflicted defeats on a number of armies sent against them, including those of the consuls of 72.

95. Marcus Licinius Crassus, son of the consul of 97 BC, supported Sulla. Forced by Cinna's proscriptions to flee to Spain, he went to Africa after Cinna's death and attached himself to Sulla's supporters there. He then joined Sulla in Italy and played an important role in the battle of the Colline Gate (see 2.27). He made a fortune in the proscriptions that Sulla initiated and thus became an important figure after Sulla's death. He financed and raised the army that he used to crush Spartacus' rebellion. The subsequent attempt by Pompey to steal credit for the victory was the source of much bitterness.

96. In 67 BC the tribune Aulus Gabinius enacted a law to give Pompey command against the pirates and threatened another tribune, Trebellius, with expulsion when he tried to oppose him. Gabinius later held the consulship (in 58) and was fiercely opposed by Cicero.

97. Marcus Antonius Creticus, father of Mark Antony, was praetor in 74 BC and for the following year had the extraordinary command to clear the Mediterranean of pirates and thus assist operations against Mithridates. There is a quiet humor in Velleius' words. Antonius was a dismal failure; he exploited the provinces he was supposed to protect and attacked Crete, which was allied with the pirates, but he suffered a major defeat and could save himself only with a dishonorable peace; he died there in 73. The honorific cognomen Creticus, first mentioned by writers much later than Antonius, was ironic.

the case of Antonius people accepted the situation with equanimity, for one rarely begrudges honors to those whose power one does not fear. By contrast, people fear extraordinary powers in the hands of those who look as if they will capriciously relinquish them or hold onto them, the only thing restraining them being their own whims. The *optimates* opposed the bill, but their advice foundered in the prevailing fervor.

32. The authority and modesty of Quintus Catulus deserve to be put on record.[98] When he spoke against Gabinius' bill in a popular assembly, Catulus observed that while Gnaeus Pompey was a man of distinction, he already had too much power for a free state, and that everything should not be placed in the hands of one man. He then added: "If something happens to this person, with whom would you replace him?" to which the assembly replied in unison, "With you, Quintus Catulus."

At that Catulus left the assembly, overwhelmed by the general unanimity of opinion and such an appreciative tribute from the citizens. [2] Here I want to express my admiration for the man's self-restraint and the people's sense of fair play: in Catulus' case for not continuing his opposition, and in the people's for refusing to cheat the man out of an honest tribute despite his opposition to their wishes.

[3] In the same time period Cotta divided equally between the two orders the judicial prerogatives that Gaius Gracchus had snatched from the senate and given to the equestrians, and which Sulla had then transferred back to the senate.[99] Otho Roscius also saw a law through that restored to the equestrians their places in the theater.[100]

[4] Meanwhile, Gnaeus Pompey recruited many distinguished men for this war and deployed naval detachments in almost all the nooks and crannies of

---

98. Quintus Lutatius Catulus was the son of the distinguished general who, with Marius, defeated the Cimbri at Vercellae (see 2.12). He joined Sulla when the latter returned to Rome, and with Sulla's support he obtained the consulship in 78 BC. He played a major role in suppressing the rebellion of Marcus Aemilius Lepidus (see note 91) and became the champion of the *optimates*. He opposed the *lex Gabinia* in 67 and the *lex Manilia* in 66.

99. Lucius Aurelius Cotta was praetor in 70 BC when he introduced the *lex Aurelia,* which removed the rule restricting service as juror exclusively to the rank of senators, as enacted by Sulla. Under the new law jurors were to be recruited equally from senators, equestrians, and *tribuni aerarii* (the functions of the last are uncertain, but they seem to have been classed as equestrians). Cotta became consul in 65. He supported Cicero in his actions against Catiline (see 2.34.3) and in the period after Cicero's exile.

100. The tribune Lucius Roscius Otho in 67 BC restored privileges to the equestrians via the *lex Roscia Theatralis.* Senators occupied the orchestra in the theater and in setting aside the first fourteen rows of seats for the equestrians, Roscius' law apparently revived an old rule (about which we have no direct information).

the coast. In a short time he liberated the world by means of his invincible forces, getting the better of the pirates in many locations on many <seas> and then, after attacking them with his fleet off Cilicia, completely routing them. [5] The sooner to bring such a widespread conflict to an end, he brought together what remained of them and settled them in fixed abodes in cities that were on land far removed from the sea. [6] There are some who criticize this measure, but while it might in any case appear reasonable simply because of its deviser, the reasoning behind it would make anyone who devised it "Great." For, by giving the pirates the chance to make a living without looting, Pompey kept them from looting.

[Pompey's command against a resurgent Mithridates (66 BC). Rome is meanwhile threatened by the Catilinarian conspiracy, which is crushed by Cicero in 63.]

33. The war against the pirates was now at an end when the plebeian tribune Manilius, who was always corrupt and ready to work as a tool of someone else in power, proposed a bill assigning conduct of the Mithridatic War to Gnaeus Pompey.[101] Seven years earlier Lucius Lucullus had, following his consulship, gained by sortition the governorship of Asia, where he had faced Mithridates and achieved great and memorable successes.[102] He had inflicted several defeats on Mithridates in numerous locations; he had liberated Cyzicus with an outstanding victory; he had beaten Tigranes, a great king, in Armenia; but he had been almost unwilling, rather than unable, to put the finishing touches on the campaign. This was because, though a man in all other respects praiseworthy, and one who had hardly ever suffered defeat in battle, <he was stimulated by financial greed> and was still carrying on the same war.

101. Gaius Manilius was tribune in 67 BC and on the last day of the year carried a law distributing freedmen through all the tribes, which was nullified by the senate on technical grounds. In 66 he sponsored the law that gave command against Mithridates and Tigranes to Pompey. He was prosecuted for corruption by the anti-Pompeian forces but the case was dropped. He was later convicted of *maiestas* (treason).

102. Lucius Licinius Lucullus was the nephew of Metellus Numidicus (2.11). He campaigned with Sulla during the Social War, supported his march on Rome, and served him effectively in the east. As consul in 74 BC he secured the command against the pirates for Marcus Antonius Creticus and the command against Mithridates for himself. In the campaign he relieved the siege of Cyzicus and occupied a considerable part of Pontus, obliging Mithridates to escape to Armenia. When Tigranes II joined Mithridates' cause, Lucullus marched through Cappadocia, invaded Armenia, and inflicted a massive defeat on Tigranes, capturing the capital Tigranocerta. Unable to sustain his successes, he later faced mutinies in his armies, frustrated by the long and difficult service. His position in Rome was increasingly undermined by his brother-in-law Publius Clodius Pulcher (2.45), and he was eventually replaced by Pompey, by the *lex Manilia,* in January of 66. He was finally allowed to celebrate a triumph in 63. Lucullus' extravagant living, especially his love of food, made his name a byword for self-indulgence.

[2] The law passed, and a struggle marked by violent quarrels broke out between the two generals. Pompey charged Lucullus with a disreputable love of money, Lucullus charged Pompey with an insatiable thirst for power, and neither's allegations could be called unwarranted by the other. [3] When he first entered political life, Pompey could not abide competition, and in spheres where he should simply have been the leader, he instead wished to be unopposed. (And nobody showed a greater passion for glory, and a greater indifference to everything else, than he did. His fervor in seeking political offices was extreme but his management of them very restrained: he would start with great exhilaration but end with nonchalance, following his own inclinations in taking up a position he wanted but laying it down at the will of others.) As for Lucullus, who was a great man in other respects, he was the original promoter of this extravagance of ours in buildings, banqueting, and furnishings. Because of the causeways he set in the sea and the way in which he drew the sea into the land by tunneling under mountains, Pompey the Great would often use of him the witty expression "Xerxes in a toga."[103]

34. At about that time the island of Crete was brought under the sway of the Roman people by Quintus Metellus.[104] (For three years it had exhausted Roman armies, the Cretan leaders Panares and Lasthenes having gathered together twenty-four thousand men of military age who were swift and nimble, well hardened to armed warfare and its rigors, and famed for their archery skills.) [2] Gnaeus Pompey could not hold himself back from capitalizing on this man's glory, either, and he tried to claim for himself a share in the victory. The triumphs celebrated by Lucullus and Metellus alike met with approval because of the two men's own exceptional merits, and also because of the dislike felt for Pompey by all decent men.

[3] It was at about this time that Marcus Cicero as consul rooted out, by his outstanding courage, determination, vigilance, and circumspection, the conspiracy of Sergius Catiline, Lentulus, Cethegus, and other men of both orders.[105] (Cicero was a man who owed to himself alone all his advancement,

---

103. Pompey's quip refers to the famous incidents during the Persian king Xerxes' invasion of Greece in the 480s BC, when Xerxes built a pontoon bridge over the Hellespont and drove a canal through the isthmus at Mount Athos. The toga is the quintessential symbol of Romanness.

104. In 67 BC the consul of 69, Quintus Caecilius Metellus Creticus, successfully reduced Crete, which had in 71 inflicted a major defeat on Marcus Antonius. Metellus was required to give way to Pompey under the *lex Manilia* and to cede authority to Pompey's lieutenant Lucius Octavius.

105. Velleius here mentions for the first time in a political context (for other contexts, see 1.17.3, 2.14.3) the orator and statesman Marcus Tullius Cicero, whom he greatly admires. Born January 3, 106 BC, into a well-to-do equestrian family, Cicero saw military service in the Social War under Pompeius Strabo. He achieved early prominence for his forensic skills and

being a very famous "new man" with a distinguished record and great intellect, one who saw to it that we were not bested in intellectual attainment by those whom we had bested in armed conflict.) Catiline was driven from the city by his fear of the consul's power. [4] Lentulus (a former consul who had twice been praetor), Cethegus, and other men of great distinction were executed in prison on senatorial authority and by order of the consul.

35. The day that this business was transacted in the senate <illustrated to a high degree> the caliber of Marcus Cato, which had already shone out conspicuously in many other situations.[106] [2] Cato, who had as his great-grandfather Marcus Cato, the leading member of the Porcian family, was the very embodiment of Virtue and in nature was in all respects closer to the gods than to human beings. He never acted properly just to be seen doing so, but simply because he had been unable to act otherwise. For him the only reasonable course of action was one that served justice, and as a man free of all human shortcomings, he always kept fortune under his control.

---

entered public life after a period of study in Athens. In 76 he was elected quaestor, serving in Sicily. He gained considerable celebrity by his prosecution in 70 of the corrupt governor of Sicily, Verres, and won a praetorship for 66. He spoke in favor of the *lex Manilia,* the first public display of his generally consistent support of Pompey. He moved up to the consulship in 63 as a new man (*novus homo;* see Book 1, note 20), the first of his family to gain the position.

Lucius Sergius Catilina (Catiline), from a patrician family, served in the Social War and later staunchly supported Sulla. Praetor in 68 BC, he governed Africa for two years afterward. Subsequently prosecuted for embezzlement, he was unable to run for the consulships in 65 and 64, though ultimately the case against him was unsuccessful. He was defeated in a bid for the consulship in 63 by Cicero. After his defeat Catiline assumed the role of champion of the oppressed, making such proposals as the cancellation of debts. He lost again in the elections for the consulship of 62 and supposedly planned a broad revolution. He was maneuvered into leaving Rome, and Cicero obtained written evidence against him. By a *consultum ultimum* of late 63, Catiline was decreed a rebel and killed in battle by the legate of Cicero's fellow consul, Gaius Antonius Hybrida. Catiline had gathered a group of followers who were supposedly planning to take Rome in a putsch.

Publius Cornelius Lentulus Sura had been disgraced as quaestor in 81. He was consul in 71 but banished from the senate by the censors in 70, and he regained entry into that body by winning reelection as praetor. Gaius Cornelius Cethegus had reputedly joined the conspiracy to have his debts canceled. He was planning to kill Cicero and set fire to Rome after Catiline's departure; arms were discovered at his house. These men and others were put to death on the night of December 5 without a judicial trial. The legitimacy of the proceedings became the subject of considerable debate and was used against Cicero by his political enemies (see 2.45).

106. Marcus Porcius Cato Uticensis was the great-grandson of the famous Cato the Censor (1.13) and nephew of Livius Drusus (2.13–14). Deeply committed to Stoic principles, he emulated his great-grandfather in his integrity and adherence to a strict code of morality. Although he aligned himself with the *optimates,* as quaestor (most likely in 64 BC) he vigorously prosecuted Sulla's informers, for which he won much acclaim. In 63 he was elected tribune of the plebs for 62 and made a vigorous intervention in the senate to secure the execution of the Catilinarians. Sallust (*Cat.* 53) provides a version of the speech given on that occasion.

[3] At this time Cato was plebeian tribune-designate and still quite a young man. Others were now recommending that Lentulus and the conspirators be kept under guard in the Italian townships, and he was one of the last invited to give his opinion. He denounced the conspiracy with great strength of purpose and intellect, and by his impassioned delivery he brought all advocating leniency in their speeches under suspicion of involvement in the plot. [4] So convincingly did he portray the dangers that would arise from the overthrow and burning of the city, and from the breakdown of the political system, and so fulsome was he in his praise for the consul's courageous action, that the entire senate went over to his view and voted in favor of executing the individuals I mentioned above, and most of the senatorial order escorted Cicero home.

[5] Catiline for his part carried out his project with no less energy than he had devoted to its planning, dying bravely and surrendering in battle the life he should have surrendered at his execution.

[The flowering of literature in this period.]

36. The birth of the deified Augustus in that year added no small measure of distinction to Cicero's consulship (that is, ninety-two years ago), since by his greatness Augustus was to put all men of all races in the shade.[107]

[2] It may now seem almost unnecessary to give the dates of men of outstanding ability—for who is unaware that in this period, with only their respective ages separating them, fell the high point of the lives of Cicero and Hortensius?[108] Who is unaware that they were preceded by Crassus, Antonius, and Sulpicius, and soon followed by Brutus, Calidius, Caelius, Calvus, and Caesar (who stands closest to Cicero), along with the men who were virtually their pupils, Corvinus, Asinius Pollio, and Sallust, the rival of Thucydides?[109] And then the writers of poetry, Varro and Lucretius, and

---

107. The fortuitous coincidence of Cicero's consulship and Augustus' birth (September of 63 BC) enables Velleius to expatiate on the great literary achievements of the Ciceronian and Augustan ages.

108. Hortensius (2.16.3) was born in 114 BC and was thus some eleven years older than his rival Cicero.

109. On Lucius Licinius Crassus and Marcus Antonius, see 2.9.1; the text here reads "Catonem"; "Antonium Cottam" was an early emendation. Some suspect here a corrupt reference to Gaius Aurelius Cotta (c. 124–74 BC), who was, according to Cicero, the finest speaker of his time. On Publius Sulpicius Rufus, see 2.18.5, 2.19.1. Marcus Junius Brutus (c. 85–42), murderer of Caesar, gave his name to one of Cicero's oratorical dialogues, the *Brutus;* Marcus Calidius (c. 94–47), praetor in 57, helped bring Cicero, who much admired him, back from exile; Marcus Caelius Rufus (82–48) was considered the master of witty invective (see 2.68); Gaius Licinius Calvus (82–47) was a close friend of Catullus, who admired his eloquence. All four represent the simple Attic style of oratory. Caesar's dates (100–44) place him chronologically close to Cicero, but as a writer of great distinction he could also be considered in Cicero's league.

Catullus, no minor poet in any genre of literary composition that he took up?[110] [3] It borders on foolishness to enumerate the talented individuals virtually still before our eyes, among whom the most famous of our time have been Virgil, the prince of poetry, Rabirius, Livy (Sallust's equal in achievement), Tibullus, and Naso, all of whom were perfect in their respective genres.[111] As for writers still alive, the great admiration they enjoy makes critical assessment difficult.

[Success of Pompey against Mithridates (63 BC).]

37. During the course of these events in Rome and in Italy, Gnaeus Pompey fought a memorable campaign against Mithridates.[112] After Lucullus left, Mithridates had put together a new and very powerful army, [2] but he was now defeated and put to flight, and divested of all his forces. He headed for Armenia, to the court of his father-in-law Tigranes, who was the most powerful king of the day, though his strength had been somewhat impaired by the campaigns of Lucullus.[113] [3] Pompey therefore entered Armenia in a

---

On Marcus Valerius Messalla Corvinus (64 BC–AD 8), see 2.71; on Gnaeus Asinius Pollio (75 BC–AD 6), see 2.63.3. They are distinguished men of letters in their own right and notable as patrons of some of Rome's greatest poets (Tibullus and Ovid in the case of the former; Virgil, Horace, and Propertius the latter). Velleius' assessment of Sallust as Rome's Thucydides, the great fifth-century historian of the Peloponnesian War, is shared by Quintilian (*Inst.* 10.1.101).

110. Varro is not the famous polymath Terentius Varro (116–27 BC), whose main reputation was as a grammarian, but Varro of Atax (85–35), author of a number of original poems and a translation of Apollonius Rhodius. Velleius' unfettered admiration of the outspoken and unfettered Catullus (87–54?) comes as something of a surprise, though Catullus was certainly admired by such poets as Lygdamus (Tibullus 3.6.41) and Ovid (*Am.* 3.9.62), who both call him *doctus* (learned), and Martial (*Ep.* 1.61.1).

111. Velleius lists some of the most celebrated writers of the Augustan age: Virgil (70–19 BC), Livy (59 BC–AD 17), Sallust (c. 86–35 BC), Tibullus (54–19 BC), and Ovid (Naso) (43 BC–AD 17), but it is striking that he omits Propertius and, even more remarkably, Horace, which is akin to his failure to mention Plautus as a comic writer (see 1.17). The omission of these two makes the inclusion of Gaius Rabirius all the more surprising. Little is known of Rabirius other than his poem on the civil wars, part of which has been identified with a fragment discovered at Herculaneum.

112. Mithridates was driven out of Pontus by Lucullus (72–71 BC), but a mutiny among the Roman troops enabled him to recover much of his territory (68–67). In 66 he fortified a position on the banks of the river Lycus in Cappadocia, which he was forced to abandon after a siege of forty-five days, losing ten thousand men in the siege and flight. Pompey founded the city of Nicopolis on the site. Mithridates made his way eventually to the Crimea where his attempts to raise a new army were thwarted by a rebellion led by his son, Pharnaces, and he died in 63 after both taking poison and being stabbed by Bituitus, a Gallic member of his guard.

113. Tigranes, king of Armenia, allied himself to Mithridates in 69 BC and became embroiled in a war with Rome. Lucullus took Tigranocerta but did not crush Tigranes. In 66 Pompey

simultaneous pursuit of the two men. It was the son of Tigranes, at odds with his father, who first came to Pompey, [4] but presently the king himself came in person as a suppliant and put himself and his kingdom under Pompey's authority. Before doing so, Tigranes declared that there was no man other than Pompey—neither a Roman nor a member of any other race—to whose authority he would have committed himself, and so he would find bearable any fate, be it harsh or congenial, if Pompey were its author. It was no dishonor, he added, to be defeated by a man whom it would be sacrilege to defeat, and no disgrace to submit to one whom Fortune had raised above all others.

[5] The king retained his royal standing but was fined a huge sum of money, all of which was, as was Pompey's practice, put in the praetor's charge and entered in the public records. Syria and the other provinces that Tigranes had seized were taken from him, some being returned to the Roman people, and others being now for the first time brought under their sway (Syria, for example, which first became a tribute-paying province at that time). The king's authority was now confined to Armenia.

[Digression on the history of Rome's territorial acquisitions.]

38. It does not seem inappropriate to the schema I have proposed for my work to give a brief survey of the peoples and races that were reduced to the status of provinces and made taxpaying subjects (and under whose generalship it happened), so that one might more easily be able to get a concise overview of what I have noted in piecemeal fashion.

[2] The first to take an army over to Sicily was the consul Claudius, but it was actually made a province some fifty-two years after that by Claudius Marcellus, with his capture of Syracuse. The first to cross to Africa was Regulus, in about the ninth year of the First Punic War, but it was 109 years after this—177 years ago—that Publius Scipio Aemilianus razed Carthage and reduced Africa to the status of a province. Sardinia had the yoke of empire firmly set on it between the First and Second Punic Wars in a campaign led by the consul Titus Manlius.[114] [3] A dreadful testimonial to our

---

succeeded in separating the two kings. Tigranes' son (also named Tigranes) went over to Pompey and joined him in marching on Artaxata. Tigranes surrendered and lost his territories outside Armenia but remained a reliable client-king of Rome until his death (c. 56).

114. Appius Claudius Caudex (consul 264 BC), led a Roman army of two legions to Sicily in response to a request for aid from Messina, which had been partially occupied by the Carthaginians. Marcus Claudius Marcellus subdued Syracuse on the east coast after a lengthy siege in 211, but the final subjugation of the island was effected by Marcus Valerius Laevinus (consul 210). Marcus Atilius Regulus led a fleet to Africa in 256. He was initially successful and conquered Tunis, but the expedition ended in disaster. Regulus was captured and famously returned to captivity after having been sent to Rome to negotiate terms that he advised the Romans to

state's warlike nature is the fact that the closing of the temple of two-faced Janus—the indicator of a lasting peace—occurred for the first time under the kings, for a second in the consulship of this Titus Manlius, and for a third only under the emperor Augustus.[115] [4] The very first men to lead armies into Spain were Gnaeus and Publius Scipio, at the beginning of the Second Punic War, 250 years ago.[116] After that the country saw varied fortunes, with parts being won and lost, and the whole being made a tribute-paying province only with the campaign led by Augustus. [5] Paulus reduced Macedonia, Mummius reduced Achaea, and Fulvius Nobilior reduced Aetolia. Lucius Scipio, Africanus' brother, tore Asia away from Antiochus, but it subsequently became the possession of the Attalid kings, thanks to the beneficence of the senate and people of Rome, until Marcus Perpenna captured Aristonicus and made it into a tribute-paying province. Nobody should be assigned the glory of conquering Cyprus.[117] [6] It was made a province by a resolution of the plebs, which was put into effect by Cato, after the suicide of its king, who chose death from a guilty conscience. Crete was penalized after the campaign led by Metellus, when the freedom it had long enjoyed was ended, and Syria and Pontus are monuments to the courage of Gnaeus Pompey.[118]

39. The Gallic lands were first penetrated with an army by Domitius and Fabius (grandson of the Paulus who was given the name Allobrogicus); later on we incurred severe losses as we repeatedly attacked them and failed to hold them. But it is here that the achievement of Gaius Caesar is to be seen

---

reject. Publius Scipio Aemilianus destroyed Carthage in 146. Titus Manlius Torquatus celebrated a triumph in 235 that brought an end to a three-year campaign to subdue Sardinia, but despite Velleius' colorful language, Manlius was obliged to return to complete the subjugation in 215.

115. The closing of the entrance to the temple of Janus had occurred under King Numa, but in fact three times in the Augustan age, as Augustus himself declared (*RG* 13): in 29 BC after the battle of Actium, in 25 after the war against the Cantabrians in Spain, and on a third occasion that is much debated but generally located in the last decade of the century.

116. Gnaeus (consul 222 BC) and Publius (consul 218) Cornelius Scipio took armies into Spain against the Carthaginians in 218; Velleius' figure of 250 years is clearly meant to be a round one. After the Second Punic War the Roman occupation of Spain was punctuated by a series of rebellions, which with some minor exceptions ended with Augustus' defeat of the Cantabrians in 19.

117. On Lucius Aemilius Paulus Macedonicus and Lucius Mummius Achaicus, see 1.9.3 and 1.12.1. Marcus Fulvius Nobilior inflicted a defeat on the Aetolians as consul in 189 BC and sent numerous plundered artworks to Rome. Lucius Cornelius Scipio Asiaticus, brother of Scipio Africanus Maior, with whom he served in Spain, was consul in 190 and early in 189 defeated Antiochus III at Magnesia, securing control of Asia for Rome. On Perpenna and Aristonicus, see 2.4.1. On Cato and Cyprus, see 2.45.4. On Metellus and Crete, see 2.34.1.

118. On Pompey and the east, see 2.37.

in all its glory; it was under Caesar's leadership and auspices that the Gallic lands were eventually crushed, and they now pay taxes <at a humiliating level,> equivalent almost to that of the rest of the world put together.[119] By the same man was made <. . .> Numidicus.[120] [2] Isauricus subjugated Cilicia, and Vulso Manlius, after the war with Antiochus, subjugated Galatia. Bithynia, as I noted above, was left to us in the will of Nicomedes. Apart from the Spanish territories, and the other races whose names add luster to his forum, the deified Augustus also made Egypt a taxpaying province at a level that enabled him to bring to the treasury almost as much revenue as his father derived from the Gallic provinces.[121] [3] Tiberius Caesar forced out of the Illyrians and Dalmatians an admission of subjection as definite as that which his father had forced out of the Spanish territories. He also brought under our sway as new provinces Raetia, Vindelicia, Noricum, Pannonia, and the Scordisci. While he defeated these in battle, it was by the exercise of his authority that he made Cappadocia a taxpaying subject of the Roman people. But let us return to our chronological narrative.[122]

[Returning to Rome from the east, Pompey disbands his army (62 BC).]

40. Next came the campaign of Gnaeus Pompey, and it is unclear which was the greater, the glory won or the hardships endured. Pompey was victorious

---

119. Gnaeus Domitius Ahenobarbus (2.10.2), consul in 122 BC, defeated the Allobroges and Arverni near Avignon. Quintus Fabius Maximus (consul 121) inflicted a massive defeat on the same coalition on August 8, 121. Their achievements led to the creation of Gallia Narbonensis specifically; Velleius uses the term "Gallic lands" imprecisely. Velleius gives little space to Caesar's campaigns in Gaul, either here or in their own context (2.44, 2.46–47).

120. There is a major problem in the text here, but almost certainly we should have a reference to Caesar's establishment of Numidia as a province with the name of Africa Nova.

121. Cilicia became a province about 80 BC. The consul of 79, Publius Servilius Vatia Isauricus, governed it in 78, with the mandate of clearing out the pirates. It was subdued but not completely. Gnaeus Manlius Vulso defeated the Galatians in 189, and the region was henceforth pro-Roman. The province of Galatia was formed after the death of its last ruler, Amyntas, who bequeathed his kingdom to Rome. Velleius has made only a passing reference to Nicomedes' bequest of his kingdom in Bithynia (2.4.1). Egypt became a Roman province in 30, after the defeat of Antony and Cleopatra, to be governed by a prefect appointed by the emperor. The reference to Augustus' father is to his adoptive father, Julius Caesar.

122. Illyricum was an imperial province from at least 11 BC, after a vigorous campaign in the region conducted by Tiberius. At some point, probably in AD 9, it was divided into two provinces that came to be known as Dalmatia and Pannonia. Augustus (in 26–25 BC), aided by Agrippa (in 19), finally subdued Spain with the completion of the Cantabrian campaign. Raetia was a region in the Alps that comprised the Tyrol and areas of modern Bavaria and Switzerland. Tiberius began his campaign there in 15. Vindelicia stretched from the southern Alps to the Danube, incorporated as the eastern part of Raetia. Noricum lay in the eastern Alps between Raetia and Pannonia. The Scordisci inhabited the region at the juncture of the Danube and the

in his invasion of Media, Albania, and Hiberia, after which he veered with his army toward those tribes that inhabit the eastern and innermost areas of Pontus: the Colchians, the Heniochi, and the Achaei. Mithridates was defeated during Pompey's leadership when he was betrayed by his son Pharnaces, and he was the last of all the independent kings apart from the Parthian.[123] [2] Pompey was then victorious over all the races he attacked, returning to Italy a greater man than his fellow citizens or he himself could have hoped he would be, after transcending human fortune in all that he did. Public opinion enhanced the popularity of his return. Most people claimed that he would not enter the city without his army, and that he would curtail public freedoms as he felt inclined. [3] The greater the public's fears of this, the more gratifying was the return of so great a general as a civilian: he disbanded the entire army at Brundisium and, retaining nothing more than his title of imperator, entered the city with only the personal retinue that he always had in attendance on him.[124] For two days he celebrated a superb triumph over all the kings he had defeated, and from the spoils he brought into the treasury far more money than anyone before him, apart from Paulus.[125]

[4] During Pompey's absence, the plebeian tribunes Titus Ampius and Titus Labienus had a law passed allowing him to wear a golden crown and the full regalia of triumphing generals at the games in the Circus, and the *praetexta* and a laurel crown at theatrical performances.[126] Pompey did not dare avail himself of this privilege more than once (and once was too much). Fortune ensured that this man rose with such gigantic steps that he triumphed first over Africa, then over Europe, and in the third instance over Asia, thus making each region of the earth a monument to his victory.[127]

Savus. By 12 they were friendly toward Rome, assisting Tiberius in his campaigns. Cappadocia in eastern Asia Minor was annexed as a Roman province in AD 17.

123. Media was a mountainous land southwest of the Caspian Sea; Caucasian Albania was north of Media, west of the Caspian. Iberia lay between the Caspian and Black seas, approximating modern Georgia. These regions were occupied in 66 and 65 BC. Velleius enumerates, selectively, regions to the west that saw Pompey's campaigns: Colchis, Achaea (in this case a region in the west Caucasus), and the lands of the Heniochi in northeastern Asia Minor. On Pharnaces, see note 112.

124. Pompey disembarked at Brundisium, on Italy's Adriatic coast, in December of 62 and disbanded his army. He was entitled to the honorific title of imperator because his soldiers had proclaimed it on the battlefield.

125. On Lucius Aemilius Paulus Macedonicus, see 1.9.6.

126. According to Dio these honors had been granted to him with the connivance of Julius Caesar and despite the opposition of Marcus Cato Uticensis (Dio 37.21.4).

127. Pompey triumphed for his victories in Africa on March 12, 79 BC. He had entered Numidia a year and a half earlier to crush Marius' forces under Gnaeus Domitius Ahenobarbus

[5] However, preeminent achievements never fail to attract envy. So it was that Lucullus (who remembered the blow he had been dealt), Metellus Creticus (who had a justified grievance in that Pompey had deprived him of captured leaders who were to have adorned his triumph), and a number of the *optimates* banded together to oppose him. Their aim was to prevent the fulfillment of promises made by Pompey to some city-states and the payment of rewards that he deemed appropriate for certain individuals.[128]

[Career of Julius Caesar up to his consulship in 59 BC.]

41. Next came the consulship of Gaius Julius Caesar, who is laying hold on me as I write and, despite my haste, compelling me to linger over his history.[129] Caesar was descended from the very noble and, it is generally agreed, very ancient family of the Julii, tracing his line back to Anchises and Venus. Preeminent among all his fellow citizens for his good looks, he was possessed of a keen and vigorous intellect and extreme generosity, and his courage transcended human nature and surpassed human belief. In the magnitude of his projects, in speed in military action, and in resolve in the face of danger, he most resembled the famous Alexander the Great, but a sober Alexander and one not given to anger; [2] he was, in fact, a man who employed food and

---

and then defeated the native king Iarbas (see note 89). On December 31, 71, he was granted a triumph for his campaign in Spain.

128. On his return Pompey sought ratification of his eastern measures and the arrangements for his veterans. The *optimates* opposed him under leadership of Quintus Caecilius Metellus Creticus (2.34). After Metellus' victories in Crete, Pompey had bypassed him and accepted the Cretans' surrender, ordering Metellus to leave the island. Metellus refused, and Pompey delayed his triumph until 62 BC. Dio claims that it was Quintus Caecilius Metellus Celer (consul 60), aided by Lucullus and Cato, who opposed the settlement, offended because Pompey had divorced his half sister (Dio 37.49–50).

129. Up to this point (59 BC) Velleius has made reference once to Julius Caesar's literary achievement (2.36.2) and twice to his political and military career (2.30.3, 2.39.1). From now to chapter 59, when Octavian enters the picture, Caesar dominates the narrative. Gaius Julius Caesar (100–44) was born into the family of the Julii, who traced their descent from Anchises of Troy, father of Aeneas, and the goddess Venus (a myth expounded in Virgil's *Aeneid*). The Julii were patrician, but Caesar was sympathetic to the *populares*. The younger Marius (consul 82) was his cousin, since Caesar's aunt Julia married the elder Marius. Caesar reinforced this political sympathy by marrying Cornelia, daughter of Cinna, and later resisted Sulla's pressure to divorce her. By contrast, Marcus Pupius Piso Calpurnianus (not consul in 61, so Velleius is in error here), who on the death of Cinna in 84 married Cinna's widow Annia, divorced her when he transferred his loyalty to Sulla. Caesar was kidnapped by pirates as a young man, in connection with a visit to either Bithynia in 81–80 or Rhodes in 76 (Suet. *Jul.* 4; cf. Plut. *Caes.* 3.1), and, in accounts that must by their nature derive from Caesar himself, he conducted himself with considerable aplomb, even telling the pirates, after he had been released for ransom, that he would return to punish them.

sleep to sustain life, not for pleasure. He had a close blood relationship with Gaius Marius and was also the son-in-law of Cinna. He could in no way be constrained by fear to divorce Cinna's daughter, whereas the ex-consul Marcus Piso dismissed Annia, who had been Cinna's wife, to please Sulla. He was about eighteen at the time that Sulla came to power, and when he was being hunted down for execution—by Sulla's henchmen and supporters of his cause rather than by Sulla himself—he changed his clothing and, dressed in a manner that belied his class, slipped out of the city at night.

[3] Later on, while still a young man, Caesar was taken prisoner by some pirates and, during the entire period that he was held by them, he behaved toward them in such a way as to inspire in them an equal degree of fear and respect. At no time, day or night, did he take off his shoes or his belt (for why omit what may be a very important detail simply because it cannot be narrated in elevated language?), his purpose evidently being to arouse no suspicion, by making any change in his usual clothing, in men whose guard amounted only to keeping an eye on him.

42. It would take too long to recount Caesar's manifold adventures and the efforts to thwart his endeavors that the magistrate of the Roman people who was governor of Asia made on his own authority. The following episode, however, should be noted as an indicator of the man's greatness soon to come. [2] He was ransomed with public money raised from city-states of Asia but only after he forced the pirates to give hostages to these city-states. On the night following the day of the payment, Caesar, who was just a private citizen, took a makeshift fleet that he had raised and attacked the spot where the pirates were located. He put some of their ships to flight, sank others, and captured a number of vessels and many men. [3] Pleased with the success of his nocturnal escapade, he returned to his own people and put the men he had taken under guard. He then headed for the proconsul Junius Iuncus in Bithynia (for the same man was governor of that province as well as Asia) and asked that he authorize the execution of the prisoners. When Iuncus refused and said that he would sell the prisoners off—for envy was now following in the wake of lethargy—Caesar returned to the coast with incredible speed and, before a letter from the proconsul addressing the matter could reach anyone, crucified all the prisoners he had taken.[130]

43. During his absence, Caesar had been appointed pontiff to replace the ex-consul Cotta (he had, when he was practically still a boy, been appointed

---

130. Marcus Junius Iuncus was governor of Asia in 75–74 BC (his precise name is far from certain). Plutarch (*Caes.* 2.6) gives his rank as praetorian and claims that he procrastinated in the hope of getting his hands on the booty Caesar had taken.

Flamen of Jupiter by Marius and Cinna but had lost that priesthood with
the victory of Sulla, who had annulled all these men's enactments).[131] He was
hurrying to Italy to enter his priesthood and, in order not to be spotted by
the pirates who at the time dominated all the seas and now had good reason
to be hostile to him, he boarded a four-oared vessel with two friends and ten
slaves and crossed the vast gulf of the Adriatic Sea. [2] On the voyage he
caught sight of some pirate ships (or so he thought) and took off his clothes
and strapped a dagger to his thigh, preparing himself for whichever turn
Fortune might take. He soon realized that his eyes had deceived him and
that a row of trees in the distance had given the appearance of ships' masts.
[3] His other dealings in the city are well enough known to have less
need of a written record. There was his famous indictment of Dolabella,
which generated more public support for the accused than defendants are
normally given; his celebrated political wrangling with Quintus Catulus
and other eminent men; and, before his praetorship, his victory over Quintus Catulus, universally acknowledged as the leading man in the senate, in
his bid for the post of *pontifex maximus*.[132] There was also, during his term
as aedile, and despite the opposition of the nobility, his restoration of the
monuments of Gaius Marius, [4] and at the same time his restitution of the
prerogatives of their rank to the children of men who had been proscribed.[133]
Then there was the praetorship and quaestorship that he discharged in Spain
with amazing courage and application.[134] (He was quaestor under Antistius

---

131. Gaius Aurelius Cotta (consul 75 BC) was the cousin of Caesar's mother Aurelia. He died
in 73, and, through Aurelia's efforts, Caesar acquired his priesthood. According to Tacitus
(*Ann.* 3.58.2) and Dio (54.36.1), Lucius Cornelius Merula, who died in 87, was the last Flamen of Jupiter for seventy-five years. Caesar may have been co-opted but never in fact inaugurated. Velleius says that the appointment happened when Marius and Cinna were consuls,
hence early in 86 (Marius died on January 13 of that year), when Caesar (born in 100) was
thirteen. But Suetonius (*Jul.* 1.1) says that Caesar was co-opted in the year after his father's
death, when he was fifteen, hence in 85.

132. In a brilliant, if ultimately unsuccessful, performance, Caesar in 77 BC prosecuted Gnaeus Cornelius Dolabella, the follower of Sulla and consul in 81, for extortion while governor of
Macedonia.
    Quintus Lutatius Catulus was a conservative senator who held a grudge against Caesar for his
defeat in the election for *pontifex maximus* in 63. They clashed in the debate over the Catilinarian
conspirators, and Catulus even suggested that Caesar himself was involved in the conspiracy.

133. In 65 BC, as aedile, Caesar proposed the restoration of the monuments of Marius. As
tribune in 73 he had introduced the vote on the *lex Plautia,* which recalled victims of the
proscriptions (Suet. *Jul.* 5). As dictator in 49 Caesar restored to the sons of the proscribed the
right to stand for office. Velleius seems to be transposing to his tribunacy a measure that belongs to the later aedileship. Dio indicates that the tribunes in 63 attempted a similar reform
but were unsuccessful (37.25.3–4).

134. Caesar served in Spain as quaestor in 69 BC and with the rank of proconsul in 61–60

Vetus, grandfather of the Vetus who is now an ex-consul and a pontiff, and who is himself the father of two men who are ex-consuls and priests, a man of integrity as great as can be imagined in a human being.)[135]

[Caesar's alliance with Pompey and Crassus during his consulship of 59 BC. The peace is disturbed by the radical tribune Publius Clodius, who secures the exile of Cicero in 58.]

44. It was when Caesar was consul that the power sharing among him, Pompey, and Crassus began, something that was deadly for the city, for the world, and no less, at different times, for the men themselves.[136] [2] Pompey's motivation for following this arrangement was to use Caesar's consulship to finally gain ratification of his measures in the overseas provinces (to which, as I noted above, many remained opposed). In the case of Caesar it was the realization that in yielding to Pompey's eminence he would be increasing his own, and that by shifting to Pompey the antipathy aroused by their joint power he would bolster his own strength. For Crassus it was the prospect of using Pompey's influence and Caesar's power to achieve a preeminence he could not achieve on his own. [3] The bonds between Caesar and Pompey were also drawn tighter by a marriage, since Gnaeus Magnus married Gaius Caesar's daughter.[137]

[4] During this consulship Caesar proposed a bill, which Pompey supported, authorizing the distribution of the Campanian lands among the plebs. The result was that roughly twenty thousand citizens were settled there and, about 152 years after it was reduced to the status of a prefecture by the Romans in the [Second] Punic War, Capua saw the restoration of its rights as a city.[138] [5] Caesar's colleague Bibulus, whose desire to obstruct Caesar's measures was greater than his ability to do so, stayed at home for most of

---

(not propraetor, as Velleius implies, but the term did follow his praetorship). In the latter period he won victories over the Gallaeci and Lusitani.

135. Gaius Antistius Vetus was praetor in 70 BC and propraetor in Spain in 69. His grandson, of the same name, was *pontifex maximus* about 16 and consul in 6. Of his sons, Gaius was consul in AD 23 and Lucius in 26.

136. Velleius dates the alliance of Caesar, Pompey, and Crassus to Caesar's consulship, though other sources place it during his candidacy (Liv. *Per.* 103.6) and after his election (Suet. *Jul.* 19.2). The first "triumvirate" did not have the strict legal formality of the second, and the name is often misleadingly applied in this earlier instance.

137. Julia, Caesar's only legitimate and acknowledged child, was married in April of 59 BC to Pompey (Gnaeus Magnus) and grew deeply attached to him. In 54 she died in childbirth, the child surviving only a few days (see 2.47.2).

138. The *lex Iulia Agraria* was carried in March of 59 BC against the fierce opposition of the *optimates*, led by Cato and Caesar's fellow consul, Marcus Calpurnius Bibulus. Capua had switched allegiance to Hannibal in 216 and was recaptured in 211. It was harshly punished and its territory seized as public land eventually distributed by Caesar. Velleius' figure of 152 years is correct.

the year.[139] By this he hoped to increase ill will against his colleague, but he succeeded only in increasing the man's power. Then Caesar was officially granted Gaul as his province for five years.[140]

45. It was at about this same time that Publius Clodius, who had passed from the ranks of the patricians to the plebs, proposed during his tribunate a bill stipulating that anyone executing a Roman citizen without trial should be "denied fire and water."[141] Clodius was well born, articulate, and irresponsible, one who recognized no constraints on what he said or did apart from his own selfish wishes. He was very keen to carry out vile projects; he was also infamous for having had sexual relations with his sister; and he had further been accused of sacrilegious behavior for attempting to commit adultery amid the Roman people's most holy observances. He was on terms of bitter hatred with Marcus Cicero—how could there possibly be friendship between people so different?—and though Cicero was not named in the wording of the bill, he was its sole target.[142]

[2] And so a man who had served the Republic well bore the misery of exile as the reward for saving his native land. Caesar and Pompey were not above suspicion in the matter of Cicero's downfall. It looked as if Cicero had

---

139. Bibulus was prevented from intervening during the meeting of the assembly that voted on the *lex Iulia Agraria*. He remained in his home for the rest of the year, where he claimed he was waiting for favorable omens before legislation could be initiated, thus making Caesar's actions technically invalid. Suetonius (*Jul.* 20.2) records that because Caesar was, thanks to Bibulus' absence from the political stage, the de facto sole consul for the remainder of that year, wits described documents as having been sealed "in the consulship of Julius and Caesar."

140. The *lex Vatinia* at the end of April of 59 BC assigned to Caesar for five years the government of Cisalpine Gaul and Illyricum, with three legions. Transalpine Gaul was subsequently added.

141. Publius Clodius Pulcher (c. 92–52 BC) lived a life of considerable notoriety. A member of the haughty patrician Claudian family, he showed his contrary political leanings by adopting the popular spelling of his name. He was almost constantly embroiled in scandal. He was suspected of incest with his three sisters, most notably Clodia, wife of Metellus Celer (probably Catullus' Lesbia; see 2.68). In December of 62, dressed as a woman, he infiltrated the ceremony of the Bona Dea, presided over by Pompeia, Caesar's second wife, with whom Clodius was believed to be having an affair. Caesar immediately divorced her on the celebrated grounds that Caesar's wife should be above suspicion (Plut. *Caes.* 10.9). As a consequence of the incident, Clodius was charged in 61 with *incestum* (lewd behavior, rather than incest specifically) but bribed the jurors to secure an acquittal. He subsequently wished to stand as tribune of the plebs but as a patrician was ineligible. Once adopted by the plebeian Fonteius, he held the office in 58. The law of Clodius to which Velleius here alludes, the *lex Clodia de Capite Civis,* was passed early in his term. On fire and water, see note 73.

142. Laws against individuals were technically disallowed in Rome, but after Cicero's departure Clodius successfully introduced a second bill that did explicitly name him, formalizing his exile and confiscating his goods. Cicero's recall was enacted in 57 BC. The senate decreed that anyone impeding his return would be considered a state enemy (*hostis*).

brought it upon himself by his refusal to sit on the Board of Twenty established to distribute the Campanian lands. [3] Within two years, however, he was restored to his erstwhile standing and his country, thanks to the belated efforts of Gnaeus Pompey (belated, but strenuous once started), to the wishes of Italy and decrees of the senate, and to the courage and exertions of the plebeian tribune Annius Milo.[143] Nor, since the time of the exile and return of Numidicus, was anyone's banishment more unpopular or restoration more joyfully welcomed. The ruthlessness with which Cicero's home had been destroyed by Clodius was matched by the grandeur with which it was rebuilt by the senate.

[4] In the course of his tribunate this same Publius Clodius also removed Marcus Cato from the political scene with an ostensibly honorable objective. He proposed a bill authorizing Cato to be sent to the island of Cyprus with the rank of quaestor, but with praetorian authority and with a quaestor as his colleague, to deprive Ptolemy of his throne—and Ptolemy was a man worthy of such an indignity, given all his moral shortcomings.[144] [5] In fact, Ptolemy committed suicide just before Cato's arrival; and Cato then brought from Cyprus to Rome money far in excess of what was expected. To praise the man's incorruptibility would be sacrilege, but there may be grounds for charging him with arrogance: when all the citizens, along with the consuls and members of the senate, flooded out to meet him as he approached, by the Tiber, with his ships, Cato did not disembark until he arrived at the spot where the money was to be put ashore.

[Julius Caesar's successful campaign in Gaul. Crassus' disastrous defeat in Syria (53 BC). Publius Clodius' murder in 52.]

46. In Gaul Gaius Caesar was achieving enormous successes that one could scarcely cover in several volumes.[145] Not content with his very numerous and very decisive victories, with the countless thousands of enemies killed

---

143. Titus Annius Milo supported Pompey. He conducted a violent campaign of opposition against Clodius, making use of armed slaves and gladiators. This ultimately led to Clodius' death and Milo's temporary exile. As tribune of the plebeians he actively pushed for Cicero's recall (see also 2.47, 2.68).

144. In 58 BC Clodius succeeded in removing Cato from Rome by obliging him to undertake the complicated annexation of Cyprus. Cato was apparently given the rank of the highest magistracy he had held (quaestorship) and thus would have been proquaestor; but he required full *imperium* and so held the position of proquaestor as praetor, or *proquaestor propraetore*. Ptolemy, king of Cyprus, was the younger brother of Ptolemy XII Auletes of Egypt (see 2.53). He committed suicide in 58.

145. Velleius devotes little space to Caesar's campaigns in Gaul (58–50 BC) and even less to the two seasons he spent in Britain (55, 54). He possibly intended to cover them in greater detail in his major work.

and captured, he even took his army over to Britain, virtually seeking a second world for our empire, and for his own. Meanwhile, the former consular pair, Gnaeus Pompey and Marcus Crassus, entered their second consulship, but their campaign for it was not honorable nor their administration praiseworthy <. . .>. [2] Under a law that Pompey brought before the people, Caesar had his provincial governorship extended for the same time period as before, and Crassus, who was contemplating a war with Parthia, was assigned Syria.[146] Crassus was a man who was in other respects blameless and free from sensual appetites, but his thirst for money and fame knew no limits and observed no bounds. [3] As he set off for Syria, the plebeian tribunes tried in vain to hold him back with reports of dire omens. If the curses they foretold had affected only Crassus, the state would have suffered the insignificant loss of a commander, but his army would have been saved.[147] [4] He had crossed the Euphrates and was heading for Seleucia, when King Orodes surrounded him with an immense body of cavalry and killed him along with most of the Roman troops.[148] [5] What remained of the legions was saved by Gaius Cassius, then a quaestor, a man who was soon to be the perpetrator of a most atrocious crime. Cassius managed to keep Syria under the control of the Roman people, to such an extent that, when the Parthians crossed into the province, he, thanks to a fortunate development of circumstances, defeated them and put them to flight.[149]

---

146. Pompey and Crassus had held the consulship in 70 BC. Their new mandate came out of a meeting between Caesar and Crassus at Ravenna, then between Caesar and Pompey, perhaps also with Crassus, at Luca in northern Italy, which reaffirmed the alliance of the three men. As a consequence Pompey and Crassus were consuls in 55 and held commands in Spain and Syria, respectively, while Caesar was reconfirmed in Gaul. Pompey and his followers used tribunician intercession to delay the election until January of 55, when the previous consuls, who opposed their candidacy, had left office, and the presence at the election of soldiers from Caesar's army encouraged Pompey's chief opponent, Lucius Domitius Ahenobarbus, to give up his candidacy (Plut. *Pomp.* 52.1–2; Dio 39.31).

There were two separate laws: the *lex Trebonia*, which granted Crassus Syria and Pompey the two Spains united as a single province, and the *lex Licinia Pompeia*, which extended Caesar's term in Gaul. Velleius would presumably have referred to Pompey's command in Spain, but if he did the passage seems to have been lost from the text.

147. Crassus left Rome in November of 55 BC for Syria; his enterprise was unpopular and there were supposedly bad omens (App. *BC* 2.18; Dio 39.39.5–7; cf. Plut. *Crass.* 16.5).

148. The battle of Carrhae (modern Harran, in southeast Turkey) occurred in June of 53 BC. When Crassus' army arrived, the Parthian king Orodes was away leading an army against Armenia. The Parthian troops at Carrhae were in fact commanded by Orodes' senior official, Surenas.

Seleucia was a major city on the Tigris, founded by Seleucus I as the capital of his satrapy of Babylonia in about 312. Under the Parthians the main administrative center was located in Ctesiphon, on the river's opposite bank.

149. The situation was salvaged by Gaius Cassius Longinus, who won fame later as one of

47. In this period, and in the period that followed and the one I have already dealt with, more than four hundred thousand of the enemy were killed by Gaius Caesar and a larger number taken prisoner. His fighting was often in the form of pitched battles, or of battles on the march, or of lightning strikes; he twice went into Britain; and, in fact, of his nine campaigning seasons there was scarcely one which did not merit a richly deserved triumph, and his exploits around Alesia were of a magnitude that hardly any human would dare to undertake, and almost no one but a god could bring to fruition.[150]

[2] It was in about the fourth year of Caesar's time in Gaul that Julia, wife of Magnus, died.[151] She had been the guarantee of the agreement between Gnaeus Pompey and Gaius Julius Caesar, which even then was holding together badly because the two jealously eyed each other's power. And now Fortune severed all ties between a pair of leaders who were destined for a conflict of such great proportions, for within a short time Pompey's small son, Julia's child, also died. [3] Then an orgy of electoral graft, for which no end or limit could be found, precipitated armed violence and the spilling of citizen blood; and Gnaeus Pompey was presented with his third consulship, this time as sole consul, with the support even of those men who had earlier opposed his advancement. It was the prestige of this office, suggesting as it did Pompey's reconciliation with the *optimates,* that more than anything else alienated him from Gaius Caesar. Pompey, for his part, brought all the force of his consulship to bear on the suppression of electoral corruption.

[4] At this juncture Publius Clodius was killed by Milo, then a candidate for the consulship, in a brawl that arose near Bovillae as the result of a chance encounter.[152] The precedent was a bad one, but the actual event proved beneficial to the Republic. Milo, on trial, was convicted less because

---

Caesar's assassins (2.56). He escaped from the battlefield and organized the defense of Syria. In 51 BC he repelled an invasion by the Parthians, under Pacorus, son of Orodes, outside Antigoneia. Pacorus died in the action.

150. In 52 BC Caesar forced the surrender of Vercingetorix, the commander of a federation of Gallic tribes, at Alesia, defeating a large Gallic army that had come to relieve their chieftain.

151. Julia, the wife of Pompey, died in childbirth in September of 54 BC (see 2.44.3); the child, whose sex is unknown, did not survive. Velleius seems to attribute to Julia's death the breakup of Caesar's alliance with Pompey but goes on to give greater weight to Pompey's election as sole consul in 52. This election followed considerable political chaos and street battles between the gangs of Clodius and Milo (see 2.45), which had prevented the elections from taking place in 53. Marcus Cornelius Bibulus, Caesar's recalcitrant fellow consul in 59 (see 2.44.5), proposed Pompey's appointment, which was seconded by Cato; they had been two of his most relentless opponents. The single consulship dealt with the prevailing anarchy without resorting to the appointment of a dictator, which Cato had opposed. In the end Pompey had Scipio Nasica as his colleague for the last five months of his term.

152. The murder of Clodius by Milo, now a consular candidate, on January 18, 52 BC, in fact

of indignation over what he did than because of Pompey's wishes in the matter. [5] Marcus Cato did, indeed, support an acquittal and openly expressed his opinion; and had he done so earlier, there would have been no shortage of people to follow his example and approve the killing of one who, more than any other, had been a plague on the state and an enemy to all decent men.

[Civil war between Caesar and Pompey. Pompey, defeated at Pharsalus, flees to Egypt, where he is killed in 48 BC.]

48. It was shortly after this that civil war initially flared up, although all right-thinking individuals wished to see both Caesar and Pompey disband their armies. During his second consulship, Pompey had wanted to be assigned the Spanish provinces; and for a three-year period, while he himself was absent from them, tending to the affairs of the city, he had his legates Afranius and Petreius, an ex-consul and an ex-praetor, respectively, administer them.[153] He now sided with those who demanded that Caesar disband his army, but he opposed those demanding the same from him. [2] Had Pompey died two years before the outbreak of hostilities, when he was afflicted with a serious disease in Campania (and when all Italy made vows for his recovery as being the foremost of all its citizens), Fortune would not have had the opportunity to bring him down, and he would have carried to the underworld, unimpaired, the greatness that he had enjoyed in the upper world. For by that point he had completed his public monuments, that is, his theater and the other buildings with which he surrounded it.[154]

[3] As for the civil war, and the miseries that followed it for twenty years in a row, no one provided a more intense and incendiary stimulus than the plebeian tribune Gaius Curio.[155] He was a nobleman, eloquent and reckless,

---

preceded Pompey's election to the consulship. "At this juncture" is thus used rather loosely. Milo was defended unsuccessfully by Cicero, who rewrote the speech for publication. The copy of the *Pro Milone* that has survived was never delivered.

153. Pompey governed his province through two legates. Lucius Afranius (consul 60 BC) commanded three legions in Spain. He was pardoned by Caesar but returned to Pompey's cause. He was executed shortly after the battle of Thapsus, some 130 miles southeast of Carthage, in 46. Marcus Petreius (praetor 63) was a vigorous commander in Spain and later enjoyed some successes against Caesar in Africa. He committed suicide after Thapsus.

154. Pompey fell ill in Naples two years later, in mid-50 BC. Pompey's theater, the first of stone built in Rome, was begun in 55 but not inaugurated until 52.

155. The twenty subsequent years of civil war to which Velleius refers lasted from 49 to 29, the year of Augustus' triumphs. Gaius Scribonius Curio was a gifted orator, initially a friend of Clodius, whose widow Fulvia he later married. In the 50s BC his allegiance shifted and he joined his father in supporting the *optimates*. He was quaestor in Asia in 53 and plebeian tribune in 50. Supposedly bribed by a massive sum from Caesar, Curio proposed a scheme

prodigal with his own and with others' fortunes and honor, a very clever
scoundrel who used his speaking ability to the detriment of the state, and
one whose [4] <desires and passions could be satisfied by no amount of
wealth . . . or lusts>. He first positioned himself on the side of Pompey, that
is, on the side of the Republic (as was thought at the time), and shortly afterward he pretended to oppose both Pompey and Caesar, though his heart
was with Caesar. (The question of whether this was an unbiased choice or
whether he accepted a hundred thousand sesterces for it, as I have been told,
I shall leave unanswered.) [5] Finally, along came some constructive conditions for establishing a firm peace which Caesar very fairly demanded, and
Pompey was happy to accept, but Curio shattered and destroyed them,
while Cicero was making a sterling effort to maintain harmony in the state.

[6] These and the earlier events are set forth in order in the full-length
books of others, and an account of them will, I hope, also be given in my
full-length treatment. For now, let me return to the scope of this particular
work to which I am committed, after first congratulating Quintus Catulus,
the two Luculli, Metellus, and Hortensius.[156] These men were preeminent
in the Republic without arousing hostility, and their distinction did not
bring them danger; and their deaths came peacefully, or at least from natural causes, before the start of the civil wars.

49. The civil war flared up in the consulship of Lentulus and Marcellus
(703 years after the city's foundation, and 78 years before you entered your
consulship, Marcus Vinicius).[157] [2] The one protagonist's cause appeared
better, the other's more powerful; on the one side everything looked impressive, the other had the real strength; Pompey's chief weapon was the authority of the senate, Caesar's the confidence of his men. The consuls and the
senate conferred supreme power on his cause, <not on Pompey himself>.

---

whereby both Caesar and Pompey would give up their armies and avert the danger of civil war,
a proposal approved by the senate by 370 to 22. The consul Gaius Claudius Marcellus refused
to accept the outcome, and at the end of his term Curio threw his support behind Caesar.
Curio was killed in battle by Juba I in Africa in 49.

Appian (*BC* 2.28) claims that during his illness Pompey wrote to the senate offering to give
up his army and repeated this offer when he came to Rome. He seems to have called Curio's
bluff, but Curio denounced the offer as insincere.

156. Velleius prefaces his account of the civil wars by noting the passing of a number of
prominent individuals, men who had well-timed deaths. Quintus Catulus (see 2.32) died in
the winter of 61–60 BC; Lucius Licinius Lucullus Ponticus (2.33), in the winter of 57–56; his
brother Marcus Terentius Varro Lucullus, consul in 73 (see 2.28), soon afterward; Quintus
Caecilius Metellus Creticus (2.34), sometime after 54; Hortensius (2.16.3), in 50.

157. Velleius dates the outbreak of the civil war to 49 BC, in the consulship of Lucius Cornelius Lentulus and Gaius Claudius Marcellus. On January 7, 49, a *consultum ultimum* gave
Pompey command against Caesar.

[3] No effort was spared by Caesar in his attempts to preserve the peace, but no offer was accepted by Pompey's supporters.[158] The one consul was more aggressive than was warranted, while Lentulus' well-being was not compatible with the well-being of the state; and Marcus Cato insisted that death was preferable to having the state accept any conditions laid down by an individual citizen bearing arms. A dignified gentleman of old would have been more inclined to praise the party of Pompey, and a shrewd man more inclined to follow that of Caesar, considering Pompey's the glorious one but Caesar's the more fearful.

[4] After that, all Caesar's demands were rejected, though he was quite content to retain one pro forma province with a single legion <. . .> and the senate had decreed that he come to Rome as a private citizen and entrust himself to the suffrage of the Roman people by standing for the consulship. Caesar thought he had to go to war and crossed the Rubicon with his army.[159] Gnaeus Pompey, the consuls, and most of the senate left the city, and subsequently Italy, and crossed over to Dyrrhachium.

50. As for Caesar, after seizing Domitius and the legions with him at Corfinium, he had promptly released the commander and any others who wanted to leave to join Pompey.[160] He had then followed Pompey to Brundisium, in a way that gave the impression that his preference was for ending hostilities while the situation remained unchanged and the same terms could obtain, rather than for crushing the fugitives; [2] but when he found that the consuls had made the crossing to Dyrrhachium he returned to Rome.[161] There, in the senate and a popular assembly, he gave an explanation of the decisions he had

---

158. During the final days of December of 50 BC, Caesar had suggested that he should keep Cisalpine Gaul and Illyricum, with two legions. After negotiations dominated by Cicero, it was proposed that Caesar should retain only Illyricum and a single legion (Suet. *Jul.* 29.2). This proposal, to which Velleius here refers, was approved by Caesar and Pompey but rejected by Lentulus and Cato. The senate then voted that Caesar should give up his command.

159. The dramatic event of crossing the Rubicon, which marked the border between Italy and Cisalpine Gaul, and hence the boundary of Caesar's province, took place on January 17, 49 BC.

160. Lucius Domitius Ahenobarbus, great-great-grandfather of the emperor Nero, consistently opposed Caesar and as praetor in 58 BC threatened to prosecute him for his actions in the previous year. Consul in 54, he was involved with his colleague Appius Claudius Pulcher in an election scandal. He was assigned Transalpine Gaul by the senate as successor to Caesar but, on his march north, was forced to surrender at Corfinium, east of Rome on the eastern side of the Apennines, on February 21, 49, and allowed to leave unharmed. He continued to oppose Caesar and died in the aftermath of Pharsalus.

161. Caesar reached Brundisium on March 9, 49 BC, but was unable to arrange a meeting with Pompey, who had withdrawn his troops from Italy and transported them across the Adriatic to Dyrrhachium (modern Durres, on the central Albanian coast).

reached and the painful constraints he was under in being forced to take up arms because others had done so.[162] He then determined to head for Spain.

[3] The speed of his journey was for a time arrested by Massilia, which, with greater loyalty than wisdom, chose the wrong moment to arbitrate in the fight between the two leaders—intervention should be a role restricted to those able to apply pressure to a party refusing to comply. [4] Then the army that had been under the command of the ex-consul Afranius and the ex-praetor Petreius surrendered to Caesar on his arrival, taken by surprise by his dynamism and lightning speed. Both legates, and anyone else wanting to join them, regardless of rank, were sent back to Pompey.[163]

51. The following year Dyrrhachium and the environs of the city were occupied by the forces of Pompey; he had sent for legions from all the overseas provinces, and for auxiliary cavalry and infantry, along with troops from the various kings, tetrarchs, and princes, and thus had put together a mighty army. He had also used his fleets to mount what he thought was an effective blockade of the seaways to make it impossible for Caesar to ferry over his legions. [2] Caesar, however, with characteristic speed and good fortune, allowed nothing to stop him and his army from reaching their destination by sea (and at a time of his choosing) and from setting up his camp (which was at first almost touching Pompey's, and presently he even encircled Pompey with siege installations). However, the shortage of supplies proved more serious for the besiegers than for the besieged.[164] [3] Then Cornelius Balbus, with bravado a man could scarcely credit, entered the enemy camp and had a number of discussions with the consul Lentulus, who hesitated only over the price of his betrayal. This was how Balbus made a way for himself to those career steps by which a man who was not just a Roman born in Spain but a genuine Spaniard could rise to a triumph and the position of pontiff and reach consular rank from private status.[165] There followed battles with

---

162. The meeting of the senate took place on April 1, 49 BC, on the Campus Martius. The process was particularly difficult, since Caesar as commander of troops was technically not allowed to enter the city. Caesar then went to Spain, where he defeated Pompey's legates, Lucius Afranius and Marcus Petreius (2.48.1), at the battle of Ilerda, on August 2, 49.

163. On the way to Spain Caesar was detained for a month at Massilia (Marseille), which was under siege by his lieutenants, Decimus Brutus and Gaius Trebonius. Massilia did not in fact fall until October 10, 49 BC.

164. In mid-December 49 BC Pompey installed himself at Dyrrhachium. Caesar made the crossing with a detachment of troops on January 4, 48, and disembarked on the next day (Caes. *BC* 3.6), but the remainder of his army was held up by bad weather for a number of weeks.

165. Lucius Cornelius Lentulus Crus was not in fact consul at this time but rather proconsul, since he had held the consulship in the previous year. There were two men called Cornelius Balbus. The elder was born in Gades (Cadiz) about 100 BC and distinguished himself in the

mixed results, but one of them particularly favored the Pompeians, with Caesar's men suffering a serious defeat.[166]

52. Caesar then headed with his army for Thessaly, which was fated to give him his victory.[167] [2] Pompey's advisers made widely conflicting recommendations, most urging him to cross over to Italy (and, in truth, no suggestion would have been more beneficial for his side), but others recommending that he drag out the conflict, which, thanks to the respect his side enjoyed, was every day turning more and more in their favor. Pompey, however, with his natural impulsiveness, set off in pursuit of the enemy.[168]

[3] The restricted scope of my composition does not allow a detailed account of the battle of Pharsalus and the day that was the goriest for the Roman race, with so much blood spilled by both armies; of the clash of the two leading men of the Republic, when the Roman empire had one of its eyes gouged out; and of the massacre of so many men, and men of such caliber, on the Pompeian side.[169] [4] But this fact must be recorded: as soon as Gaius Caesar observed that the battle line of the Pompeians had given way, he thought nothing was more pressing or more important than to dispatch to all fronts (if I may follow my practice of using a military expression) <a tablet ordering that citizens' lives be spared>.[170] [5] Immortal gods, what a price this merciful man later paid for his kindness to Brutus! [6] Nothing in that victory was more remarkable, magnificent, and glorious than the fact that the fatherland suffered the loss of no citizen apart from those killed in battle. But the gift of mercy was frustrated by obstinacy, since the conqueror was at that point more willing to grant life than the conquered were to accept it.

---

war against Sertorius, receiving citizenship as a result in 72. He was a supporter of Caesar and then of Octavian and became consul in 40 without holding previous office. His nephew, the younger Balbus, was quaestor in 44 and seems to have been adlected to consular rank by Octavian. He later used his adventurous missions as the subject of a play that he put on in his hometown (Cic. *Fam.* 10.32.3). It is possible that Velleius has conflated the two men.

166. Pompey succeeded in inflicting a major defeat on Caesar when Caesar attempted to blockade him at Dyrrhachium (Caes. *BC* 3.41–72).

167. Caesar made the lengthy journey to Pharsalus almost immediately following the defeat at Dyrrhachium.

168. Plutarch claims that it was in fact the followers of Pompey who urged him to pursue Caesar, despite his own misgivings (Plut. *Pomp.* 66.1–3, *Caes.* 40–41.5).

169. The battle of Pharsalus occurred on August 9, 48 BC (June 28, by the Julian calendar). Caesar reputedly lost 200 men and 30 centurions, in contrast to massive losses for Pompey (the figures as reported range from 6,000 to 15,000 dead).

170. The text is clearly corrupt at this point, and a section seems to be missing (the restoration offered here is a tentative suggestion of Watt). Velleius does seem to be contrasting the magnanimous behavior of Caesar after the battle with the ingratitude of Brutus, one of his chief assassins.

53. Pompey fled with the two Lentuli, who were former consuls, and with his son Sextus and the ex-praetor Favonius, men whom chance had brought to him as his companions.[171] Some of them urged him to make for the Parthians, and others for Africa, where he would have King Juba as a loyal supporter of his cause.[172] However, Pompey bore in mind the services he had rendered to the father of the Ptolemy who was then ruling in Alexandria (and who was a boy rather than an adult), and instead he proposed to make for Egypt.[173] [2] But who in times of trouble keeps alive the memory of services received? Or who thinks gratitude is owing to those struck by calamity? Or when does shifting fortune not alter loyalties? So it was that, on the advice of Theodotus and Achillas, men were sent by the king to welcome Gnaeus Pompey on his arrival (he at this point had his wife Cornelia, whom he had taken on board at Mytilene, as his companion in his flight), and to encourage him to transfer from the freighter he was on to the ship that had come to meet him.[174] Having done this, the leading figure of the Roman race was, in the consulship of Gaius Caesar and Publius Servilius, murdered on the authority, and by the personal decision, of an Egyptian slave.

[3] Such was the end of a man of the greatest integrity and distinction, after three consulships and the same number of triumphs, and after he had conquered the world and reached a point beyond which it is impossible to

---

171. The two Lentuli were Lucius Cornelius Lentulus Crus (consul 49 BC) and Publius Cornelius Lentulus Spinther (consul 57). Marcus Favonius, born in 90, was praetor in 49 and a vigorous opponent of Caesar. Taken prisoner after the battle of Philippi in 42, he was put to death. Pompey's route after Pharsalus took him to Larisa, Amphipolis, Mytilene, Rhodes, Attaleia, and then Syhedra in Cilicia. At this point he stopped to ponder his future plans.

172. Juba I of Numidia was roughly treated by Caesar, who had reputedly grabbed his beard in a tussle, and Juba never forgave him for the slight (Suet. *Jul.* 71). He was an ally of Pompey and in 49 BC the senate, in a pro-Pompeian mood, moved that the king be declared *socius et amicus* (ally and friend), but the tribune Marcellus blocked the measure (Caes. *BC* 1.1.6). Later in 49 Juba defeated Caesar's lieutenant Curio in battle.

173. Ptolemy XII Auletes had been driven out of Egypt by his own subjects in 58 BC and had regained his throne in 55 through the help of Aulus Gabinius, with the support of Pompey (Dio 39.55.2). He was succeeded in 51 by his daughter Cleopatra VII and his son Ptolemy XIII, who was about twelve at this time.

174. Theodotus of Chios was Ptolemy's tutor in rhetoric. He later displayed Pompey's head to Caesar (Plut. *Caes.* 48.2) and was then executed by Brutus. Achillas was the commander of Ptolemy's armies.

Cornelia was the daughter of Quintus Metellus Scipio (who had joined him late in 52 BC as his fellow consul). Her marriage to Pompey occurred in 50 (Velleius) or 52 (Plut. *Pomp.* 55.1). Pompey was joined by Cornelia and his son Sextus at Mytilene, their residence during the campaign that led up to Pharsalus. Velleius seems to suggest that (2.72.4) was with Pompey at Pharsalus but may simply mean that Sextus joined his father before he reached Cilicia. A number of authorities (Plut. *Pomp.* 76.4–6; App. *BC.* 2.83; Dio 42.2.5) indicate that Pompey preferred Parthia but allowed himself to be won over by others in favor of Egypt.

rise further. He died in his fifty-eighth year and on the day before his birthday. Fortune was in the case of this man so capricious that, recently lacking land to conquer, he was now lacking land for his burial. [4] (There are some who have made a miscalculation of five years in the age of a man who was so important and was also almost of our own generation. What else could I say of these men other than that their attention must have been too preoccupied elsewhere? For calculating the years from the consulship of Gaius Atilius and Quintus Servilius was so easy! I have added this not to criticize anyone but to avoid criticism myself.)[175]

[Caesar's campaign against the Pompeian loyalists and his assassination (44 BC), which precipitates a power struggle.]

54. The king and those by whose influence he was guided showed no greater loyalty to Caesar than they had to Pompey. When Caesar arrived there they first tried to trap him and then ventured to challenge him on the battlefield, and by their deaths they paid a well-deserved penalty to the two great commanders, the one dead, the other still living.[176]

[2] Physically, Pompey had ceased to exist, but in name he was still alive everywhere. The enormous support his cause enjoyed had sparked the African War, which was being prosecuted by King Juba and the ex-consul Scipio (the man chosen by Pompey, two years before his death, as his father-in-law). [3] Their troop numbers had been increased by Marcus Cato with the addition of legions that he brought to them despite enormous logistical difficulties and lack of provisions in the region. Cato was presented with supreme command by his men but preferred to remain subordinate to the man with the higher rank.[177]

55. My commitment to my promise of brevity reminds me of how cursory my treatment of everything has to be. Following up his good fortune, Caesar sailed over to Africa, which Pompeian troops had held in their power

---

175. Pompey died in 48 BC. The eve of his birthday was September 28 (Pliny *NH* 37.13). Both Tacitus (*Ann.* 13.6.3) and Valerius Maximus (5.2.9) imply that he was born in 101. Velleius dates his birth to 106, which concurs with the biographical information provided by Appian (*BC* 2.86).

176. Caesar reached Egypt on October 1, 48 BC, and was informed of Pompey's murder. He became involved in an exhausting campaign there during the winter, which finally ended on March 27, 47, with the death of Ptolemy on the Nile and the establishment of Cleopatra VII as queen.

177. Cato was propraetor and so deferred to Quintus Metellus Scipio, who had been consul in 52 BC and thus held the rank of proconsul. Cato reached Utica after an extraordinary journey by sea from Corcyra to Crete, then to Berenice, in Egypt, and finally, after a grueling journey across the desert, to Utica. He (famously) committed suicide there, acquiring the

since Curio, leader of the Julian party, had met his end.[178] There he fought, with mixed fortunes initially, but he was then attended by his usual good fortune, and the enemy forces were driven back.[179] [2] There, too, Caesar's clemency toward the defeated was no different from that which he had shown earlier to others.

Victorious in the African War, Gaius Caesar now faced a more serious war in Spain (for his conquest of Pharnaces added hardly anything to his reputation).[180] This was a mighty and frightful conflict to which Gnaeus Pompeius, son of Pompey the Great, had put the torch. He was a young man with a great propensity for warfare, and to him flooded auxiliary troops from the world over from people who still kept up their support for the great name of his father. [3] Caesar's usual good fortune went with him into Spain, but never did he engage in any battle more fierce or perilous. In fact, when the outcome was more than doubtful, he got off his horse, stood in front of his retreating battle line, and, after denouncing Fortune for having preserved him to face such an end, declared to his men that he would not take a single step back. So, he said, they should bear in mind who the commander was that they would be deserting and in what circumstances.

[4] The battle line was reestablished more as a result of their shame than their courage, and by the general rather than by the men. Gnaeus Pompeius was found seriously wounded in some remote wasteland and was dispatched, and Labienus and Varus fell during the battle itself.[181]

---

epithet Uticensis, after the failed final stand of the Pompeians in Africa at Thapsus in 46. Curiously, Velleius omits mention of Cato's celebrated death. Scipio also committed suicide, with far less acclaim.

178. Curio (2.48.3) was killed by Juba on August 20, 49 BC, at the Bagrada River in Africa.

179. Caesar arrived at Hadrumetum on December 28, 47 BC. He harried the Pompeians and Numidians in the winter of 47/6 and defeated them decisively at Thapsus on April 6, 46 (February 6 by the Julian calendar).

180. Caesar had defeated Pharnaces II, son of Mithridates and king of the Cimmerian Bosporus, at the battle of Zela on August 2, 47 BC (June 12 in the Julian calendar), with the help of King Deiotaurus of Galatia. This occurred before his African campaign and led Caesar to make his famous claim "Veni, vidi, vici" (I came, I saw, I conquered; Plut. *Caes.* 50; Suet. *Jul.* 37).

181. Gnaeus Pompeius, thirty-one at the time, was Pompey's eldest son. He had proved an able commander, destroying Caesar's transport ships before the battle of Dyrrhachium. He had occupied the Balearic Islands and crossed from there to Spain, where the battle of Munda on March 17, 45 BC, ended the war. In this particularly bloody engagement 33,000 Pompeians are said to have died. Gnaeus Pompeius fled and was put to death in a cave near Lauro. Titus Labienus, the tribune who had proposed special honorifics for Pompey in 63 (see 2.40.4), supposedly with Caesar's agreement, went on to serve the latter ably in Gaul, essentially as his second in command. He threw in his lot with Pompey in 49. Publius Attius Varus had been a former governor of Africa and had served under Quintus Metellus Scipio at Thapsus.

56. Victorious over all his opponents, Caesar returned to Rome where—in a gesture surpassing anyone's belief—he pardoned all who had borne arms against him. He then filled the city with the most magnificent shows—a gladiatorial contest, a naval engagement, cavalry and infantry battles, and, in addition, fights between elephants—and hosted a banquet that lasted many days. [2] He celebrated five triumphs. The ornaments for his Gallic triumph were made of citron wood; those for the Pontic from shittimwood; those for the Alexandrian from tortoiseshell; those for the African from ivory; and those for the Spanish from polished silver. The money raised from the spoils and carried in the procession amounted to slightly more than 600 million sesterces.[182]

[3] But it fell to this great man, who had been so merciful in all his victories, to have peaceful enjoyment of supreme power for no more than five months. He returned to the city in the month of October and was murdered on the Ides of March in a conspiracy led by Brutus and Cassius, the first of whom he had not managed to conciliate with the guarantee of a consulship, while Cassius he had alienated by postponing that office.[183] There were even a number of Caesar's closest friends involved in the plot to kill him, men who had been elevated to the highest positions thanks to the good fortunes of his party—Decimus Brutus, Gaius Trebonius, and others of great renown.[184] [4] Considerable animosity had been roused toward Caesar thanks to Mark Antony, a man ready for any reckless venture and Caesar's colleague in the consulship.[185] Antony had set a royal diadem on Caesar's head as he sat before the

182. Caesar had returned to Rome after Thapsus on July 25, 46 BC, and after Munda, in March of 45, made his final return to the city in October of 45. The first four triumphs, for Gaul, Africa, Egypt, and Pontus, were celebrated in August and September of 46 and the fifth, for Spain, in October.

183. Caesar died on March 15, 44 BC, as the result of a conspiracy led by Marcus Junius Brutus and Gaius Cassius Longinus. Brutus had in 58 accompanied Cato to Cyprus (see 2.38.6). He had been a Pompeian supporter during the civil war but received a pardon from Caesar after Pharsalus. He was governor of Cisalpine Gaul in 46 and urban praetor in the year of the assassination, which he seems to have championed for idealistic reasons. Gaius Cassius Longinus had fought with distinction after the battle of Carrhae in 53 when he organized the defense of Syria (see 2.46). He served as a naval commander in support of Pompey, mainly off Sicily, but on the news of Pharsalus ceased operations and was later given a pardon. He held the office of foreign praetor in 44.

184. Decimus Junius Brutus had been a consistent supporter of Caesar before the assassination, serving under him in Gaul and then commanding, with Trebonius, his fleet at the siege of Massilia in 49 BC. Afterward he was appointed proconsul of Cisalpine Gaul. Urban praetor in 44, he was clearly favored by Caesar and had been designated consul for 42. Gaius Trebonius had known Caesar's favor as his legate in Gaul and at the siege of Massilia. He held a consulship in 45 BC and had been designated proconsul of Asia by Caesar before Caesar's death.

185. Velleius here introduces the figure of Marcus Antonius (Mark Antony). He was born in

Rostra during the Lupercalia, and though it was refused by him, the refusal was given in such a way as to suggest no offense on Caesar's part.[186]

57. As events showed, praise is due to the advice of Hirtius and Pansa, who had always declared to Caesar that he should hold by arms a principate won by arms.[187] Caesar kept saying that he preferred death to living in fear, and, while he was expecting to meet in turn the clemency he had himself shown, he was caught off guard by ungrateful wretches. The immortal gods had, however, revealed to him a large number of portents and omens of his forthcoming peril. [2] The soothsayers had warned him to be particularly wary of the Ides of March, and his wife Calpurnia, thoroughly alarmed by a dream at night, also kept begging him to stay home that day.[188] Moreover, some papers informing him of the conspiracy were given to him but not immediately read by him. [3] But for sure the power of the Fates cannot be avoided; they destroy the judgment of anyone whose fortunes they have decided to change.

58. In the year in which they committed this crime, Marcus Brutus and Gaius Cassius were praetors and Decimus Brutus was consul-designate. [2] Along with the band of the conspirators, and escorted by a troop of gladiators belonging to Decimus Brutus, these three seized the Capitol. At that point Antony, the consul, convened the senate. (Cassius had actually suggested that Antony be killed along with Caesar and that Caesar's will be destroyed, but Brutus had rejected the suggestion, insisting that their goal as citizens should

---

83 BC, the eldest son of Marcus Antonius Creticus (2.31.3), and served under Caesar in Gaul until late 50; later, as tribune in Rome, he was Caesar's spokesman in the senate. He served at Pharsalus and in 44 was Caesar's fellow consul. He will play a key role in the next thirty or so chapters of Velleius' narrative.

186. The Lupercalia was an ancient festival of purification celebrated on February 15. Participants assembled at the Lupercal, the cave on the Palatine where the she-wolf (*lupa*) supposedly suckled Romulus and Remus (see 1.15.3). Magistrates ran through the street ritually striking passers-by with thongs; Antony participated as consul in 44 BC, his gesture one of the most striking events of Caesar's career. The motives of Antony and Caesar in this famous incident have been much discussed; it might well have been a ruse to test the crowd's reaction to the notion of monarchy, or perhaps to allow Caesar the opportunity to reaffirm his republican credentials.

187. Gaius Vibius Pansa was a committed Caesarian, governor of Bithynia in 47–46 BC and Cisalpine Gaul in 45, and designated by Caesar to be consul in 43. He joined Hirtius against Antony in March of 43 and died after Mutina (Modena, on the south side of the Po valley), allegedly poisoned on Octavian's orders. Aulus Hirtius was an officer of Caesar in Spain and in the east, propraetor in Gaul in 45. He was the author of a book attached after Book 8 of Caesar's *Bellum Gallicum* and perhaps of the *Bellum Alexandrinum*. He died at Mutina.

188. Calpurnia was the daughter of Lucius Calpurnius Piso Caesoninus (consul 58 BC). She married Caesar in 59 to strengthen the ties between him and her father, though Piso maintained neutrality in the civil war. The story that she sought to keep him from the senate meeting is found also in Plutarch (*Caes.* 63.10). She handed Caesar's papers over to Antony after the assassination.

be nothing more than the blood of the "tyrant"; using this expression for Caesar lent support to their coup.) [3] Dolabella, whom Caesar had marked out to succeed him as consul, had by now seized the fasces and insignia of consulship, and Antony, as if to broker a peace, sent his own children as hostages to the Capitol and gave Caesar's assassins his word that they could come down without harm.[189] [4] The precedent of the famous Athenian decree was cited by Cicero, and its application to the present situation was approved by the senate with a decree granting amnesty for past actions.[190]

[Octavian's earlier career, before his adoption by Caesar, and his decision to pursue high office after the adoption. Rivalry with Antony, leading to Antony's defeat at Mutina (early 43 BC).]

59. There followed the opening of Caesar's will, by which he adopted Gaius Octavius, grandson of his sister Julia.[191] A short account of the ancestry of Octavius should be given, <even if it is premature at this point>.

[2] Gaius Octavius <the father>, while not of patrician stock, was nevertheless born into a very distinguished equestrian family, and was a man who was dignified and honest, ethical and affluent. In a field of candidates of the highest nobility, he was in first place among those elected praetor (while the respect he enjoyed earned for him as a wife Atia, daughter of Julia).[192] After

---

189. Lucius Cornelius Dolabella (69–43 BC) was the former son-in-law of Cicero, whose daughter Tullia he had married in 50 and divorced in 46. Dolabella joined the side of Caesar during the civil wars. Tribune of the plebs in 47, he fought alongside Caesar in Africa and then in Spain. In the face of Antony's opposition, Caesar designated him as suffect consul to succeed him in 44.

  Cicero (*Phil.* 1.31) claims that on March 17, 44 BC, Antony sent only his two-year-old son by Fulvia, Marcus Antonius Antyllus (later to be executed by Octavian in Alexandria after the death of Antony; Plut. *Ant.* 87); his other son Iullus Antonius (consul 10 BC) was probably not yet born. Velleius' plural here may be rhetorical or he may intend to include Antony's daughter with his second wife Antonia Hybrida.

190. To avoid, for a time, the danger of civil war, the conspirators were granted amnesty after Caesar's death. The historical parallel cited here is to the pardon proposed in 403 BC, when the Thirty Tyrants were expelled from Athens and democracy was restored by Thrasybullus. Cicero, in a lost speech *De Pace*, given on March 17, 44, promised amnesty to the murderers, ratification of Caesar's acts, and a consulship for Dolabella.

191. This is the first reference to the future emperor Augustus, born 63 BC, in a period that may be the best documented in Roman history. Velleius is clearly sympathetic toward him, following Cicero in demonstrating a clear bias against Antony. But he does not show the enthusiasm that he does for Tiberius, apologizing, for instance, for Octavian's participation in the proscriptions. Caesar had no surviving offspring, and Octavian became Caesar's son by testamentary adoption, which does not seem to have been regarded as full and "regular" adoption (a son adopted by this process normally maintained the family name of his biological father), which explains why Octavian had his status as Caesar's son ratified by the *comitia curiata*.

192. Augustus was born Gaius Octavius, on September 23, 63 BC, the son of his father's

that office he gained Macedonia by sortition and was acclaimed as imperator in the province. He was returning from there to stand for the consulship when he died, leaving behind a son still in the *toga praetexta*.[193] [3] This boy was then brought up in the home of his stepfather Philippus, and his great-uncle Gaius Caesar loved him as his own son. When he was eighteen Octavius went with Caesar on the Spanish campaign, after which Caesar kept him at his side, never having him stay in anyone else's quarters or travel in anyone else's carriage, and he honored him with the priestly office of pontiff though he was still a boy.[194] [4] After bringing the civil wars to an end, he had, in order to give the exceptional young man's character a training in the liberal arts, sent him to Apollonia for his studies, and had planned to take him along later as his associate in his wars against the Getae and then the Parthians.

[5] When Octavius was brought the news of his uncle's assassination, the centurions of the legions nearby assured him of their support and that of their men, and Salvidienus and Agrippa told him he should not reject their offer.[195] He therefore made haste for Rome and at Brundisium received a detailed account of both the murder and the will. [6] As he approached Rome a huge crowd of well-wishers flocked to meet him, and when he entered the city the sun's orb was seen forming a perfectly rounded, <rainbow-colored> circle above his head, as though placing a crown on a man soon to be so great.

60. Octavius' mother Atia and his stepfather Philippus were opposed to his assuming the Caesar's name with the hatred that attended its fortunes, but

---

second wife Atia. She was the daughter of Marcus Atius Balbus (praetor 60) and Julia, Caesar's sister. Hence Octavius was Caesar's great-nephew.

193. Gaius Octavius Thurinus, the father, died in 59/8 BC, probably in the summer of 59, before the consular elections. He was proconsul of Macedonia in 60/59 and was saluted as imperator for defeating the Bessi. Octavius the son was almost four at the time of his father's death. Octavius' mother Atia subsequently married Marcius Philippus (consul 56).

194. In November of 46 BC Caesar left Rome to face the Pompeians in Spain. He had intended to take Octavius on the campaign, but the latter was detained by a major illness and was obliged to join him later, by which time Caesar had ended the campaign. He most likely had Octavius with him in Spain during the summer of 45. When they traveled from Spain to Gallia Narbonensis, Caesar did indeed allow Octavius to share his quarters and transported him on his ship (Nic. Dam. *Aug.* 11), but traveling through Italy afterward Antony rode with Caesar and Octavius followed with Decimus Brutus Albinus (Plut. *Ant.* 11.1). He succeeded Lucius Domitius Ahenobarbus, who died in 47, in the pontificate.

195. Marcus Vipsanius Agrippa, born, like Octavian, in 63 BC and consul in 37, was Octavian's most loyal supporter, the architect of his victory at Actium, and later his son-in-law, with his marriage to his only daughter Julia. He died in 12. Quintus Salvidienus Rufus was elevated later to high station by Octavian. He served (unsuccessfully) against Sextus Pompeius and played a major role in the Perusine War. He later negotiated secretly with Antony and was denounced by Octavian as a public enemy and executed or forced to commit suicide (2.76.4).

the Fates that protect the Republic and the world laid claim to the founder and savior of the Roman race.[196] [2] His divine spirit therefore rejected human recommendations and proposed to follow the dangerous path of greatness rather than the safe one of mediocrity. He chose to trust the judgment made of him by his uncle, who was a Caesar after all, rather than that of his stepfather. It was not right, he would say, for him to consider himself unworthy of the name of which Caesar had considered him worthy.

[3] The consul Antony from the start gave him a condescending welcome—but that was fear, not disdain—and after receiving him in the gardens of Pompey barely granted him time for a conversation.[197] Soon Antony began to make unconscionable allegations that he was the target of plots directed at him by the young man, and this was where his dishonesty was shamefully exposed. [4] After that, the insane plans for an unspeakable tyranny hatched by the consuls Antony and Dolabella burst into the open.[198] Gaius Caesar had placed 700,000 sesterces in the temple of Ops. This was seized by Antony, and the records of Caesar's acts were doctored by the insertion of falsified grants of citizenship and <amnesty>. Everything was modified for financial gain, with the consul putting the Republic up for sale. [5] Antony also decided to seize for himself the province of Gaul, which had been assigned by decree to the consul-designate Decimus Brutus, while Dolabella assigned to himself the overseas provinces.[199] The two were men of very dissimilar temperament and they had different agendas, with the result that hatred began to grow between them, and the young Gaius Caesar found himself every day the target of Antony's plots.[200]

196. Velleius' account of the parental opposition to the adoption is reflected in Nic. Dam. *Aug.* 18, who says that Atia and Philippus wrote to Octavius while he was in Italy.

197. Antony left Rome for Campania close to the end of April 44 BC but returned about a month later for a meeting with Octavian. Appian (*BC* 3.14) adds the detail that Octavian had to meet him in the vestibule.

198. Dolabella, Caesar's own choice as suffect consul for 44 BC, behaved ruthlessly in the office and vigorously suppressed the pro-Caesarians. His actual term in office was marked by arrests and executions.

199. In early April of 44 BC Decimus Brutus left for Cisalpine Gaul, to which he had been appointed by Caesar. Antony and Dolabella were assigned the provinces of Macedonia and Syria, Dolabella's through an appeal to the popular assembly (App. *BC* 3.7). Antony was not satisfied with Macedonia and planned to introduce a proposal on June 1 that would assign Brutus' Cisalpine Gaul as well as Gallia Comata to himself, with him surrendering the governorship of Macedonia but not its army. This proposal met with intense disapproval and an insufficient number of senators turned up on June 1 to vote for it, but Antony appealed instead to the popular assemblies. Brutus, claiming that he had been authorized by the senate, was unwilling to accede; he clashed with Antony and was besieged by him at Mutina, Cisalpine Gaul, at the end of 44.

200. After his adoption Gaius Octavius became Gaius Julius Caesar Octavianus, the last element being the standard adaptation of the name of one's *gens* (family) carried as a traditional element

61. The state was oppressed and languishing under the despotic rule of Antony (all felt indignation and distress, but none had the power to resist), when Gaius Caesar, barely entering his twentieth year, embarked on a remarkable enterprise that achieved outstanding success, and with a plan of his own exhibited on behalf of the state greater courage than did the senate. He called in his father's veterans, [2] first from Calatia and shortly afterward from Casilinum. Others followed these men's example and in a short time they coalesced to form a regular army.²⁰¹ Soon Antony met the army he had ordered to come to Brundisium from the overseas provinces, but the Legion of Mars and the Fourth Legion, when they learned of the wishes of the senate and of the character of the great young man, struck camp and joined Caesar. [3] The senate honored Caesar with an equestrian statue, which, set up in the Rostra, to this day records his age with its inscription. (This was an honor that, in a period of three hundred years, had fallen to no one apart from Lucius Sulla, Gnaeus Pompey, and Gaius Julius Caesar.) The senate then ordered him, in partnership with the consuls-designate Hirtius and Pansa, to wage war on Antony with the rank of propraetor. [4] This war he conducted with great courage near Mutina, when he was in his twentieth year, and he freed Decimus Brutus from a blockade. Antony was forced to leave Italy in an ignominious and destitute flight, but one of the consuls died in battle and the other of his wounds a few days later.²⁰²

in the new name, though in fact Octavian seems to have dropped it. He is conventionally referred to as Octavian from this point until his receipt of the name/title Augustus in 27 BC.

201. Throughout 44 BC the tensions between Octavian and Antony abated from time to time but did not disappear. The situation worsened after October of 44, when Antony made his trumped-up claim of an assassination attempt (see 2.60.3). As Antony made plans to transfer his legions from Macedonia to Italy to wrest Cisalpine Gaul from Decimus Brutus, Octavian took the bold step of calling Caesar's veterans to arms by appealing to the loyalties of those troops who had settled in Campania. The raising of the army took place in October. In the *Res Gestae* (1.1) Augustus indicates that he raised his army when he was nineteen, confirming that it occurred after September 23, 44. Thus Velleius is mistaken in saying that it happened in his nineteenth year, that is, just after his eighteenth birthday. Octavian made an ill-judged attempt to force events by bringing troops into Rome in November but prudently desisted when the desired outcome was clearly not attainable.

202. Of the four legions brought over from Macedonia by Antony, two declared eventually for Octavian and the commitment of the other two was far from secure. Antony moved his troops against Decimus Brutus, and Cicero carried a resolution in the senate on December 20, 44 BC, that Brutus was authorized to stay in his province for as long as he could. Cicero claimed that, in defecting, the legions of Antony were conforming to the senate's will (*Phil.* 3.8). The senate was reluctant to break with Antony, but it gave Octavian a commission with the rank of propraetor to order the consuls Hirtius and Pansa to raise extra troops. Velleius' account, while not inaccurate, is misleading, since at the same time that the statue was voted for Octavian in early January of 43, Cicero made a successful motion that one should be made for Marcus Aemilius Lepidus. On April 14, Octavian and Hirtius defeated Antony at Forum Gallorum, close to Mutina. A few

[Triumvirate of Octavian, Antony, and Lepidus (late 43 BC). The triumvirs reintroduce proscriptions, for which Velleius blames Antony and Lepidus.]

62. Before Antony took to flight, all manner of decrees honoring Caesar Octavian and his army were passed by the senate, mostly thanks to the efforts of Cicero. When the threat receded, however, the senate's true feelings suddenly burst into the open and morale was immediately restored to the Pompeian party.[203] [2] Brutus and Cassius were now formally assigned by decree the provinces that they themselves had taken over without senatorial authorization; whatever armies had joined them received commendations; and all overseas jurisdictions were put under their control.[204] [3] In fact, Marcus Brutus and Gaius Cassius had earlier issued public statements declaring that they would be happy to live in perpetual exile as long as the state could enjoy a harmonious stability, that they would furnish no grounds for civil war, and that the greatest honor for them lay in the recognition of what they had done. This they did at one time from fear of Antony's military strength, and at another with a pretense of fear in order to heighten resentment against him. On leaving the city and Italy, however, they had— the two of them being determined <and like-minded>—commandeered provinces and armies, without official authorization; and, on the pretext that the state was situated wherever they themselves happened to be, they had even taken over monies that were being conveyed to Rome by the quaestors (who willingly surrendered them) from the overseas provinces.[205]

[4] All these acts of theirs were now dealt with and ratified by decrees of the senate, Decimus Brutus was decreed a triumph although he owed his life to another's services, and Hirtius and Pansa were honored with a state funeral. [5] Of Caesar Octavian there was no mention, and in fact the envoys sent to his army were told to ensure that he was excluded from their

---

days later Antony was defeated at Mutina and the siege of the city was lifted. Hirtius was killed in the battle and Pansa died shortly afterward of wounds received in the earlier engagement. Antony chose to withdraw to Gallia Narbonensis and on April 26 was declared a public enemy.

203. The senate had instructed Octavian to combine his forces with those of Decimus Brutus, which Octavian was unwilling to do since he saw himself as his father's avenger. This led to a rift between Octavian and the senate, which refused to provide him with the huge funds that he had promised his soldiers as bounty.

204. Velleius indicates that republican feelings were running high following Mutina and that the commands of Brutus and Cassius were confirmed by the senate.

205. Gaius Antistius Vetus, propraetor in Syria, and Marcus Appuleius, proquaestor of Asia, both handed over public funds, and possibly troops, to Brutus (Plut. *Brut.* 25.1; App. *BC* 3.63, 4.75) while Publius Cornelius Lentulus Spinther, *proquaestor propraetore* (former quaestor with the authority of a praetor; compare the rank of Cato at 2.45.4) in Asia, handed over money and troops to Cassius (Cic. *Fam.* 12.14.6).

conversation with the troops. The army, however, was not as ungrateful as the senate had been, for while Caesar bore the insult by concealing his feelings, the men declared that they would accept no instructions without their commander being present. [6] This was the time that Cicero, because of his ingrained attachment to the Pompeian party, gave as his opinion that Caesar Octavian "should be commended and taken out," thereby saying one thing but with another meaning understood.[206]

63. Meanwhile Antony had crossed the Alps in his flight but was at first rebuffed in his negotiations with Marcus Lepidus.[207] (Lepidus had been covertly appointed *pontifex maximus* in Gaius Julius Caesar's place, and though Spain had been decreed as his province, he was still loitering in Gaul.) Presently, however, Antony made quite frequent appearances before Lepidus' men, and since all generals were better than Lepidus, and since Antony was better than most, when he was sober, he was let in by the soldiers at the rear of the camp, where they had broken down the fortifications. He then yielded titular command to Lepidus, but supreme authority actually rested with him.[208] [2] Iuventius Laterensis had been strongly advising Lepidus not to join up with Antony, who had now been pronounced an enemy of the state, but he could see that his advice was in vain; and just before Antony's entrance into the camp, he stabbed himself with his sword, the man's death being consistent with the life he had led.[209]

[3] Plancus, then, with dubious loyalty (that is, his own brand of loyalty), was long conflicted over which side to support and had difficulty making up his mind.[210] At one point he was aiding his colleague, the consul-designate

206. The witticism arises from the double meaning of the Latin *tollo*, "elevate" or "remove/kill." The famous assessment of Cicero appears in a somewhat different form, with the addition of *ornandus* ("should be distinguished"), in Cicero (*Fam.* 11.20.1).

207. Marcus Aemilius Lepidus earned his place in history as the third member of the "second" triumvirate. As praetor in 49 BC he supported Caesar and was appointed governor of Nearer Spain, becoming involved in the disturbances in Further Spain and consequently celebrating a triumph. He was consul in 46 and had been appointed by Caesar, just before his death, as proconsul of Gallia Narbonensis and Nearer Spain. He became *pontifex maximus* after Caesar's death—it was Antony who had transferred that election from the people to the priests. In May of 43, following Mutina, he was evidently determined to resist Antony but lacked the courage and ability to do so.

208. After Mutina, Antony retired by forced marches into southern Gaul, but there his fortunes turned, since he was able to win over the governors of Gaul and Spain (Plancus and Pollio). Lepidus in Gallia Narbonensis had an army of seven legions, which along with two powerful armies in Further Spain and Gallia Comata came under Antony's control, though he conceded to Lepidus the formality of equal rank. He was then able to reenter Italy at the end of the summer of 43 BC.

209. Marcus Iuventius Laterensis, who belonged to a distinguished family from Tusculum, was a man universally admired by the ancient sources. He was aedile in 55 BC and praetor in 51.

210. Lucius Munatius Plancus was legate of Caesar in Gaul in 54 BC and supported Caesar

Decimus Brutus, and was insinuating himself into the senate's good graces with dispatches, but he soon betrayed that very same man. Asinius Pollio, on the other hand, stuck to his decision: he remained loyal to the Julian party and opposed the Pompeian.[211] Both men handed over their armies to Antony.

64. First abandoned by Plancus, Decimus Brutus then also became the target of his intrigues. As his army gradually deserted him, he took to flight, only to be murdered by assassins sent by Antony, in the home of a certain nobleman who had offered him shelter (the man's name was Camelius). And so he paid a well-justified penalty to Gaius Julius Caesar, who had deserved the best from him.[212] [2] Of all Caesar's friends, Brutus had been the foremost, and he became his murderer; the resentment felt toward the fortune from which he himself had benefited he directed against the man who had amassed it; and he thought it fair for him to hold onto what he had accepted from Caesar, and for Caesar, who had given it to him, to die.

[3] These were the days when Marcus Tullius Cicero, in a series of speeches, branded with everlasting infamy the memory of Antony.[213] It was, however, with flashes of his divine oratory that he tore Antony to shreds, whereas the tribune Cannutius did so with the fury of a rabid dog.[214] [4] Their championship of freedom cost both men their lives, but the proscription commenced with the tribune's blood and virtually ended with Cicero's, as though Antony now had his satisfaction.

---

in a number of campaigns in Spain and Africa. He became praetor in 45 and governor of Gallia Comata in 44/3. He was the consul-designate for 42 with Decimus Brutus. He was the father or grandfather of Plancina, who was implicated in the death of Germanicus (see note 411). This is the first of several references to Plancus by Velleius (see also chapters 64, 67, 74, 76, 83.3, 91, 95), who clearly despised him. Velleius may have derived this hostile portrait from the writings of Asinius Pollio, whom he much admired.

211. Gaius Asinius Pollio (76 BC–AD 4) was with Caesar when he crossed the Rubicon and also at Pharsalus, Thapsus, and Munda. He was propraetor in Spain in 44. He became an adherent of Antony and was appointed legate in Transpadane Gaul and consul in 40. He was a distinguished patron of literature, admired by both Virgil and Horace. His own writings included an account of the civil wars that was used by Plutarch and Appian, and perhaps by Velleius. See also 2.86.3.

212. Decimus Brutus, abandoned by Plancus, planned to join Marcus Junius Brutus in Macedonia but was deserted by his army. He was captured by a Gallic chief and executed on Antony's orders. The name of his slayer is given variously: Capenus, said to be one of the Sequani, in Livy (*Per.* 120.2); Camillus in Appian (*BC* 3.98); Furius in Valerius Maximus (4.7.6, 9.13.3).

213. Cicero delivered his famous series of *Philippics* against Antony between September 2, 44, and April 21, 43 BC. Brutus died sometime after the end of June of 43, so Velleius' chronology ("these were the days") is rather casual.

214. Tiberius Cannutius (tribune 44 BC) was a vitriolic opponent of Antony. He was taken prisoner after the fall of Perusia (modern Perugia) in central Italy in 41 by Octavian and executed along with three hundred equestrians and a number of senators. Velleius glosses over this by suggesting that Antony's bloodlust was sated with the death of Cicero at Formiae, on December 7, 43.

Lepidus was then judged an enemy of the state by the senate, as Antony had been earlier.[215]

65. There followed correspondence by dispatches between Lepidus, Caesar Octavian, and Antony in which terms were mentioned, while Antony continually reminded Caesar of how hostile the Pompeian party was to him, what heights it had now reached, and with what enthusiasm Brutus and Cassius were being extolled by Cicero.[216] Antony actually threatened to join forces with Brutus and Cassius, who were now in command of seventeen legions, should Caesar reject any accord with him, adding that Caesar had a greater duty to avenge his father than Antony did to avenge a friend. [2] Then began the power sharing, and in response to the exhortation and pleas of their armies a family connection was even formed between Antony and Caesar, with the betrothal of Antony's stepdaughter to Caesar.[217] Caesar entered the consulship, with Quintus Pedius as his colleague, on September 22, the day before he completed his twentieth year, that is, 709 years after the city's foundation, and seventy-two before you entered your consulship, Marcus Vinicius.[218]

[3] This year saw Ventidius add the consular *toga praetexta* to that of a praetor, and that in a city through which in the past he had been led in a triumphal procession as one of the captives from Picenum. He also later celebrated a triumph.[219]

---

215. Lepidus was outlawed on June 30, 43 BC, and the senate at the same time decreed the destruction of his statue on the rostra.

216. Other sources (Plut. *Ant.* 19.1; App. *BC* 3.97; Dio 46.52.2) reflect the notion that it was Octavian who sought the alliance, from fear of Brutus and Cassius.

217. The agreement was made late in 43 BC and the formal triumvirate was confirmed by the *lex Titia* on November 17. Velleius describes the alliance between the three men as a *societas,* the same term he uses of the earlier association between Caesar, Pompey, and Crassus. The stepdaughter of Antony was Claudia, the daughter of Publius Clodius and Fulvia.

218. In July of 43 BC, Octavian had forced an open rupture with the senate, demanding one of the vacant consulships, which they inevitably refused. Thereupon Octavian marched into Rome, which he occupied without opposition, an action glossed over by Velleius. He instituted elections in which he and Quintus Pedius were returned as consuls, in succession to Hirtius and Pansa. Octavian undertook two important measures: he had his testamentary adoption as Caesar's son legally confirmed and he rescinded the amnesty given to the conspirators, all of whom were declared enemies of the state. Octavian took the consulship on August 19, 43. This date seems to be firmly established by Dio (56.30.5) and Tacitus (*Ann.* 1.9.1) but at variance with Velleius' very precise dating of September 22. One of the terms of the triumvirate was that Octavian resign the consulship, and he and Pedius be succeeded by Publius Ventidius Bassus and Gaius Carrinas.

219. Ventidius was in fact serving his term as praetor when he was elevated to the consulship. He was a Picenian who had raised soldiers from his native region in support of Antony. He and his mother had been taken prisoner in the Social War and had been led in the triumph of Pompeius Strabo in 89 BC. He went on to celebrate a triumph over the Parthians in 38 (see 2.78.1).

66. Then came the proscriptions, a repeat of the disaster on the Sullan model. They arose out of the rage of Antony as well as Lepidus, both of whom, as I noted above, had been adjudged public enemies, and both of whom preferred to be told what they had suffered rather than what they had deserved. Caesar Octavian opposed the idea, but against two his opposition was futile. [2] Nothing was more scandalous in this period than Octavian's being forced to proscribe anyone or Cicero's having been proscribed by anyone. Through the criminal act of Antony the people's voice was severed, with no one defending the life of a man who for so many years had, in the public sphere, defended the life of the state and, in the private, the lives of citizens.[220] [3] But you achieved nothing, Mark Antony—the indignation that bursts forth from my mind and heart forces me to go beyond the parameters I set for my work! Yes, you achieved nothing in counting out the payment for cutting off that heavenly voice and celebrated head, and with a deadly fee inciting people to murder a man who had earlier been the savior of the state and such a great consul! [4] What you stole from Marcus Cicero was a life that would have been full of anxiety, some years of senility, and an existence that would have been for him more wretched with you in power than death with you as triumvir. But the fame and glory of his acts and words you did not take from him, and in fact you magnified them. [5] He lives and will live in the memory of all the ages to come. As long as this physical world remains intact (whether its structure was due to chance or providence or whatever else), a world that he alone of the Romans, one might almost say, saw through the eyes of his mind, grasped with his intellect, and illuminated with his eloquence, it will carry along with it the praise of Cicero as its partner through time. All posterity will admire his writings directed against you and will curse what you did to him. The human race will disappear from the world before Cicero's <name will> fade away.

67. No one has been able even to deplore in an adequate manner the misfortunes of this whole period, and certainly one cannot properly describe them in words. [2] This fact, however, must be noted. Toward the proscribed the loyalty of their wives was consummate, that of their freedmen passable, that of their slaves slight, and that of their sons nonexistent. So difficult for human beings is the deferment of whatever hopes they may have conceived. [3] To leave nothing sacred for anyone and, as it were, <to give a signal for> and inducement to atrocities, Antony had proscribed his

---

220. The first consequence of the triumvirate was a wave of proscriptions during which thousands of political opponents were eliminated. Velleius' attempt to exonerate Octavian entirely from the exactions rings hollow. Antony posted a reward for Cicero's death and paid out a bonus to his slayer, called Popilius Laenas (App. *BC* 4.20) or Herennius (Plut. *Cic.* 48.6).

uncle, Lucius Caesar, and Lepidus had proscribed his brother, Paulus; nor was Plancus lacking the influence to have his brother Plancus Plotius proscribed.[221] [4] So it was that, as part of their traditional soldiers' banter, those following Lepidus' and Plancus' triumphal chariot would repeatedly chant, amid boos from the citizens, the following verse: "It is over the germans, not the Gauls, that our two consuls are triumphing."[222]

[The fates of some minor political figures.]

68. Mention must now be made of something omitted from its proper context—the individual in question does not permit only a rough sketch of his actions. Marcus Caelius was a man very much like Curio in his oratorical ability and in spirit, but in both he was his superior and he was no less clever a scoundrel than Curio.[223] He could not be rescued even with an inordinate amount of money—Caelius' financial situation was in a worse state than his character—and while Caesar was fighting for the state's interests at

---

221. Antony's father, Marcus Antonius Creticus (2.31.3), had married Julia, the daughter of Lucius Julius Caesar (consul 90 BC; see 2.15.1). Julia's brother, also Lucius Julius Caesar (consul 64), had opposed Antony after Caesar's death and was saved after the proscription by the intervention of his sister.

    Lucius Aemilius Paulus (consul 50) had been an *optimate* early in his career but was won over to Caesar with the help of a considerable bribe. He had supported the resolution declaring his brother a public enemy, and after being proscribed he was allowed to escape, whereupon he joined Marcus Junius Brutus. He was pardoned after Philippi.

    Gaius Munatius Plancus, brother of Lucius, had been adopted by Lucius Plautius. He was designated praetor by Caesar for 43. Pliny the Elder reports that when he tried to escape the proscriptions he was betrayed by the powerful odor of his perfume (*NH* 13.25).

222. Plancus, proconsul of Transalpine Gaul, triumphed on December 29, 43 BC, over the Gauls or the Raeti; Lepidus, proconsul of Gallia Narbonensis and Nearer Spain, triumphed on December 31 for victories in Spain. The joke depends on the pun, *Germanus* = "German," *germanus* = "brother." As often happens in these situations, the soldiers sacrificed constitutional nicety on the altar of wit; neither man was consul until 42 and during the triumph were strictly consuls-designate for the following year.

223. Marcus Caelius Rufus was born into an equestrian family about 88 or 87 BC and acquired a reputation for witty eloquence, and for extravagant and dissolute behavior (see 2.36.2). Caelius was at one time the lover of Clodia, sister of Publius Clodius (2.45) and almost certainly the Lesbia of Catullus' poetry. In 56 he was prosecuted for involvement in a plot to murder an embassy from Alexandria representing Ptolemy XII. He was defended by Cicero, whose famous speech, the *pro Caelio*, has survived; Cicero suggested that Caelius' prosecution was all part of a plot by Clodia, and Caelius was acquitted. Caelius supported Caesar during the civil war and was urban praetor during Caesar's absence from Rome in 48 when he proposed a moratorium of six months for the repayment of debts, and another measure that would have canceled debts. He recalled Milo from his exile in Massilia and was subsequently suspended from office (Caes. *BC* 3.20–21). In 48 he raised an insurrection against Caesar along with Milo, during the course of which both Milo and Caelius died. Curio's eloquence is alluded to at 2.48.3.

the battle of Pharsalus, [2] he gained prominence in his praetorship as the proponent of a law canceling debts. He could not be put off by the authority of the senate and the consul. He even called to his assistance Annius Milo, who was hostile to the Julian party because of his failure to secure a recall from exile, and incited sedition in the city and, <just as openly>, disorder on the scale of a war. Caelius was first of all banished from the state, and subsequently, on the orders of the senate, he was crushed by the consuls' army near Thurii. [3] Milo met a similar fate in a venture of the same kind. He was struck by a stone during his attack on the Hirpinian city of Compsa and simultaneously paid the penalty to Publius Clodius and to his fatherland, on which he was launching an armed attack. He was a restless man, more impetuous than courageous.

[4] Inasmuch as I am looking back to what I have omitted, reference should be made to the extraordinary and unbecoming liberties that the plebeian tribunes Marullus Epidius and Flavus Caesetius took with regard to Gaius Julius Caesar in seeking to prove that he harbored regal aspirations (for which they almost felt the force of his absolute power!). [5] However, although the princeps was often provoked by them, his anger went only to the length of removing them from politics. He was satisfied with castigating them as a censor rather than inflicting a dictator's punishment, and he declared that it was to his great regret that he had to choose between departing from his nature and having his dignity undermined.[224] But I must now return to the regular order of events.

[Brutus and Cassius raise armies in the east but are defeated by Octavian and Antony at Philippi in 42 BC. Sextus Pompeius, with his powerful naval forces, remains a threat.]

69. In Asia Dolabella had by now duped the ex-consul Gaius Trebonius, whom he was trying to supplant, with a stratagem and had killed him at Smyrna.[225] (Trebonius was an individual who had shown himself very

---

224. The activities of Gaius Epidius Marullus (or Marcellus) and Lucius Caesetius Flavus are clothed in obscurity and remain so in Velleius' narrative. At some point in January they removed the diadems that someone had put on the statues of Julius Caesar in the Rostra. When Caesar entered Rome on January 26, 44 BC, he was greeted as king and the tribunes arrested the persons who had placed them there. Caesar objected, for reasons unknown, to their behavior (the sources suggest that they in fact drew attention to Caesar's ambitions to become king) and they proclaimed that he was interfering with their freedom of speech. Caesar spoke against them in the senate and had their powers removed, on the motion of their colleague Gaius Helvius Cinna. Caesar was appointed censor at the same time as he was made dictator.

225. After his digression Velleius resumes his narrative with activities outside the city. Gaius Trebonius, one of Caesar's assassins, had been plebeian tribune in 55 BC. He had fought in Gaul and taken part in the siege of Massilia and was again at Caesar's side in Spain. He was

ungrateful for the generous treatment he had received at Caesar's hands, and had been party to the assassination of the man by whom he had been promoted all the way to the consulship.) [2] Gaius Cassius had then taken over the very powerful legions stationed in Syria from Staius Murcus and Crispus Marcius, both of whom were ex-praetors and commanders.[226] He had blockaded Dolabella (who had come into Syria after previously seizing Asia) at Laodicea and then, after taking that city, brought about his death (inasmuch as Dolabella did not hesitate to offer his neck to a blow from his own slave). Cassius had thus brought under his control the ten legions in that quarter, [3] while Marcus Brutus had wrested legions (who went over to him willingly) from Gaius Antonius, brother of Mark Antony, in Macedonia, and from Vatinius in the environs of Dyrrhachium, and was now seven legions strong.[227] (While Brutus had opened hostilities against Antony, Vatinius he had overwhelmed with the force of his reputation.[228] For Brutus appeared to be better than any commander, and there was none to whom Vatinius could not be regarded as inferior: [4] his physical ugliness competed with his depravity, to the point that his spirit appeared to be shut in a dwelling that was most appropriate for it.) [5] And by the Pedian law that the consul Pedius, Caesar's colleague, had proposed, all those who had murdered the elder Caesar were denied water and fire.[229] At that time Capito, my uncle, a man of the senatorial order, supported Agrippa in his prosecution of Gaius Cassius.

[6] During these events in Italy, Cassius had, after a bitterly fought and very successful campaign, captured Rhodes, an immense achievement, and

suffect consul from October 1, 45, and received the governorship of Asia for 44–43. On Caesar's death Dolabella became consul (see 2.58.3) and played both sides, negotiating with Antony and also with the supporters of the tyrannicides. He obtained the governorship of Syria for five years and crossed over to Asia, where he assassinated the governor Gaius Trebonius. The senate at this point outlawed Dolabella and, moving into Syria, he was besieged by one of Caesar's assassins, Cassius Longinus (2.56.3), and forced to commit suicide.

226. Lucius Staius Murcus was praetor probably in 45 BC, Quintus Marcius Crispus in 46.

227. Gaius Antonius, Antony's brother, was appointed proconsul in Macedonia for 43 BC, but the appointment was revoked late in 44. He failed to win over the three legions of Vatinius, proconsul in Illyricum, which fell to Marcus Junius Brutus, who besieged Gaius in Apollonia. Gaius surrendered in March of 43; Brutus took him hostage and had him executed in 42, though Velleius does not mention the death.

228. Publius Vatinius, described by Catullus as a *struma* (tumor), was tribune in 59 BC when he proposed the law to grant Julius Caesar the governorship of Cisalpine Gaul and Illyricum for five years (see 2.44.5). He obtained the consulship in 47 and was proconsul in Illyricum in 45, where he campaigned successfully; despite surrendering to Brutus he triumphed in 42.

229. In August of 43 BC Quintus Pedius and Octavian became suffect consuls in succession to Hirtius and Pansa, and Pedius carried a law to make provision for the trials of Caesar's assassins.

Brutus had brought the Lycians to heel. The two had then transported their armies over to Macedonia, and Cassius in all circumstances defied his own nature and outdid even Brutus in clemency.[230] One could not find men whom Fortune attended with such favor as Brutus and Cassius, or men whom she—as though exhausted—abandoned more quickly.

70. Caesar and Antony then took their armies over to Macedonia, and at the city of Philippi they clashed in battle with Brutus and Cassius.[231] The wing that Brutus commanded drove back the enemy and took Caesar Octavian's camp. (Octavian himself, despite severe health problems, was still performing all the duties of a commander; his doctor Artorius had actually pleaded with him not to remain in camp, frightened as he was by an unambiguous warning that came to him in a dream.) The wing where Cassius had been in command, however, was routed and badly mauled and had retreated to higher ground. [2] At that point Cassius, gauging his partner's success on the basis of his own misfortune, sent off a special-service veteran under orders to bring back to him information on the identity and strength of the large body of men advancing toward them.[232] The man was slow in reporting back, and as the column of men was heading toward him at a running pace and was close at hand, and recognition of faces or standards was made impossible by the dust, Cassius thought it was the enemy bearing down on him. He therefore threw his cloak over his head and fearlessly stretched out and offered his neck to his freedman. [3] Cassius' head had just fallen when the veteran arrived with the news of Brutus' victory. When he saw his commander stretched out on the ground, the veteran said: "I shall follow the man my tardiness has killed," and with that he fell on his sword.

[4] A few days later Brutus once more engaged the enemy. Defeated in the battle, he fell back to a hill by night and there persuaded his friend Strato of Aegeae to lend a hand in his suicide. [5] He threw his left arm back above his head, and with his right he held the point of the man's sword to

---

230. Velleius' account of Cassius' clemency is not echoed in other sources. Appian (*BC* 4.73) says that after taking Rhodes he put to death fifty leading citizens and plundered the temples of all of their funds.

231. Antony had initially arranged to counter Brutus and Cassius single-handedly but was obliged to seek assistance from Octavian. Together they advanced to Macedonia where they met the joint armies of their opponents. The first battle of Philippi in reality consisted of two clashes. In the first, on October 3, 42 BC, the forces of Cassius were defeated and he took his life in despair, but Brutus had in the meantime got the better of Octavian's wing. Three weeks later, on October 23, Brutus was tempted into a second engagement where he was severely defeated.

232. On completion of their military service veterans could, on the invitation of the commander, reenlist. They were generally promoted, often to the rank of centurion, and granted remission from standard duties.

his left nipple, to the very spot where the heart beats. He then thrust himself on the sword and died immediately, transfixed with the single stroke.

71. Messalla Corvinus, an outstanding young man, was next in line to Brutus and Cassius in authority in that camp, and, though there were some who were clamoring for him as their leader, he preferred deliverance through Caesar Octavian's beneficence than to put war with its dubious prospects to the test again.[233] For Caesar nothing was more gratifying in his victories than having saved Corvinus, nor was there a better example of a grateful and loyal man than Corvinus in his relationship with Caesar.

[2] No other war saw the spilling of the blood of so many distinguished men. Cato's son fell at that time, and the same fate carried off Lucullus and Hortensius, the sons of very eminent citizens. [3] As for Varro, when he was about to die and was being mocked by Antony, he made some very outspoken though appropriate predictions about Antony's death that turned out to be true. Livius Drusus, father of Julia Augusta, and Quintilius Varus did not even try to win mercy from their enemy. Drusus did away with himself in his tent, and Varus, after putting on the insignia of his offices, was cut down by the hand of his freedman, whom he had forced into the deed.[234]

---

233. Marcus Valerius Messalla Corvinus became a leading figure of the Augustan age. Proscribed in 43 BC, he escaped to the camp of Brutus and Cassius; after Philippi he supported Antony but later shifted his allegiance to Octavian. He was consul in 31, in place of Antony, and took part in the battle of Actium. He suppressed a rebellion in Aquitania, for which he was granted a triumph, in 27. He was a famous literary patron, most notably of Ovid and Tibullus, and uncle of the poetess Sulpicia.

234. After Messalla, Velleius lists a number of other victims, all of whom were fathers or sons of famous Romans. He begins with Marcus Porcius Cato, son of Cato Uticensis, who emulated his father's courage. Refusing to flee after the defeat at Philippi, he died leading a small band of loyal followers. Marcus Licinius Lucullus was the son of the great commander of the Mithridatic War (see 2.33) and his second wife Servilia. He was raised by Cato Uticensis and died at Philippi or shortly afterward. Quintus Hortensius was the son of the great orator. Praetor in 45 BC, he was proconsul of Macedonia in 44. He was responsible for the assassination of Antony's brother Gaius and was in turn executed on Antony's orders. Varro's identity is uncertain, perhaps Marcus Terentius Varro Gibba, quaestor in 46 and plebeian tribune in 43. This is Velleius' first reference to Livia, wife of Octavian/Augustus. Her name at that time was Livia Drusilla; she became Julia Augusta on Augustus' death, when she was adopted into the *gens Julia* and received her husband's honorific. She had Claudian connections: her father Marcus Livius Drusus Claudianus had almost certainly been adopted by Marcus Livius Drusus, the famous tribune of 91 (see 2.13–15). Livia's father initially supported Caesar and was selected for a mission to Alexandria in 59 BC to raise funds. After Caesar's assassination he evidently switched his loyalty to Brutus and Cassius and in 43 sponsored a decree to give two legions to Brutus. Late in the year he was proscribed and joined the tyrannicides at Philippi. After the battle he refused to seek mercy and committed suicide in his tent. Sextus Quintilius Varus, quaestor in 49 BC, was the father of the Varus who later brought on the disaster at the Teutoburg Forest.

72. Such was the end that Fortune decided on for the party of Marcus Brutus, who was in his <thirty-seventh> year.[235] Brutus had maintained an unblemished character up to the day that swept away all his virtues with a single act of recklessness. [2] Cassius, however, was the better commander of the two as Brutus was the better man. You would prefer to have Brutus as a friend, but you would fear Cassius more as an enemy. In the one there was more dynamism, in the other more virtue. It was more beneficial for the state to have Caesar Octavian than Antony as princeps; similarly, if these two had prevailed, it would have been better to have Brutus rather than Cassius.

[3] Gnaeus Domitius took possession of some ships and, accompanied by a large group of men who went along with his plans, entrusted himself to the vagaries of flight, content with assuming personal leadership of his party.[236] (Domitius was the father of the Lucius Domitius who was our recent contemporary, a man of outstanding and famed integrity, and the grandfather of our Gnaeus Domitius, a distinguished young man.) [4] Staius Murcus, who had been in charge of the fleet and responsible for the protection of the seaways, made sail for Pompey the Great's son Sextus Pompeius (who, returning from Spain, had occupied Sicily by force of arms) with the entire force of troops and ships that had been put at his disposal.[237]

---

235. Brutus died on October 23, 42 BC. If, as Velleius suggests, he was in his 37th year (that is, 36 years old), he would have been born between October 24, 79, and October 22, 78. Cicero (*Brut.* 324) says that Brutus was born 10 years after Hortensius gave his first speech, an event Cicero (*Brut.* 329) places in 95 BC, suggesting that he was in fact born in 85. To reconcile the two accounts scholars have suggested emending the text of Cicero to read 17 years instead of 10, or Velleius' text to read 43 instead of 37.

236. Gnaeus Domitius Ahenobarbus, son of Lucius (see 2.50.1), was the great-grandfather of the emperor Nero. He was besieged by Caesar with his father at Corfinium in 49 BC and like his father was allowed to leave unharmed. He followed Brutus to Macedonia after Caesar's assassination; he inflicted a naval defeat on the triumvirate in the Ionian Sea at the time of Philippi and later fought a naval campaign independently of Sextus Pompeius. He became reconciled to Antony in 40 and took part in his Parthian expedition. Consul in 32, he defected to Octavian just before the battle of Actium in 31 and died shortly afterward. His son Lucius was named as executor of Augustus' will. Velleius' high opinion of Lucius is echoed by Tacitus, who calls him a noble individual (*Ann.* 4.44). Suetonius (*Ner.* 4), on the other hand, claims that Lucius was arrogant and cruel and that his gladiatorial shows were too bloodthirsty even for Roman tastes. On Lucius' son Gnaeus, father of Nero, see 2.10.2.

237. Lucius Staius Murcus (see 2.69.2) was commander of the republican fleet and patrolled the Adriatic after Philippi. Sextus Pompeius was the youngest son of Pompey, born about 67 BC. He was present when his father was struck down in Egypt. He eventually joined the anti-Caesarians in Africa and after the battle of Thapsus (46) campaigned with his brother Gnaeus Pompeius in Spain. After Munda he continued operations, with some success, against Caesar's commanders, including Gaius Asinius Pollio (2.73.2). In the summer of 44 Lepidus arranged a settlement between Sextus and the senate, which necessitated his departure from Spain, but he remained in Massilia rather than returning to Rome. In April of 43 he was made commander

[5] Proscribed men whom Fortune had whisked out of immediate danger were now coming in droves to Pompeius from the camp of Brutus, as well as from Italy and other parts of the world. Naturally, for men with no political status, any leader, no matter who, would suffice: their circumstances gave them no choice but did reveal to them a refuge, and to those running from a deadly storm a simple anchorage was a harbor.

73. This young man was uneducated, uncouth in his language, vigorous in his undertakings, enterprising, quick-thinking, and in loyalty very unlike his father; he was the freedman of his own freedmen, and a slave of his own slaves, envying impressive people only to be deferential to the very mediocre. [2] The senate was then made up almost entirely of members of the Pompeian party, and after Antony's flight from Mutina, and at the very same time that it had assigned the overseas provinces to Brutus and Cassius, it had also restored Sextus to his father's estate and given him command of the coastal waters. (This was following his recall from Spain, where the ex-praetor Asinius Pollio had waged a very impressive campaign against him.)[238] [3] Sextus had then, as I noted above, seized Sicily, and by admitting slaves and fugitives into his army he had created a substantial legionary strength. He also used his father's freedmen, Menas and Menecrates, who were in command of his fleet, to infest the seaways with piracy and looting, using the plunder to maintain himself and his army.[239] He felt no shame at infesting with criminal freebooting the seas that had been freed from it by the military leadership of his father.

[Octavian takes responsibility for Italy, where he defeats Antony's brother Lucius Antonius in late 41 BC.]

74. Now that the party of Brutus and Cassius was crushed, Antony stayed behind in order to visit the overseas provinces. Caesar went back to Italy

---

of the fleet but was outlawed in August and occupied Sicily, using it as a base for naval raids. Sextus proved a doughty foe of Octavian; despite short-lived reconciliations, he continued his resistance until 36, when Agrippa defeated his fleet at Naulochus. Sextus was executed in Miletus in 35 on the order of Mark Antony.

238. Asinius Pollio (see 2.36, 2.63) commanded in Spain, where after Caesar's assassination he was involved in the campaigns against Sextus Pompeius.

239. Menas (also known as Menodorus) was a freedman of Pompey the Great and under his son became a naval officer of some reputation. In 40 BC he captured Sardinia for Sextus and advised him against the Treaty of Misenum. In 38 he switched loyalty and surrendered the island to Octavian. In 36 he switched back briefly to Sextus but later joined Octavian's cause once again. He was killed in the Illyrian campaign in 35. The background of Menecrates was similar. In 38 he was engaged in a naval battle between Ischia and Cumae against Octavian's commander Calvisius Sabinus and the renegade Menas. He was severely wounded and, when obliged to surrender his ship, committed suicide by leaping overboard.

and found it in a much more turbulent condition than he had anticipated. [2] This was because of the consul Lucius Antonius, who shared all of his brother's vices but none of the virtues occasionally seen in him. Antonius had at one moment been denouncing Caesar Octavian before the veterans, and at the next inciting to arms those of them who had lost their land when the distribution of properties had been put into effect and colonists designated, and he had brought together a large army.[240] [3] On the other hand, Mark Antony's wife Fulvia, who had nothing of the woman about her apart from her body, was promoting armed insurrection everywhere.[241] She had chosen Praeneste as her military base. Antonius, driven back at all points by Caesar's forces, had retreated to Perusia, and Plancus, a supporter of Antony's party, had held out the prospect of assistance without actually furnishing him with any aid.[242]

[4] With characteristic valor and good fortune, Caesar reduced Perusia. He released Antonius unharmed, and the savagery wreaked on the people of Perusia resulted from the anger of the soldiers rather than the wishes of their leader. The city was burned, the fire started by a leading citizen of the place, one Macedonicus, who, having set alight his belongings and home, stabbed himself with a sword and threw himself into the flames.[243]

75. At this same time a war had flared up in Campania, fomented by Tiberius Claudius Nero, a man of great character and learning, who was also an ex-praetor and a pontiff and the father of Tiberius Caesar.[244] Nero claimed

---

240. After Philippi, Antony went to the east. Octavian had the task of confiscating land from several Italian cities to found colonies for the veterans. He encountered the resistance of Lucius Antonius, who took up the cause of the dispossessed and in 41 BC gathered his troops at Praeneste to launch an attack on Rome.

241. Fulvia had been married first to Publius Clodius Pulcher, the demagogue (2.45), and married Antony after the death of Gaius Scribonius Curio, her second husband. She was a vigorous supporter of Antony and joined Lucius at Praeneste where she supposedly wore a sword and took part in councils of war and harangued the troops. The city was besieged, and when it fell she was allowed to rejoin Antony in the east but was received with little respect and died not long afterward. Octavian forced the surrender of Lucius' forces at Perusia (Perugia).

242. Lucius Munatius Plancus (see 2.63.3) was consul in 42 BC. Velleius' contempt for him is apparent in this reference to his unreliability.

243. Velleius is clearly faced with the embarrassment of the supposed brutal treatment of the population after the fall of Perusia, when Octavian is said to have executed three hundred citizens at the altar of Divus Julius (Sen. *Clem.* 1.11; Suet. *Aug.* 15; Dio 48.14.4). Lucius Antonius was allowed free passage and went to Spain, where he died. Appian (*BC* 5.49) names the arsonist as Cestius and gives his nationality as Macedonian (doubtless an echo of the other version of his name).

244. Velleius digresses on events in Campania in order to highlight the fate of Tiberius' father, whom he describes fulsomely (and somewhat undeservedly), and also to bring in the fate of his own grandfather. Tiberius Claudius Nero is first heard of in 54 BC, when he conducted

to be the champion of those who had lost their lands. This war was also suppressed and snuffed out by the arrival of Caesar Octavian. [2] Who could sufficiently marvel at the changes of fortune and the uncertain fluctuations in human affairs? Who would not hope for, or else dread, circumstances different from what one is experiencing, and the opposite of what one expects? [3] Livia was the daughter of Drusus Claudianus, a man of great distinction and courage, and she was the most outstanding of Roman women in birth, virtue, and beauty, a lady we later saw as the wife of Augustus, and as his priestess and daughter after Augustus passed over to join the gods. At that time she fled before the weapons of Caesar Octavian, soon to be her husband, bearing in her arms, when he was less than two years old, the present Tiberius Caesar, who was to become the defender of the Roman empire and the son of that very same Caesar Octavian. Following back roads and avoiding the swords of soldiers, and with only one attendant so that her flight might more easily go undetected, she reached the sea and with her husband Tiberius Nero sailed over to Sicily.[245]

76. I shall not cheat my own grandfather of a tribute I would pay to the grandfather of anyone else. Gaius Velleius had been chosen by Gnaeus Pompey for a very honorable position among the famous 360 judges; and he had also been prefect of engineers under Pompey as well as under Marcus Brutus and Tiberius Nero. He was a man second to none in Campania, and on the departure of Nero from Naples—he had been a supporter of Nero's cause because of his close friendship with him—he was unable to go with him because of his age and poor physical condition. He therefore stabbed himself with his sword. [2] Caesar Octavian permitted Fulvia to leave Italy unharmed, and Plancus along with her, to attend the lady in her banishment. Asinius Pollio, who

---

an unsuccessful prosecution of Aulus Gabinius, governor of Syria. By 50 he was a serious contender for the hand of Cicero's daughter Tullia. In 48 he put his support behind Caesar, serving as quaestor and commanding the fleet at Alexandria.

245. Tiberius Claudius Nero's wife Livia, whom Velleius admires unreservedly, later married Octavian and, by an extraordinary process for which there are no clear parallels, was adopted by him in his will, thus technically becoming his daughter. Livia was at birth the daughter of Marcus Livius Drusus Claudianus, who died at Philippi (see 2.71.3). She was born on January 30, 59/8 BC, and married Tiberius Nero sometime before November 16, 42, when her son Tiberius was born. He eventually was adopted by Augustus (hence Velleius' reference to him as "the son of that very same Caesar") and become Rome's second emperor. Livia's husband had shown his support for the tyrannicides, even voting special honors for them and, after Philippi backed the wrong side yet again, joining the cause of Antony. After the fall of Perusia he made his way to Naples where he tried to instigate a slave uprising. He was helped in this by Gaius Velleius, the historian's grandfather, who committed suicide when the venture failed. Tiberius' family, including his infant son, the future emperor, and Livia, made a narrow escape to Sicily where they sought the protection of Sextus Pompeius.

had long kept Venetia in Antony's power and had brought off some great and spectacular exploits around Altinum and other cities in the region, now headed for Antony with seven legions.[246] Domitius, as I mentioned above, had left Brutus' camp on his commander's death and had become the admiral of his own fleet. Pollio found him still in a quandary after being forced to abandon his plan <. . .> and by giving him a guarantee of safety brought him over to Antony's side. [3] On the basis of this act anyone claiming to be a fair judge would be perfectly sure that Antony benefited no less at the hands of Pollio than Pollio did at those of Antony. Antony's subsequent return to Italy, and Caesar's preparations against him, raised fears of war, but a peace treaty was negotiated in the area of Brundisium.[247]

[4] At this time the unconscionable plans of Salvidienus Rufus came to light.[248] Rufus, who had very humble origins, thought it too little to have been given the greatest honors, and to have been the next man to have been elected consul from the equestrian order after Gnaeus Pompey and Caesar himself. He needed to climb to heights from which he could have looked down upon Caesar and the Republic!

[A peace treaty with Sextus Pompeius (39 BC) proves to be short-lived; Octavian defeats Pompeius decisively in 36 BC.]

77. Then, in response to the united demands of the people, who were suffering from the high price of grain because the seaways were disrupted, peace was also made with Pompeius, in the environs of Misenum.[249] When Pompeius received both Caesar and Antony to dinner on his ship, he observed, not inappropriately,

---

246. When Fulvia and Plancus went into exile Asinius Pollio remained to support Antony. He was later much criticized by Antony for his lack of loyalty, and Velleius is clearly determined here to defend him.

247. In 40 BC Pollio brokered the Treaty of Brundisium (which effected a reconciliation between Antony and Octavian) and entered the consulship. According to one widely accepted interpretation of the poem, Virgil's mysterious fourth *Eclogue,* written in that year, clearly saw the moment as the beginning of a new golden age.

248. Quintus Salvidienus Rufus was a man of humble origins who rose, along with Marcus Agrippa, to be one of Octavian's closest companions. He was engaged in campaigns against Sextus Pompeius and Lucius Antonius in the Perusine War, after which he was sent to govern Gaul and was consul-designate for 39 BC, even though he still had equestrian status. When Antony returned from the east in 40, Salvidienus offered his support. Antony supposedly revealed the treachery to Octavian after the Peace of Brundisium; the senate denounced Salvidienus as a public enemy, and he either was executed or committed suicide.

249. The Peace of Misenum was concluded between Octavian, Antony, and Sextus Pompeius in the first half of 39 BC, in part, as Velleius indicates, because of public concerns over the grain shortage, but also because Antony was anxious to launch his expedition against Parthia. It granted Sextus control over Sardinia and Corsica, in addition to Sicily and Achaea, which he already held.

that he was giving them dinner "in his own Carinae," making a reference to the district of his father's house, at that time owned by Antony.[250]

[2] In this peace treaty it was agreed that Sicily and Achaea should be ceded to Pompeius, but his restless disposition could not adhere to the pact. There was only one advantage that he brought to his country by appearing there, and that was that he negotiated a recall and immunity for all the proscribed, and for others who had sought refuge with him for various reasons. [3] This restored to the state many distinguished individuals, including Claudius Nero, Marcus Silanus, Sentius Saturninus, Arruntius, and Titius. Staius Murcus, however, who had doubled Pompeius' strength by joining him with his powerful fleet, had become the target of groundless accusations because Menas and Menecrates had been averse to having a man of such quality sharing the command, and Pompeius had had him executed in Sicily.[251]

78. It was in this time period that Mark Antony took as his wife Caesar Octavian's sister Octavia.[252] Pompeius had returned to Sicily and Antony to the overseas provinces, which Labienus had thrown into turmoil by his great efforts. Labienus had left the camp of Brutus to join the Parthians and

---

250. The Carinae (literally, "keels") was the name of a fashionable quarter of Rome's Fourth District, between the Caelian and Esquiline hills.

251. Some of the figures recalled went on to distinguished careers as adherents of Octavian. The recall of Tiberius Claudius Nero had major consequences for the later history of Rome, since as a result Octavian met and fell in love with Tiberius' wife Livia. Marcus Julius Silanus had gone over to Antony at Mutina in 43 BC but fell out of favor and fled to Sextus Pompeius. He was appointed directly to the senate in 30 and was consul in 25. Gaius Sentius Saturninus joined Sextus Pompeius' cause as a young man. He was consul in 19, proconsul of Africa in 14, and later a commander in Germany under Tiberius. Lucius Arruntius was proscribed in 43 BC and escaped to Sextus Pompeius. After his return to Rome he commanded the left wing of Octavian's fleet at Actium and was consul in 22.

   Marcus Titius was proscribed along with his father in 43 BC. His father joined Sextus Pompeius while the son raised a private fleet and was captured by Sextus' lieutenant Menas but spared for the sake of his father. After Misenum, Titius initially supported Antony, but in 32, along with his uncle Lucius Munatius Plancus (2.63.3), he deserted to Octavian. He was consul in 31 and later governed Syria. He was responsible for the execution of Sextus Pompeius (see 2.79.5).

   Lucius Staius Murcus was a legate of Caesar in Africa but was sympathetic to the tyrannicides and was sent by the senate to govern Syria in 44 BC. There he was joined by Cassius, who put him in command of the fleet, where he was joined by Gnaeus Domitius Ahenobarbus. Lucius fell out with Domitius and joined Sextus Pompeius, who grew to distrust him and had him killed.

252. Octavia, Augustus' much-admired sister, was first married to Gaius Claudius Marcellus (see note 301), but Marcellus' death in 40 BC made it possible for her to marry Antony and seal the Peace of Brundisium. She proved to be a strikingly loyal spouse, a strong force for reconciliation between husband and brother, and an active player in negotiations between them. Like Antony's previous wife Fulvia, Octavia was in the end treated contemptuously by her husband.

had then led an army of theirs all the way into Syria and had put Antony's legate to death. Thanks to Ventidius' courageous leadership, he was killed along with the Parthian troops and the most famous of their young warriors, Pacorus, the son of their king.[253]

[2] To prevent inactivity—military discipline's greatest enemy—from doing harm to his men, Caesar in the meantime mounted frequent operations in Illyricum and Dalmatia, toughening up his army by exposing them to danger and giving them experience in combat. [3] At this same time Domitius Calvinus, gaining Spain as his province after his consulship, provided an example of harsh discipline comparable to those of days of old. He had a senior centurion named Vibillius clubbed to death for dishonorable flight from battle.[254]

79. Pompeius' fleet and reputation were both increasing every day, and Caesar Octavian decided to shoulder the burden of this war. Authority for building the ships, assembling soldiers and oarsmen, and giving them training in naval engagements and maneuvers was assigned to Marcus Agrippa.[255] Agrippa was a man of outstanding courage who could not be overcome by toil, lack of sleep, or danger. He knew very well how to give obedience, but to one man alone; when it came to others he was very eager to command, and he avoided delay in everything, making decisions and their implementation a single act.

[2] On Lake Avernus and Lake Lucrinus Agrippa built a magnificent fleet, and with daily training he brought the fighting men and rowers to the point where they had superb military and naval expertise. It was with this fleet that Caesar Octavian went on the offensive against Pompeius in Sicily, but only after taking as his wife Livia, whom Nero, to whom she was earlier married, pledged to him—the omens of that wedding being propitious for

---

253. Quintus Labienus, son of the famous Titus Labienus (2.55.4), joined the Parthians after Philippi and, along with Pacorus, invaded Syria and won over a number of Roman troops. They took Apamea in Syria, then Labienus turned to Asia and conquered much territory before his defeat by Publius Ventidius Bassus. Subsequently Ventidius inflicted an overwhelming defeat on Pacorus in the region of Cyrrhestica, west of the Euphrates, for which he was awarded a triumph.

254. Gnaeus Domitius Calvinus was a consistently loyal adherent of both Caesar and Octavian. Consul in 53 BC, he served at Pharsalus and later went on to be governor of Asia, where he suffered a defeat at the hands of Pharnaces, king of the Bosporus, who exploited the chaos of the civil war to invade Pontus. Despite the defeat, he retained Caesar's respect and assisted him in Africa. He held a second consulship in 40 and was sent by Octavian to govern Spain, where his successes led to a triumph. The date of his death is unknown but he was still alive in 20 BC. Velleius here refers to the *fustuarium,* the clubbing to death of a soldier for desertion.

255. Sextus Pompeius proved a difficult foe. Agrippa (2.59.5) established a major naval base near Puteoli by creating a passage between Lake Lucrinus and the sea, and another between Lucrinus and the very deep Lake Avernus. Octavian tried to take Sicily but was defeated first at the battle of Messina in 37 BC, then at Tauromenium in 36.

the state. [3] But this man who could not be conquered by human power was now severely shaken by Fortune. A violent southwesterly wind arising off Velia and the promontory of Palinurus badly damaged and scattered what was by far the greater part of the fleet. That delayed termination of the war, which was afterward fought with wavering fortunes, the outcome sometimes hanging in the balance. [4] In fact, the fleet was again battered by a storm in the same area; and, in addition, despite success in the first battle, which was fought off Mylae under Agrippa's command, there was a disastrous defeat off Tauromenium, before Caesar Octavian's very eyes, because of the unexpected arrival of the enemy fleet, and Caesar himself was exposed to danger there. The legions that were with Caesar's legate Cornificius were almost crushed by Pompeius after they were set ashore.[256]

[5] However, the misfortune of this critical juncture was quickly set to rights by sheer courage. After the fleets of both sides had been deployed for battle, Pompeius lost nearly all his ships and made for Asia in flight. There, as he dithered between playing the general and playing the suppliant, at the one moment trying to maintain his dignity and at the next begging for his life, he was—on the orders of Mark Antony, whose aid he had come to seek—murdered by Titius.[257] [6] The hatred that this outrage earned for Titius lasted for so long that later, when he was putting on games in the theater of Pompey, he was driven from the spectacle that he was hosting by the catcalls of the people.

[Octavian strips Lepidus of power in 36 BC and ends a mutiny of the troops.]

80. While he was conducting his war on Pompeius, Caesar Octavian had sent for Lepidus to come from Africa with twelve legions that were at half strength.[258] This man was the most unreliable person alive, and it was not

---

256. Lucius Cornificius was a close friend of Octavian and former prosecutor of Brutus, after the murder of Caesar. He was cut off with three legions at Tauromenium but succeeded in withdrawing them and joined Agrippa at Tyndaris.

257. Sextus was finally defeated by Agrippa on September 3, 36 BC, off Naulochus in northern Sicily, after which he escaped to Asia and was able to exploit his father's name to raise a private army of three legions. He was forced to surrender at Miletus in 35. On hasty instructions from Antony he was put to death without trial by Marcus Titius, even though he was a Roman citizen. Antony in fact later rescinded his instructions, but his subsequent letter arrived too late (Dio 49.18.4–6).

258. The triumvir Lepidus (2.63) was consul in 42 BC and in control of Rome and Italy during the Philippi campaign. He subsequently took Africa and managed to avoid getting caught up in the quarrels between Antony and Octavian. After Naulochus in 36, Agrippa and Lepidus besieged the land forces of Sextus at Messina. Lepidus disobeyed the instructions of Agrippa and united the forces of Sextus with his own. This high-handed action provided Octavian with an excuse to act against him, ten years after Lepidus' first consulship (in 46), forcing him into

through any redeeming quality that he had gained Fortune's indulgence for so long. Lepidus had arrogated to himself the army of Pompeius because it lay closer to him, despite the fact that it accepted Caesar Octavian's authority, not Lepidus', and was loyal to Octavian. [2] Full of bravado now through having more than twenty legions under him, Lepidus reached such a pitch of madness as to regard the entire victory as his own, though he was really only a useless associate in another man's victory (one that he had long delayed by opposing Caesar Octavian's plans and by always opposing what others were agreed upon). He even had the audacity to order Caesar out of Sicily!

[3] No bold stroke ever ventured and brought off by the Scipios or other Roman generals of old was more courageous than the action then taken by Caesar Octavian. He was unarmed and dressed in his cloak, bearing no weapon other than his name. He went into Lepidus' camp and, dodging projectiles hurled at him on the orders of that scoundrel (though his cloak was pierced by a lance), dared to seize a legionary eagle. [4] You could see the difference between the leaders. Armed soldiers followed the lead of the unarmed man; and, in the tenth year after attaining a level of power that his career had certainly not warranted, Lepidus was abandoned by both his men and Fortune. Wearing a dark cloak, he hid at the back of a crowd that was flocking to Caesar and then fell at his knees. He was granted his life and continued possession of his belongings, but he was stripped of his rank, which he was incapable of maintaining.

81. There followed a sudden mutiny of the army (which, observing the strength of its own numbers, often discards discipline and cannot bring itself to make a request for what it thinks it can gain by force). It was put down partly by severe measures, and partly by the generosity of the princeps.[259] [2] At this time an impressive addition was made to the colony of Capua <. . . its lands> had remained public property. In return, they were given lands far more fertile on the island of Crete that yielded 1,200,000 sesterces, and they were promised the aqueduct that to this day makes a unique contribution to public health, as well as adding to the charm of the place.

[3] In this war Agrippa earned the honor of a naval crown—an honor never previously awarded to any Roman—by virtue of his outstanding courage.[260] The victorious Caesar then returned to Rome. There he announced

---

exile in Circeii in Latium. He was relieved of his offices, except that of *pontifex maximus;* he died in obscurity in 13/12 BC.

259. Octavian was not technically princeps until 27 BC; Velleius' use of the term here reflects the de facto situation after the demise of Lepidus. Dio (49.14) provides a clearer account of these events, noting that veterans were settled on lands near Capua in Campania.

260. The *corona navalis* was a gold chaplet decorated with miniature beaks of ships. It seems that it could be presented to two different categories of recipients, the first man to board ship

that he had, by purchases made through agents, bought up several homes in order to increase the area of his own, but that his intention now was that they should be public property, and he promised to erect a temple of Apollo with porticoes around it (which was subsequently built with extraordinary munificence on his part).[261]

[Antony's campaign in the east is initially unsuccessful, though he later restores the situation. He becomes infatuated with Cleopatra. The hostility between Antony and Octavian culminates in the battle of Actium in 31 BC.]

82. The summer in which Caesar Octavian so successfully <Libium in Sicilia . . . Fortune fought well in the case of Caesar and the state> in the east.[262] Antony entered Armenia and then Media with thirteen legions and, as he passed through these regions while making for the Parthians, he encountered their king.[263] [2] He first of all lost two legions along with all their baggage and siege equipment, plus his legate Statianus. Later, putting his entire army at very serious risk, he on numerous occasions exposed himself to dangers from which he despaired of being delivered; and after losing no less than a quarter of his men he owed his salvation to the loyal advice of a man who was a captive, but a Roman one. The man had been taken prisoner in the debacle suffered by Crassus' army, but his sympathies had not altered along with his fortunes. He approached a Roman guard post at night with a warning that the Romans not take the route they had decided upon but rather make their way by another path through the woods.

---

during a sea battle or a commander who had destroyed an enemy fleet. Agrippa may have been preceded by Marcus Varro, who, according to Pliny (*NH* 16.7), received the award from Pompey the Great for his contribution to the war against the pirates.

261. The Palatine Hill was a prime residential area for well-to-do Romans. Octavian was born on the Palatine and made arrangements to reside there after his marriage to Livia. In 36 BC, on the grounds that part of his house had been destroyed by lightning, and that it was required by the gods, he dedicated the site to a new temple of Apollo; to compensate him for his generosity, the senate voted him a new house to be constructed at public expense. Livia's name has been found inscribed on lead pipes in the building, suggesting that part of the original residence remained her private quarters, where she probably lived after Augustus' death.

262. This sentence is hopelessly corrupt.

263. In 36 BC Antony initiated a major invasion of Parthia (ruled at the time by King Phraates IV) with an army of a hundred thousand men. His mission was to recover the standards lost by Crassus at Carrhae. The campaign proved to be a disaster. He was deserted by his Armenian allies under Artavasdes II, and two legions under his lieutenant Oppius Statianus were destroyed. His failure to take the key stronghold of Phraapsa, which he reached too late in the season, convinced him to withdraw. He then had to suffer great hardships as he retreated through Armenia in the winter. On the grounds that the Armenians had deserted him in 36, he annexed their territory in 34. He celebrated a triumph in Alexandria, in the course of which Artavasdes II was displayed in gold chains (he died in captivity in 30).

[3] This proved to be the salvation of Mark Antony and all those legions. Even so, no less than a quarter of these men and of the army as a whole was lost, as I noted above, and a third of the camp followers and slaves, as well; and hardly any of the baggage survived. Antony, however, still called that flight of his a victory because he had emerged from it with his life. When he returned to Armenia two summers later, he caught its king Artavasdes by trickery and put him in shackles (but, so he should not be denied his due respect, shackles of gold).

[4] Then the ardor of his passion for Cleopatra increased, as did the magnitude of his vices (which are always nourished by power, license, and flattery), and he decided to make war on his native land. He had earlier given instructions that he be called "New Father Bacchus," and he had ridden in a chariot in Alexandria with a garland of ivy and a crown of gold on his head, holding a thyrsus, and wearing high boots like Father Bacchus.[264]

83. During the preparations for this war Plancus defected to Caesar Octavian.[265] This was not because he judged that he was choosing the right side, nor was it from any love for the state or for Caesar Octavian (he was always critical of them both), but because in his case treason was a disease. He had been the most abject flatterer of the queen, and a "client" who was beneath the level of slaves; he had been Antony's secretary, and the instigator and abettor of his most obscene acts; and he was on hire for anything and to anyone. [2] At a banquet he had, on his knees, played the part of Glaucus in a dance in which, painted blue and naked, he had reeds around his head

---

264. Cleopatra VII Philopator was the last independent Ptolemaic ruler of Egypt. She came to the throne on the death of her father in 51 BC, at the age of eighteen, ruling in conjunction with her husband (who was also her brother), the twelve-year old Ptolemy XIII Theos Philopator. Disputes with Ptolemy led to the intervention of the Romans; by 48 she had been ousted. After the murder of Ptolemy in Egypt, Caesar reestablished Cleopatra as ruler with her younger brother Ptolemy XIV. Cleopatra and Caesar became lovers and she bore him a son named Caesarion (little Caesar).

Antony first met Cleopatra in 41 at Tarsus where they contracted an alliance and began an affair. She bore twins to him after his departure (their lives were ultimately spared by Octavian while Caesarion was put to death). Four years later he visited Alexandria again, on his way to Parthia, and supposedly married Cleopatra in an Egyptian rite. By adopting the guise of Dionysus/Bacchus, Antony was perhaps trying to convey the notion that he and Cleopatra, in the form of Isis, could rule as a divine pair.

265. The much-despised Lucius Munatius Plancus (2.63.3) escaped with Fulvia to join Antony in Greece after the Perusine War. He was governor of Asia in 40 BC, and of Syria, as Antony's deputy, during the latter's campaign against Parthia. He was a notorious flatterer of Cleopatra but, along with his nephew Marcus Titius (2.77.3), abandoned her before Actium and joined Octavian. It was Plancus who in 27 suggested that Octavian assume the title Augustus, in preference to Romulus (Suet. *Aug.* 7.2). The charge that he had performed in a mime reflects a standard weapon of disparagement in the Roman world, in which actors generally enjoyed little status.

and dragged a tail behind him. His defection came after he was given the cold shoulder by Antony because of some clear evidence of his thieving. Later on he even interpreted the victor's clemency as recognition of his merits, insisting that Caesar had approved of what he had merely pardoned. Presently Titius, whose uncle he was, followed his example. [3] When Plancus' desertion was recent, and he was reproaching the absent Antony in the senate with numerous monstrous acts, Coponius, father-in-law of Publius Silius and a very earnest ex-praetor, declared, quite aptly, "Heavens! Antony must have done a lot the day before you left him!"[266]

84. Subsequently, in the consulship of Caesar Octavian and Messalla Corvinus, the war was brought to an end at Actium, where the victory of the Caesarian camp was in no doubt at all long before the fighting began.[267] On this side there were soldiers and a commander full of energy; on the other there was total listlessness. On this there were robust oarsmen, on the other oarsmen much weakened by supply shortages. Here the ships were of modest size that did not restrict speed; there they were more menacing in appearance alone. From this side no one was deserting to Antony; from that someone was deserting to Caesar every day.[268] [2] King Amyntas joined the better side, which also offered greater practical advantages.[269] As for Dellius, he stuck to his usual ways, so that < he defected from Dolabella to Caesar>; and the very distinguished Gnaeus Domitius, who stood alone in Antony's party in greeting the queen only by name, faced very great and imminent danger in going over to Caesar.[270] Finally, right before the faces and eyes of Antony's fleet,

---

266. Gaius Coponius was a former Pompeian, praetor in 49 BC. Publius Silius Nerva (consul 20) was a friend of Augustus and legate in Nearer Spain and proconsul in 17–16.

267. The battle of Actium, fought in 31 BC at the mouth of the Ambracian Gulf in western Greece, marked the end of the conflict between Octavian and Antony and Cleopatra.

268. Antony had about 230 vessels of different types, Octavian 400. When the battle started Agrippa tried to outflank Antony's right wing, which parted from the rest of the fleet to cover the opponents, and Cleopatra's fleet of some 60 ships escaped through the gap. Antony's left wing was ineffective and much of it was forced back into the gulf where it was destroyed or burnt.

269. Amyntas was the former secretary of Deiotarus, a tetrarch of western Galatia. He commanded the Galatian troops of Brutus and Cassius, but deserted before Philippi. Deiotarus died in 40 BC and Antony made Amyntas ruler of what became a considerable kingdom in Asia Minor. He joined Antony at Actium but switched sides, and afterward Octavian further expanded his kingdom. He died fighting unruly border tribes in 25.

270. Quintus Dellius was a famous opportunist, who earned the nickname of *desultor,* a trick horse rider who leapt from mount to mount, for his skill at switching sides. He deserted Dolabella for Cassius in 43 BC, then in 42 moved over to Antony, to be used by him as a negotiator on different occasions with Cleopatra, Herod, and Artavasdes of Armenia. Just before Actium he moved over to Octavian's side and revealed Antony's battle plans to him. He was held in high regard by Octavian (Sen. *Clem.* 1.10.1).

Leucas was stormed by Marcus Agrippa, Patrae was captured, and Corinth taken, while the enemy fleet was twice defeated before the final battle.

85. Then came the day of the decisive encounter, when Caesar Octavian and Antony brought forward their fleets and did battle, one for the salvation of the world, the other to destroy it. [2] The right wing of the Caesarian fleet was entrusted to Marcus Lurius, the left to Arruntius, and overall supervision of naval operations to Agrippa.[271] Caesar Octavian assigned himself to whichever sector he might be called by Fortune, and was omnipresent. Command of Antony's fleet was put in the hands of Publicola and Sosius.[272] As for land forces, Taurus commanded Caesar's and Canidius those of Antony.[273]

[3] When the fight began, everything—leader, oarsmen, soldiers—was to be found on one side, and on the other nothing but soldiers. The first to flee was Cleopatra. Antony preferred to attend the queen in her flight rather than his men in battle, and the commander, who was under an obligation to deal fiercely with deserters, became a deserter from his own army. [4] Even with their chief removed, however, his men long maintained their resolve to battle on valiantly, and though they had no hope of victory they kept fighting to the death. Caesar could have finished them off with the sword but preferred

---

On Domitius, see 2.72.3. Velleius suggests that he addressed Cleopatra merely by her name, without her title.

271. Plutarch (*Ant.* 65.1) claims that Agrippa commanded the left wing and Octavian the right. Lucius Arruntius (2.77.3) went on to become consul in 22 BC. He was instrumental in obtaining a pardon for Gaius Sosius after Actium (2.86.2). Marcus Lurius had as governor of Sardinia attempted to hold the island in 40 against Menas, the naval commander of Sextus Pompeius (Dio 48.30.7).

272. Lucius Gellius Publicola had been a supporter of the tyrannicides and had deserted them for the triumvirs, holding the consulship in 36 BC. No reference is made to him after Actium, where he might have died. Gaius Sosius, praetor in 49, joined Antony after Caesar's assassination. He was made governor of Syria and Cilicia in 38, and in 37 he supported Herod against Antigonus and placed him on the throne of Judaea. He was consul in 32. At Actium he put the squadron of Lucius Arruntius to flight. He was later pardoned by Octavian.

273. Titus Statilius Taurus was probably second only to Agrippa among Octavian's steadfast commanders. His first recorded service was in a naval command against Sextus Pompeius in 36 BC. He later held Africa, celebrating a triumph in 34, and fought in Illyricum. After Actium he served in Spain, was consul in 26 as a new man (*novus homo*), and was appointed city prefect in 16, when Augustus left Rome to visit the western provinces. His descendant Statilia Messalina was Nero's third wife.

Publius Canidius Crassus served initially under Lepidus in Gaul, then supported Antony; he is probably the Crassus recorded by Appian (*BC* 5.50) as serving in the Perusine War. He went with Antony to Parthia and was left in command in Armenia, bringing an army to assist him in 32 BC. He commanded Antony's land forces at the time of Actium and urged a land battle, where he would have an advantage, rather than a naval one. After Antony's defeat he was accused of deserting his army. He joined Antony in Egypt, where he was executed by Octavian in 30.

instead to win them over with words. He repeatedly shouted to them and showed them that Antony had taken to his heels, and he kept asking them for whom they were fighting and against whom. [5] After putting up a protracted struggle on behalf of their absent leader, they reluctantly put down their weapons and ceded the victory; and Caesar guaranteed them their lives and merciful treatment before they were persuaded to sue for such terms. It was, indeed, generally admitted that the soldiers had functioned like an excellent general, and the general like the most cowardly soldier. [6] One might well wonder, then, whether Antony in victory would have followed his own judgment or that of Cleopatra, given that it was in accordance with her wishes that he took to flight. The army on land followed suit after Canidius rushed off in headlong flight to join Antony.

86. What that day gave to the world, and how the fortunes of the state were transformed—who could describe all that in this cursory treatment of such limited scope? [2] The victory was certainly characterized by great clemency, and nobody was executed <except for a very small number, mostly those who could not even bear to beg for mercy>. From such leniency on the commander's part one could have gathered what limitations he might have placed on his victory, either at the start of the triumvirate or on the fields of Philippi, had he been allowed to do so. In Sosius' case, it was the loyal friendship of Lucius Arruntius, a man well known for an old-world dignity, that came to his rescue, as did Caesar Octavian later, though he long struggled against his characteristic clemency.[274]

[3] Nor should the memorable conduct and pronouncement of Asinius Pollio be passed over in silence.[275] After the Treaty of Brundisium, Pollio had stayed on in Italy. He had never seen the queen, nor had he associated himself with Antony's party after Antony's spirit had been sapped by his passion for her. When Caesar then asked him to join him in the war at Actium, Pollio replied: "My services to Antony have been too great, and his kindnesses toward me too well known, and so I shall keep out of your dispute and be the prize of the winner."

[Octavian pursues Antony and Cleopatra to Egypt, where they both commit suicide. In Rome the son of Lepidus is executed for planning the assassination of Octavian.]

87. Then, the next year, Caesar Octavian pursued the queen and Antony to Alexandria and put the final touches on the civil wars. Antony was no coward in dispatching himself, so that by his death he compensated for the

---

274. On Gaius Sosius, see 2.85; on Lucius Arruntius, see 2.77.3.
275. On Gaius Asinius Pollio, see 2.63.3.

many charges of spinelessness leveled at him. Thwarting her guards, Cleopatra had an asp brought in to her and so ended her life—at least lacking a woman's fear in facing its bite.[276]
[2] It was consistent with Caesar's fortune and clemency that none of those who had borne arms against him was put to death by him or on his orders. Decimus Brutus' death came from Antony's ruthlessness.[277] Sextus Pompeius was defeated by Caesar, but again it was Antony who, although he had given his word that the man's rank as well as his life should be preserved, robbed him of his life as well. [3] Brutus and Cassius died by suicide before sounding out the disposition of their conquerors. How Antony and Cleopatra died I have narrated. Canidius died in greater fear than was in keeping with the declarations he had always made.[278] The last of Caesar's assassins to make atonement with his death was Cassius Parmensis—Trebonius had been the first.[279]

88. While Caesar Octavian was putting the final touches on the wars of Actium and Alexandria, Marcus Lepidus—a young man with more looks than brains—had embarked on a project to kill him as soon as he returned to the city.[280] (Marcus was the son of the Lepidus who had been triumvir for the organization of the state, and of Brutus' sister Junia.) [2] At the time Gaius Maecenas, a man of an equestrian but illustrious family, was in charge of maintaining security in the city.[281] Maecenas was the sort of man who

276. After Actium, Octavian invaded Egypt. As he approached Alexandria Antony's troops, despite some initial successes, deserted their commander, who then committed suicide as Octavian entered the city. A few days later Cleopatra also reputedly committed suicide. Most of the ancient sources report that she died from the bite of an asp, though Strabo (*Geog.* 17.10) mentions the alternate theory that she used a poisonous ointment. Modern scholars are generally skeptical about her supposed methods of suicide.

277. On Decimus Brutus, see 2.64.

278. On Publius Canidius Crassus, see 2.85.

279. Gaius Cassius Parmensis (quaestor 43 BC) supported Brutus and then Sextus Pompeius, whom he abandoned for Antony after the battle of Naulochus. He was a poet of some reputation (Hor. *Sat.* 1.10.60). He supposedly taunted Octavian with being the grandson of a baker and a money changer (Suet. *Aug.* 4.2). On Gaius Trebonius, see 2.56.3.

280. Marcus Aemilius Lepidus was the son of the triumvir and Junia, a sister of Marcus Junius Brutus. In 44 BC he was betrothed to Antonia Major, daughter of Mark Antony, but the union did not last. He was executed in 30 by Octavian as leader of a conspiracy.

281. Maecenas (c. 70–12 BC), an equestrian of Etruscan stock, was one of Octavian/Augustus' staunchest supporters. He remained an equestrian, as characterized by the wearing of a tunic with a narrow purple band, and never held formal office but was the princeps' most intimate friend and trusted adviser and represented him at the Peace of Brundisium and of Tarentum. He acquired great wealth, probably from the proscriptions. He was a considerable patron of writers and enjoyed a particularly warm relationship with Horace. In 31 he was placed in charge of Rome and Italy while Octavian was in the east.

would be alert when the situation demanded vigilance and would use fore-sight and know the action to be taken, but who, as soon as there could be respite from active service, would be awash in idleness and extravagant liv-ing, almost more than a woman. He was no less dear to Caesar than Agrip-pa was, but he was given fewer honors—he lived his life <almost> happy with the narrow stripe—and while he could have achieved no less distinc-tion than Agrippa, he did not have such aspirations. [3] With the utmost composure, and concealing his investigation, Maecenas kept the reckless young man's schemes under surveillance and, with amazing dispatch and without upsetting anything or anyone, he collared Lepidus and snuffed out at its horrendous start the recommencement of civil war. Lepidus paid the penalty for his ill-conceived plans. Lepidus' wife Servilia may be put on the same level as Antistius' wife, whom I have already mentioned. She swal-lowed burning coals and in return for her premature death gained immortal remembrance for her name.[282]

[Octavian's triumphant return to Rome (29 BC) ushers in an era of order and stability.]

89. Caesar Octavian then returned to Italy and to Rome. Not even within the scope of a full-scale work (and much less a restricted one like this) could the size of the gathering and the enthusiasm with which he was welcomed by everyone—by people of all <classes>, all ages, and all ranks—be ade-quately described. Nor could the magnificence of his triumphs and the pub-lic shows he staged.[283] [2] From then on there was nothing that men can ask of the gods, nothing that the gods can confer upon men, nothing that can conceivably be wished for, no happiness that can be brought about that Augustus did not after his return to the city restore to the state, the Roman people, and the world.[284] [3] The civil wars were at an end after twenty years, foreign wars extinguished, peace restored, and the fury of armed conflict everywhere lulled to sleep; the laws were given back their force, the law courts their authority, and the senate its sovereignty; the powers of the

---

282. Servilia was the daughter of Publius Servilius Vatia Isauricus (consul 48 BC). She had at one time been engaged to Octavian, who put her aside to marry Claudia, daughter of Publius Clodius and Fulvia. Her manner of death is traditionally ascribed to Porcia, wife of Brutus (Val. Max. 4.6.5; Plut. *Brut.* 53.5); Velleius is the only source to ascribe it to Servilia. On Calpurnia, wife of Antistius, see 2.26.3.

283. Octavian celebrated a triple triumph during the period of August 13–15, 29 BC, for his campaigns in Illyricum, Actium, and Alexandria.

284. On January 16, 27 BC, Octavian received the name of Augustus. This is the first time that Velleius applies it to him.

magistrates were again restricted to their former limits; there was merely an addition of two praetors to the earlier eight. [4] The old and venerable form of the Republic was brought back. Agriculture returned to the farmlands, respect to religion, security to men, and to each person the assured ownership of his property. Laws were usefully revised and new ones passed to beneficial effect; and senate membership was reviewed without harshness but not without rigor.[285] Leading men, those who had celebrated triumphs and held the highest offices, were swayed into beautifying the city by exhortations from the princeps.[286] [5] In the matter of the consulship, despite his frequent and strenuous objections to accepting it, all Caesar could achieve was continuing in the office only up to his eleventh tenure of it.[287] In the case of the dictatorship, his refusal was as steadfast as the people's insistence on conferring it on him.[288] [6] An account of the wars fought under his command, the peace brought to the whole world by his victories, and all his achievements outside Italy and at home—that would exhaust a writer even if he intended to devote the whole span of his life exclusively to such a work. I, keeping my declared commitment in view, have set before my readers' eyes and minds only a general outline of his principate as a whole.

90. With the civil wars extinguished, as I noted above, and with the individual members of the state starting to bond together, those elements that such a long series of conflicts had torn to shreds also now began to coalesce. Dalmatia, recalcitrant for 220 years, was subdued to the point of unconditionally acknowledging our rule.[289] The Alps, famed for their wild

---

285. After the death of Julius Caesar, entry into the senate had not been scrupulously monitored. Augustus undertook a series of purges, bringing the number to six hundred.

286. Most notably, Agrippa built the Pantheon, the baths of Agrippa, the Saepta Julia, the Aqua Virgo aqueduct, a bridge over the Tiber, and a portico on the Campus Martius; Titus Statilius Taurus built the first stone amphitheater; Gnaeus Domitius Calvinus restored the Regia; Lucius Cornificius rebuilt the temple of Diana; Lucius Marcius Philippus repaired the temples of Hercules and Saturn; Lucius Cornelius Balbus built the third stone theater in Rome; and the Aemilii restored the Basilica Aemilia.

287. In 23 BC Augustus gave up the permanent consulship, which he himself records was offered to him, perhaps as compensation for his refusal of the dictatorship (Dio 53.32.3; *RG* 5). Dio (54.10.5) suggests that he received consular *imperium* for life, but this may reflect the senatorial rule of the same year that he not have to remit his proconsular *imperium* when he entered the city. He was consul twice more, in 5 and 2 BC.

288. Augustus (*RG* 5) records his refusal to accept the post of dictator, which he may have felt would have reinforced the sense of monarchical aspirations (Dio 54.1.4).

289. Dalmatia was reduced by Octavian in 35–33 BC and became a senatorial/public province in 27. Velleius must have in mind here the conclusion of the Pannonian War of 9 BC, which came two hundred years after Rome's first campaign in Illyricum. It is surprising that he did not date its subjugation to the end of Tiberius' successful campaign in AD 9.

and uncivilized tribes, were totally subdued.[290] The Spanish provinces were brought to heel in numerous wars fought with mixed outcomes by the princeps in person at one point, and at another by Agrippa, whom the princeps' friendship had elevated all the way to a third consulship and presently to holding tribunician authority as his colleague.[291] [2] Roman armies had initially been sent into these provinces in the consulship of Scipio and Sempronius Longus, during the first year of the Second Punic War (250 years ago). They were commanded by Gnaeus Scipio, uncle of Africanus, and for two centuries the struggle there was marked by great bloodshed on both sides, with the result that the loss of the Roman people's commanders and armies often brought shame, and sometimes even danger, to the Roman empire.[292] [3] In fact, it was those provinces that swallowed up the Scipios; they put our ancestors under pressure in the humiliating fifteen-year war when Viriathus was their leader; and they struck panic into the Roman people in the Numantine War.[293] It was in those provinces that Quintus Pompeius struck his disgraceful treaty, and Mancinus his even more disgraceful one, both of which the senate rescinded, handing the latter general over to the foe as a mark of his disgrace.[294] That was the land responsible for the loss of so many ex-consuls and ex-praetors, and which in the time of our fathers so elevated Sertorius by its armed might that for a five-year period it was impossible to judge whether it was the Spaniards or the Romans who had greater military strength, and which people was going to be subject to the other.

290. The Alps were subdued in 25 BC with the subjugation of the Salassi in the Val d'Aosta by Aulus Terentius Varro Murena. The campaign actually went on until 7.

291. A campaign had been launched in Spain in 29 BC by Statilius Taurus (see 2.85). Augustus campaigned there in person in 26–25 and then returned to Rome, leaving Agrippa with the task of final pacification, completed by 19. Armies had first been sent into Spain in 218 (consulship of Publius Cornelius Scipio and Tiberius Sempronius Longus), so Velleius is using very round figures. Agrippa was consul first in 37, and subsequently in 28 and 27. He received *tribunicia potestas* for five years in 18 and a further five years in 13. Augustus acquired some of the constitutional rights of the plebeian tribunes without holding the actual office, which was one of the fictions that allowed the Republic to function as a monarchy. His *tribunicia potestas* gave him the right to convene the senate and the popular assemblies, and to initiate or veto legislation. This authority in many ways lay at the heart of the principate, and emperors dated their reigns from the point when their *tribunicia potestas* was assumed. By conferring the power on another individual the princeps was in a sense marking out his successor.

292. Gnaeus Cornelius Scipio Calvus (consul 222 BC) won a victory over the Carthaginians in 218, at the battle of Cissa, the first Roman campaign in Spain. He and his brother Publius (consul 218, father of Africanus Maior) died in Spain in 212 or 211 within a short space of time.

293. The Lusitanian War engaged the Romans in 154–139 BC, and the opposition was led by Viriathus (see 2.1.3) from 147 to his death in 139. The text here reads XX (20), which has been variously emended as X or XV (the reading accepted here). If the first edition reading is retained it means that Velleius is being very casual with his figures.

294. On the disgrace of Quintus Pompeius and Gaius Hostilius Mancinus, see 2.1.

[4] Such, then, were the provinces—provinces so widespread, so populous, and so wild—which, some fifty years ago, Caesar Augustus brought to such a level of peace that, though never before free from the most violent of wars, they remained free even from banditry under the governorship of Gaius Antistius, then under Publius Silius and the others that followed.[295]

[Octavian receives the title of Augustus (27 BC) and suppresses a number of conspiracies.]

91. While the west was being pacified, the Roman standards that Orodes had captured when Crassus was vanquished, and those that Orodes' son Phraates had taken after defeating Antony, were sent back from the east by the king of the Parthians to Augustus.[296] This cognomen (Augustus) was accorded to that <god-on-earth>, on a motion from Plancus, by the unanimous agreement of the senate and of the people of Rome.[297]

[2] There were, however, some who hated this happy situation. Indeed, Lucius Murena and Fannius Caepio, men of different character (without this particular crime Murena could have passed for a good man, but even before it Caepio was the worst type of scoundrel), formed plans to assassinate Caesar.[298] They were, however, caught by the public authorities and themselves suffered under the law what they had intended to inflict with violence. [3] Not much later, too, came Egnatius Rufus, a man in all respects more like a gladiator than a senator.[299] During his aedileship he had acquired some popular support, which, by using his private band of slaves to put out house fires,

---

295. On Gaius Antistius Vetus, see 2.43. Quaestor in Further Spain in 61 BC, plebeian tribune in 56, consul in 30, he defeated the Cantabri as Augustus' legate in 25. Publius Silius Nerva (consul 20) succeeded Antistius as legate of Nearer Spain.

296. The standards were handed over by Phraates in 20 BC to Tiberius, who was present in the east to reestablish Tigranes on the throne of Armenia. They were placed in the temple of Mars in the forum of Augustus in 2 BC (see note 305). On Crassus' disaster at Carrhae, see 2.46; on Antony's defeat by Phraates, see 2.82.

297. The bestowal of the name Augustus took place at a meeting of the senate on January 16, 27 BC. Lucius Munatius Plancus (2.63.3) was the senior consular.

298. Lucius Murena is probably to be distinguished from the Aulus Murena mentioned in note 290 (though some emend and argue that they are one and the same). He was the brother of Terentia, wife of Maecenas. Little is known of Fannius Caepio, except that he was condemned to death, tried to escape, and was captured through treachery and executed. The date of their plot is uncertain, either 23 (especially if there is only one person with the cognomen Murena) or 22 BC.

299. Marcus Egnatius Rufus was the son of a friend of Cicero. He established a private fire brigade in Rome. Aedile in 21 BC and praetor in 20, he became a candidate for the consulship for 19 but was prevented from standing by Gaius Sentius Saturninus (2.92), who refused to recognize his candidacy. His supporters rioted; Egnatius was accused of conspiring against Augustus and executed in 19.

he had then increased every day, so much so that he moved directly from that office to the praetorship and soon had the temerity to stand for the consulship. He was, however, overwhelmed by his awareness of all his crimes and misdeeds, and his financial situation was in no better condition than his character. He brought together men like himself and decided to murder Caesar. Unable to achieve security while Caesar was secure, he would remove him first and then die himself. [4] For such is people's nature: they prefer to die creating general disaster rather than be crushed in a personal one, and to be less noticed when facing the same fate as others. But Egnatius was no more successful than his predecessors in keeping his secret; he was shut up in a prison with his fellow conspirators and died a death most appropriate to his life.

92. The exemplary measure taken by the excellent Gaius Sentius Saturninus, consul at around this time, must not be cheated of notice.[300] [2] Caesar Augustus was away settling matters in Asia and the east, delivering around the world by his very presence the benefits of the peace he had brought about. At this time Sentius, who happened to be sole consul in Caesar's absence, had generally been exercising old-fashioned severity and unwavering firmness, in the manner of the consuls of old, bringing into the open the fraudulent practices of the tax collectors, punishing their greed, and restoring public moneys to the treasury. In particular, he truly showed himself a consul in presiding over the elections. [3] He forbade those he considered unfit candidates for the quaestorship to put their names forward; when they insisted on doing so, he threatened to use his discretionary power as consul to punish them if they went down to the Campus. [4] Egnatius was then enjoying the people's support, and hoping to have his consulship immediately follow his praetorship, as he had had the praetorship follow his aedileship. Sentius, however, forbade him to put his name forward and, when he failed to get Egnatius' agreement, swore that even if he were elected consul by the votes of the people he would not proclaim him returned.

[5] This, I think, invites comparison with any of the glorious actions taken by the consuls of old; but the fact is that we are by nature more inclined to praise those acts that we have heard about than those we have witnessed. We regard those of the present with envy, those of the past with

300. Gaius Sentius Saturninus (2.77, 2.105) was a Pompeian but was allowed to return to Rome after the Treaty of Misenum in 39 BC. He is much admired by Velleius. He was consul, as a new man (*novus homo*), in 19. Augustus was to be the other consul for that year but was absent on a tour of the east from 22 or 21 to 19 and did not take up the office (which gave Egnatius the incentive to run). Sentius was sole consul until August, when he took Quintus Lucretius Vespillo as his colleague. Late in the year Sentius resigned, to be replaced by Marcus Vinicius, grandfather of Velleius' patron.

veneration; and we believe we are put in the shade by the one category but enlightened by the other.

[Augustus' nephew and intended heir Marcellus dies and his stepson Tiberius begins his public career (23 BC).]

93. About three years before the crime of Egnatius burst onto the scene, that is, about the time of the conspiracy of Murena and Caepio, fifty years ago, Marcus Marcellus died when he was still a relatively young man.[301] Marcellus was the son of Augustus' sister Octavia, and people assumed that should anything happen to Caesar Augustus he would succeed to his power, though they did not believe that Marcus Agrippa would let that happen without giving him some trouble. He was, they say, well endowed with noble qualities and possessed of a cheery character and disposition, and well qualified for the high position for which he was being brought up. His death occurred just after a magnificent spectacle that he had staged to mark his aedileship.

[2] Agrippa had left for Asia, ostensibly on some imperial errands, though rumor had it that he had withdrawn himself for the moment because of the latent hostility between him and Marcellus.[302] After the latter's death, however, he returned and married Caesar's daughter Julia, who had been Marcellus' wife, a woman whose womb brought happiness neither to Julia herself nor the state.

94. As I explained above, Tiberius Claudius Nero was three years old when Livia married Caesar Octavian.[303] [2] He was brought up with an education divinely inspired, a young man well blessed in breeding, good looks, a tall stature, the finest studies, and great intelligence, one who had from the start

---

301. Marcus Claudius Marcellus was the son of Gaius Claudius Marcellus and Augustus' sister Octavia and was thought to represent Augustus' hopes for the succession. His sister Marcella married Agrippa. In 25 BC Marcellus married Julia, the daughter of Augustus and Scribonia, and became aedile in 23. He died at about the age of nineteen in the same year (Plut. *Marc.* 30.6; Pliny *NH* 19.24; Dio 53.30.4). It is difficult to reconcile this date with Velleius' reference to fifty years.

302. Agrippa was supposedly offended that Marcellus was given preference and left Rome for Mytilene in a form of self-imposed exile. Whatever his motives, he was recalled in 21 BC and married Julia that same year, after divorcing Marcella. His marriage to Julia produced Gaius and Lucius Caesar, both of whom died in their youth (see 2.96, 2.102); Julia the Younger, wife of Lucius Aemilius Paulus, who would, like her mother, be involved in scandal and exiled; Agrippina the Elder, mother of Caligula, exiled for political reasons by Tiberius; and Agrippa Postumus, exiled under Augustus and executed on Tiberius' accession.

303. Velleius makes only the most fleeting reference to the marriage of Octavian and Livia, which took place on January 17, 38 BC. This is hardly surprising: the event occasioned much scandal, since Livia was at the time pregnant with her second son Drusus (the Elder).

been able to raise hopes of the greatness he now has, and in his features had the cut of a princeps. [3] Now, in this period, he began his public career, as a quaestor, when he was in his nineteenth year. On the orders of his stepfather he tackled the enormous problem of the food supply and the shortage of grain both at Ostia and in the city, and he made it clear from the job he did how great a man he was going to be.[304]

[4] Moreover, he was not long afterward sent out with an army by his stepfather to inspect and organize the provinces in the east.[305] After outstanding displays of all his virtues in that area, he marched into Armenia with his legions, brought it under the power of the Roman people, and conferred its throne on <Artavasdes, whose . . .>. The king of the Parthians, too, intimidated by the eminence of such a great name, sent his own children to Caesar Augustus as hostages.

[The campaigns of Tiberius and his brother Drusus in Germany and Pannonia. Drusus dies in 9 BC. Lucius Piso subdues a rebellion in Thrace in 11.]

95. When Tiberius returned from Asia, Caesar Augustus decided to put him to the test by giving him charge of a war of some importance and he assigned to him as his assistant in the enterprise his brother Drusus Claudius, to whom Livia had given birth in Caesar's house.[306] [2] The two divided their responsibilities and launched an offensive against the Raeti and the Vindelici.[307] They attacked many towns and strongholds, and also had successes in pitched battle; and they crushed tribes that enjoyed great protection from the terrain, were very inaccessible, had large populations, and were pitilessly cruel. This they did with greater risk than actual loss to the Roman army, but with much blood shed by the two enemy tribes.

[3] This was preceded by the censorship of Plancus and Paulus, which was spent in wrangling that was neither to their credit nor to the advantage

---

304. Tiberius was elected quaestor in 24 BC and charged with overseeing the grain problems. Suetonius (*Tib.* 8) claims that he was also charged with the regulation of slave penitentiaries.

305. Tiberius went to the east in 20 BC to settle the succession in Armenia. He bestowed it in fact on Tigranes III, son of Artavasdes, supposedly in response to a request from the Armenians that Augustus send Tigranes from Rome, where he was resident, to rule them. At the time Phraates IV restored to the Romans the standards lost by Crassus at the battle of Carrhae. Velleius surprisingly makes no mention here of the return of the Roman standards, which would have redounded to Tiberius' credit.

306. Both of Livia's sons, Tiberius and Drusus, proved to be military commanders of genuine and considerable ability. Drusus was born in 38 BC amid rumors that he was Octavian's son. He was quaestor in 18, praetor in 11, and consul in 9, the year of his death. In 16 he married Antonia Minor, daughter of Mark Antony and Octavia.

307. In 16/15 BC Drusus and Tiberius undertook campaigns against the Raeti, in the east of what is now Switzerland, and against the Vindelici, in the south of present Bavaria.

of the state.[308] One of the two lacked the stringency of a censor, the other the requisite lifestyle: Paulus was barely able to carry out the duties of the censorship, while Plancus should have feared them—there was no accusation he could make against the young, or hear others make, that he could not recognize as applying to himself, old though he was.

96. Then came the death of Agrippa.[309] He was a man who had, by his many achievements, added nobility to his "new man" status and raised it to the point of becoming Tiberius' father-in-law and seeing the deified Augustus adopting his sons, giving them the forenames Gaius and Lucius.[310] The death brought Tiberius closer to Caesar, since his daughter Julia, formerly married to Agrippa, now married Tiberius.[311]

[2] Shortly after this the Pannonian War was fought under the leadership of Tiberius.[312] It had been fought initially under the commands of Agrippa and Marcus Vinicius, your grandfather; and being a major and bloody conflict, and very close at hand, it posed a threat to Italy.[313] [3] The tribes of

---

308. Paulus Aemilius Lepidus and Lucius Munatius Plancus were appointed censors in 22 BC. They were the last censors to hold office who did not belong to the imperial family. Plancus (2.63.3) has been mentioned several times by Velleius, always in tones of contempt. Lepidus was consul in 34, clearly well connected, as he first married Cornelia, daughter of Scribonia, then the younger Marcella, daughter of Augustus' sister Octavia.

309. Agrippa went to Campania in 12 BC to recover his health and died there on March 20. Augustus gave the funeral oration and Agrippa was buried in the mausoleum of Augustus.

310. Despite Velleius' laudatory comments, Agrippa's lowly birth haunted him after his death, when some of the nobility refused to attend his funeral. He had become father-in-law to Tiberius through the latter's marriage to Vipsania Agrippina, Agrippa's daughter by his first wife Pomponia, daughter of Titus Pomponius Atticus, the celebrated correspondent of Cicero.

Gaius and Lucius Caesar, who were adopted by Augustus in 17 BC and given accelerated privileges, occupied an important position in the plans for the succession. Gaius was born in 20 BC, received the *toga virilis* in 5 BC, and was consul-designate for AD 1 and admitted to the senate. He married Livilla, daughter of Drusus the Elder, in 1 BC and was sent on an eastern mission, where he was fatally wounded, dying on February 21, AD 4. Lucius Caesar was born in 17 BC. He received the *toga virilis* in 2 BC and received honors similar to those of Gaius. He died on his way to Spain on August 20, AD 2.

311. Tiberius was obliged to divorce Vipsania, with whom he had enjoyed a happy marriage, to marry Julia. This second marriage became acrimonious, Julia reputedly believing that Tiberius was her inferior.

312. Pannonia, which became a province in AD 9, is seen by modern Hungary as its predecessor. It actually comprised what is now southwest Hungary, southeast Austria, and northwest Croatia.

313. Marcus Vinicius was in Pannonia at the outset of the revolt, charged with handling it until Agrippa arrived. The text of Velleius as transmitted in the first edition ("when Agrippa and Marcus Vinicius, your grandfather, were consuls") suggests that the war started when Agrippa and Marcus Vinicius were consuls. But they held the office at different times (Agrippa's final term, 27 BC; Vinicius' sole term, 19), and in any case the campaign did not start until

Pannonia and Dalmatia, the topography of the region and its rivers, the number and composition of their forces, and the outstanding and numerous victories won by such a great commander—all this I shall describe elsewhere. This work must hold to its proper format. For winning this victory Tiberius celebrated an ovation.[314]

97. However, while all was going very successfully in this part of the empire, there was a disastrous defeat in Germany. The leader there was the legate Marcus Lollius—a man always more interested in money than proper conduct and a total degenerate, though he made every effort to conceal his degeneracy—and the loss of the Fifth Legion's eagle took Caesar Augustus from Rome into the Gallic provinces.[315] [2] The arduous conduct of the war in Germany was then delegated to Drusus Claudius, Tiberius' brother, a young man with qualities as many and great as a man's nature can acquire, or energy bring to perfection. It is not clear whether his talents were better suited to the rigors of war or the arts of civilian life; [3] at all events, his endearing and pleasant nature is said to have had no equal, nor his way of appreciating his friends fairly and putting himself on the same level as them. His good looks stood next to those of his brother. But an unjust fate snatched this man from us during his consulship, when he was in his thirtieth year, a man who was the conqueror of most of Germany and who had spilled a great deal of its people's blood in various locations.[316]

[4] The burden of that war was then transferred to Tiberius' shoulders. He conducted the campaign with his usual courage and good fortune, and he made his way through all parts of Germany with no serious losses to the army that had been entrusted to him, something that was always of particular

---

much later, in 13 (possibly 14 at the earliest). The text adopted here accepts Watt's judgment that the reference to the consulship is a later interpolation.

314. An ovation was essentially a "lesser" triumph. The senate in fact voted Tiberius a full triumph (Dio 54.31.4), but Augustus reduced the honor, celebrated on January 16, 9 BC.

315. Marcus Lollius was a strongly committed supporter of Augustus. He was legate in Galatia in 25 BC and consul in 21 as a new man (*novus homo*); he served in Macedonia about 19–18, probably as proconsul, and then in Gaul. A number of Germanic tribes entered Gaul in 16; Marcus Lollius sent his cavalry against them but was defeated by the Germans, who entered the Roman camp and took away the standards. The defeat involved shame rather than serious loss, according to Suetonius (*Aug.* 23.1), and Velleius perhaps exaggerates its significance. In 1 BC Lollius was appointed to accompany Gaius on his eastern mission and as a bitter enemy of Tiberius poisoned Gaius' mind against him (see also 2.102). It was thus inevitable, perhaps, that Velleius would regard him with contempt.

316. Drusus carried out a number of successful campaigns in Germany between 12 and 9 BC and advanced as far as the Elbe. He celebrated an ovation in 10. In 9 he suffered a serious fall from his horse and died. Tiberius rushed to his side but arrived too late, then accompanied his funeral cortege to Rome on foot.

concern to this commander. He subjugated the country to the point of almost reducing it to the level of a tribute-paying province. He was then awarded another triumph along with another consulship.[317]

98. In the course of the events in Pannonia and Germany that I mentioned above, a fierce war broke out in Thrace, where all the tribes of that nation had been roused to arms.[318] What suppressed the war was the courage of Lucius Piso, a man whom even today we regard as a very diligent and at the same time very humane protector of our urban security.[319] [2] (As Caesar Augustus' legate, Piso fought a three-year war with the Thracians, and in pitched battle as well as by storming strongholds he inflicted severe losses on them and reduced them to a state of peace on their former terms.) By finishing off the war, he restored security to Asia and peace to Macedonia. In the case of this man everyone must think and admit this: his character is a superb mix of dynamism and clemency, and there is hardly anyone to be found more intensely fond of his leisure or, on the other hand, more ready and capable in his undertakings and more painstaking in getting done what is needed, without any exhibitionism.

[Tiberius leaves Rome for Rhodes in 6 BC. The scandal of Julia erupts in 2 BC.]

99. A short time after this, Tiberius revealed a filial piety that was amazing, unbelievable, and downright indescribable. He had already held two consulships and celebrated as many triumphs; he had been put on a level with Augustus through sharing his tribunician authority; he was the most eminent of all citizens apart from one (and that because he wanted it that way); he was the greatest commander of all, and the most famous in terms of reputation and fortune; and he was truly the second light and head of the state.[320] He now requested from the man who was at the same time his

---

317. In 7 BC Tiberius held his second consulship (the first in 13) and celebrated what was, strictly, his first triumph, since he had previously been granted only an ovation.

318. The Thracian rebellion broke out in 13 BC, incited by Vologaeses, a priest of Dionysus, with the intention of driving out King Rhoemetalces (Dio 54.34.5). It was crushed by Lucius Calpurnius Piso, consul in 15 and later possibly governor of Galatia-Pamphylia and legate in Thrace. His three-year campaign lasted from 13 to 11 and earned him the triumphal ornaments.

319. Lucius Piso was the third to occupy the newly reformed office of city prefect, in AD 13. Marcus Valerius Messalla Corvinus (2.36.2) did so for a few days in about 25 BC, followed by Titus Statilius Taurus (2.85) in 16 BC (Tac. *Ann.* 6.11).

320. Tiberius had been consul in 13 and 7 BC and had celebrated an ovation in 9, for Illyricum, and a full triumph in 7 for Germany. In 6 he received *tribunicia potestas,* which brought considerable recognition of his status (on this power, see 2.90). This makes his decision to retire from public life especially baffling, though Tacitus claims that in making the second award

father-in-law and his stepfather a respite from his ongoing labors. [2] His motivation was as follows (though he concealed the reason for his decision).[321] Gaius Caesar had already assumed the *toga virilis,* and Lucius was also going to assume it shortly, and he did not want his own prestige to be an obstacle to the early progress of these rising young men. [3] The sentiments of the state at that time, the feelings of individuals, the tears of everybody taking leave of such a great man, and how his fatherland almost laid claim to him—let me keep all that in reserve for my full-scale history. [4] Even in this overview, however, the following must be said. During his seven-year stay on Rhodes, all proconsuls or legates who set off for overseas provinces <came to see him and on meeting him> they always lowered their fasces before him, private citizen though he was (though such majesty never belonged to a private citizen), thereby acknowledging that his furlough carried greater honor than their command.[322]

100. The entire world felt aware of Tiberius' resignation from the guardianship of the city: the Parthian laid hands on Armenia, abandoning his Roman alliance, and Germany rebelled, now that its conqueror's eyes were turned away.[323]

[2] In Rome, meanwhile, during the consulship that he held with Gallus Caninius (that is, thirty years ago), the deified Augustus filled the minds and eyes of the Roman people with the most magnificent entertainments—a gladiatorial show and a mock sea battle—on the dedication of the temple of Mars.[324]

---

of *tribunicia potestas* Augustus used the occasion to make disparaging comments about Tiberius (Tac. *Ann.* 1.10.4).

321. Velleius attributes Tiberius' departure to a concern for the position of Gaius and Lucius, which, according to Suetonius (*Tib.* 10), was the reason Tiberius himself later provided. But Suetonius also suggests other possibilities: the hope that his exit would strengthen his position, if it was found that he was needed, and his need to get away from Julia, which Tacitus also claims (*Ann.* 1.53). Dio (55.9.5–8), admitting all sorts of conjectures, provides a number of motives: contempt for Julia, fear of Gaius and Lucius, anger at not being made coemperor, or even expulsion by Augustus.

322. The respect supposedly shown to Tiberius while on Rhodes may owe much to Velleius' imagination. Suetonius (*Tib.* 13) gives a quite different account, suggesting that Tiberius was held in considerable contempt.

323. In 20 BC the Romans had placed Tigranes III on the throne of Armenia (see 2.91). On his death (c. 6), Tigranes was replaced at the instigation of pro-Parthian elements by his son Tigranes IV and his daughter Erato. The Romans rejected this arrangement and imposed Artavasdes, who was in turn driven out in 2 BC by the Parthian king Phraates V. It is not clear what German rebellion Velleius refers to but there could well have been problems with the Chauci and Cherusci, who had already rebelled in 6.

324. On August 1, 2 BC, Augustus consecrated the temple of Mars Ultor (Mars the Avenger) that he had promised to build after Philippi (Dio 60.5.3). He was consul for the thirteenth

But in that very year a storm burst out within his own household that is terrible to relate and frightful to remember. [3] Augustus' daughter Julia, with no thought whatsoever for so great a father and husband, did not in her debauched excesses refuse to indulge in any disgusting activity in which a woman could partake either actively or passively.[325] She gauged the extent of her fortune by the freedom she had to sin, claiming as legitimate whatever took her fancy. [4] Iullus Antonius, who was a prime example of Caesar Augustus' clemency, then became a defiler of that man's household and was himself the avenger of the crime he had committed. (After defeating Iullus' father, Caesar Augustus had not only spared Iullus' life but had honored him with a priesthood, a praetorship, a consulship, and provincial governorships and had even accepted him into the closest family relationship through countenancing his marriage to his sister's daughter.)[326] [5] Then, too, Quintius Crispus, who masked his singular depravity with a stern demeanor, Appius Claudius, Sempronius Gracchus, Scipio, and other men of lesser name and of both orders paid the penalty they would have paid for the violation of the wife of any citizen, when it was the daughter of Augustus Caesar and the spouse of Tiberius that they had violated.[327] Julia was relegated to an island and removed from the sight of her country and parents, although her mother Scribonia accompanied her and of her own will remained with her in exile.[328]

---

time. Lucius Caninius Gallus was suffect consul from July 1, in succession to Marcus Plautius Silvanus.

325. The scandal surrounding the conduct of Julia was clearly a major event but is not well understood. Seneca provides the most detailed account of Julia's behavior with her multitude of lovers, and the other sources tend also to stress the moral aspects of her conduct, but scholars generally assume that claims of sexual misconduct are essentially meant to cloak political wrongdoing, and Tacitus expresses surprise at the severity of the punishment meted out to her (Sen. *Ben.* 6.32.1–2, *Clem.* 1.10.3, *Brev. Vit.* 4.5; Tac. *Ann.* 1.53, 3.24.1–3, 4.44.3, 6.51.3).

326. Iullus Antonius was the second son of Mark Antony and Fulvia. His elder brother had been executed on Octavian's order after the victory at Alexandria, but Iullus was spared. He held the praetorship in 13 BC and the consulship in 10, and was governor of Asia from 9 to 3. He married Octavia's daughter Marcella, the second wife of Agrippa, whom Agrippa had divorced to marry Julia. He was the "avenger of the crime" in the sense that he committed suicide.

327. Titus Quintius Crispus Sulpicianus was consul in 9 BC. Tiberius Sempronius Gracchus was a writer of tragic verse who was tribune in 2. He was exiled to Cercina, a small island near the African coast, where he was executed soon after Tiberius' accession.

328. Julia was banished to the island of Pandateria off the coast of Campania. Later, in response to appeals for clemency, she was allowed to transfer to Rhegium, on the mainland, where she died in AD 14. In saying that she was separated from her "parents," Velleius is including as "parent" her stepmother Livia. The gesture of her biological mother, Augustus' second wife Scribonia, in accompanying Julia into exile says much about her character. Scribonia survived her daughter and died in 16.

[Gaius Caesar leaves for his eastern mission, accompanied for part of the time by Velleius. Lucius Caesar dies in Spain in AD 2; Gaius, in Lycia in 4.]

101. Only a short time had elapsed after this when Gaius Caesar, who had earlier visited other provinces on tours of inspection, was sent to Syria, and before leaving he met with Tiberius, to whom he paid every honor as if to a superior.[329] Gaius' performance of his duties in Syria was so uneven as to provide abundant material for praise but at the same time no small amount for criticism. He met with the king of the Parthians, a young man <of very tall stature, on> an island situated in the middle of the Euphrates, each leader attended by a retinue of the same size. [2] This spectacle was truly glorious and memorable—the Roman army standing on one bank, with that of the Parthians opposite them on the other, while two of the most eminent leaders of their respective empires and of the world came together —and it was my luck to set eyes on it as a military tribune in the early stages of my army career.[330] [3] (I had begun my service at that rank earlier, under your father, Marcus Vinicius, and Publius Silius, in Thrace and in Macedonia.[331] Later on I visited Achaea, Asia, and all the eastern provinces, as well as the mouth and both coastlines of the Black Sea, and I take much pleasure from the very sweet memories of so many events and places, and of so many peoples and cities.) It was the Parthian who dined first with Gaius on our bank, and later Gaius dined with the king on the bank held by the enemy.

---

329. Gaius (2.96) spent time in the Balkans in 1 BC (Dio 55.10.17), to which Velleius presumably refers when he speaks of "other provinces." He was engaged on his eastern mission in AD 1–4. He passed through Athens and Samos, where he met Tiberius in 2 and in fact received him very coldly (Suet. *Tib.* 12.2–3; Tac. *Ann.* 3.48.2; Dio 55.10.18–21). It is not clear why Tiberius would have been his superior, since his term of *tribunicia potestas* officially lasted from July 1, 6, to June 30, 1 BC, and would have expired by this time. An emendation of the text has been suggested (*cui* to *qui*) which would make Tiberius show respect to Gaius, but the issue is surely one of Velleius exaggerating Tiberius' status.

330. Velleius provides a fascinating firsthand account of the meeting between Gaius and the king of Parthia on the island in the Euphrates. This was followed by the installation of the Roman candidate Ariobarzanes of Atropatene as king of Armenia, which led to a revolt, during which Gaius received a fatal wound (see 2.102). The Parthian king was Phraates V (Phraataces), son of Phraates IV, who succeeded his father in 2 BC after murdering him with the help of his own mother, whom he married. He was deposed in AD 4.

   Velleius' rank was that of military tribune, of which six were assigned to each legion. Five would generally be, like Velleius, equestrians, one a young man of senatorial rank at the outset of his career.

331. On Marcus Vinicius the Elder, see Introduction, section I. Publius Silius was consul in AD 3. He and Vinicius were presumably proconsuls of Macedonia with praetorian rank or legates of Moesia.

102. Augustus had wanted Marcus Lollius to act as governor to his young son, but at this time a rumor spread that this man's treacherous schemes, full of the cunning of a wily and deceitful mind, had been brought to Caesar Augustus' attention by the Parthian.[332] Lollius' death followed a few days later, but whether it was an accident or suicide I do not know. However, while men felt joy at Lollius' passing, the state shortly felt just as much sadness over the loss of Censorinus—a man born to win people's affection—in those same provinces.[333]

[2] Gaius then entered Armenia and met with success in the first part of his incursion.[334] Later, in negotiations near Artagera, which he had imprudently attended in person, he was seriously wounded by someone called Adduus, and as a result his physical condition began to decline and his mental functioning to be less beneficial to the state. [3] Nor was there any shortage of people around him to encourage his vices with sycophancy—adulation is always there as the companion of great fortune—and the upshot was that he was induced to prefer the prospect of growing old in some far-off and truly remote corner of the world over returning to Rome. Then, as he was returning to Italy, reluctantly and under protest, he succumbed to an illness in a city of Lycia called Limyra. His brother Lucius Caesar had died at Massilia about a year earlier as he was making his way to Spain.

[Tiberius is adopted by Augustus in AD 4 and dispatched against the Germans. Velleius serves under him and testifies to the highly successful campaign.]

103. Although Fortune had withdrawn the hopes attaching to the boys' great name, she had by then restored to the state its own special protection: before the deaths of either of the young men, in the consulship of your father Publius Vinicius, Tiberius had returned from Rhodes, filling the fatherland with joy beyond belief.[335] [2] Caesar Augustus did not wait long—

332. Augustus' respect for Lollius (2.97) had been sufficient to send him as companion to Gaius, his grandson and adopted son, on his eastern mission. Lollius fell from favor, however, accused of taking bribes from the king of Parthia. He died soon after, in AD 2. In contrast to Velleius' uncertainty, Pliny the Elder explicitly states that, on losing Gaius' friendship, Lollius took a draft of poison (*NH* 9.118).

333. Gaius Marcius Censorinus was one of the *IIIvir monetales* (officials of the treasury) in 12–11 BC, consul in 8, and proconsul of Asia when he died in AD 2–3.

334. Gaius entered Armenia in AD 2. The anti-Roman party had rebelled there against Ariobarzanes, the Roman candidate. Gaius was wounded on September 9 and sought permission from Augustus to retire to Syria, but the emperor prevailed on him to return to Rome; he died on the journey, in Lycia, on February 21, 4. Lucius had died on August 20, 2. In both cases there were rumors that Livia had been responsible for their deaths (Tac. *Ann.* 1.3.3).

335. Publius Vinicius was consul between January 1 and July 1, AD 2, when he was replaced

there was no need to look for a man to choose, only to choose the man who stood out. [3] And so, after the death of both boys, he pressed ahead and did what he had wanted to do after the death of Lucius, while Gaius was still alive, but had been held back from doing by the strenuous objections of Tiberius. This was to make Tiberius his partner in his tribunician authority, over the vigorous protests of Tiberius both at home and in the senate, and also to adopt him, which he did on the <26th> of June in the consulship of Aelius Catus and Gaius Sentius, 754 years after the city's founding, that is, twenty-seven years ago.[336]

[4] The joy of that day, the citizens flocking together and almost grasping the sky with their hands in making their vows, and the hopes now conceived for everlasting safety and for the permanence of the empire—of all this I shall scarcely be able to give a full account in my proposed full-scale work, and much less would I attempt a thorough description here. <I am content to say just this, how that day was favorable to everyone.> [5] This was when definite hope shone forth, hope of parents for their children, of husbands for their marriages, of owners for their properties, and of all people for security and calm, peace and tranquility, so much so that one could not have entertained greater hopes, or seen them more happily fulfilled.

104. That same day also saw the adoption of Marcus Agrippa, whom Julia bore after the death of Agrippa, but in the case of Tiberius' adoption an addition was made to the formula with these words from Caesar Augustus: "This I do for the good of the state."[337]

---

by a suffect. Lucius died not long after Tiberius' return, Gaius some two years later. According to Suetonius, Tiberius was allowed to return on condition that he remain a private citizen (Suet. *Tib.* 13.2). Velleius suggests that the condition was set by Tiberius himself.

336. Augustus' adoption of Tiberius took place in AD 4, on June 26 according to the inscribed calendar of events of the town of Amiternum ("*Fasti Amiterni,*" in *Corpus Inscriptionum Latinarum* 1 [2], 243), not on the 27th, as posited in the text of Velleius as transmitted. Velleius provides a tortured explanation for Augustus' waiting two years after Tiberius' return, and he does not mention that after his own adoption Tiberius in turn was obliged to adopt Germanicus (2.116), son of his brother Drusus and husband of Augustus' granddaughter Agrippina the Elder. This grant of *tribunicia potestas* was for either ten years (Dio 55.13.2) or five years (Suet. *Tib.* 16.1).

337. Marcus Agrippa Postumus was born after his father's death in 12 BC and adopted along with Tiberius in AD 4. He was noted for serious personal, perhaps mental, problems (see 2.112. 7), and sources speak of his brutish behavior. He was removed from Rome and confined to the pleasant confines of Sorrento, but as his behavior grew worse he was sent to the desolate island of Planasia in 7. He supposedly spent most of his days fishing. There were rumors of a rapprochement between him and Augustus during the latter's final months, and he was executed immediately after Augustus' death. Tiberius, Livia, and Augustus were all implicated in Agrippa's death, but the circumstances were very murky and are glossed over by Velleius (see 2.112.7; also Tac. *Ann.* 1.6.1, 2.39.1–2; Suet. *Tib.* 22; Dio 57.3.5–6; *Epit. de Caes.* 1.27).

[2] The nation did not keep the champion and protector of its empire in the city for long but sent him directly to Germany where, three years earlier, an enormous war had flared up when your grandfather Marcus Vinicius, a man of great distinction, was in command.[338] The war had been conducted with success by Vinicius in some sectors while in others he had mounted a successful defense, and for that reason he had been decreed triumphal ornaments with a magnificent inscription listing his achievements. [3] This was the time that saw me as a soldier in Tiberius Caesar's camp, after my earlier service as tribune. Immediately following Tiberius' adoption, I was sent to Germany with him as a prefect of cavalry (a post in which I was succeeding my father) and for nine consecutive years I witnessed his divinely inspired operations, when I was either a prefect or a legate, and later I assisted him with them, to the best of my limited ability. And I do not think the human condition can again witness anything like the spectacle I then enjoyed. Throughout the most thickly populated areas of Italy and the whole length of the provinces of Gaul, the people were seeing again their commander of old, a man who had become a Caesar through his merits and fine qualities before receiving the name, and they were all more fulsome in congratulating themselves than they were in congratulating him! [4] Indeed, tears of joy were brought to the soldiers' eyes at the sight of him; there was animation and a strange sort of elation in their greetings; there was an eagerness to touch his hand. And they could not stop themselves from adding: "Are we really looking at you, General?" "Do we have you safely back among us?" and then, "I was with you in Armenia, Commander," "I was with you in Raetia," "I received a donative from you in Vindelicia," "And I received one in Pannonia," "And I received one in Germany." All this cannot be described in words and perhaps can scarcely be believed.

105. Tiberius straightaway entered Germany where he crushed the Canninefates, the Attuarii, and the Bructeri, and accepted the submission of the Cherusci—tribes that I would wish had not later gained so much fame from our disaster![339] The river Weser was crossed and the stretches beyond

---

The famous addendum to the declaration of Tiberius' adoption is often taken to suggest that Augustus found it personally distasteful to have Tiberius as a son. Velleius clearly takes it as a vote of confidence in Tiberius' adoption.

338. Marcus Vinicius, the grandfather of Velleius' patron, was consul in 19 BC as a new man (*novus homo*). He had been a legate in Gaul in 25 and went on to serve in Illyricum. With Agrippa he began the Pannonian campaign, which Tiberius ended successfully in 12–9. His service on the Rhine in AD 1 or 2, alluded to by Velleius, is the last item of information on him.

339. There is little information on military activities in Germany since Tiberius' earlier campaign there, but the general strategy on this occasion was likely to prepare for a major campaign against the Marcomanni in Bohemia. Tiberius advanced beyond the Weser but established his

it penetrated. Tiberius Caesar would claim for himself all the toughest and most dangerous theaters of the war, and others that were less hazardous he put under the command of Sentius Saturninus, who was at the time a legate of his father in Germany.[340] [2] Saturninus was a man of many fine qualities; he was diligent, active, foresighted, and able to bear the hardship of military duties as well as being proficient in them. But when his obligations afforded some leeway for leisure, the same man would make the most of it, liberally and unstintingly, but in such a manner that one would call him splendidly extravagant and affable rather than prodigal or idle. I have spoken above about this man's fine character and his famous consulship.

[3] The campaigning season of that year was extended into the month of December, and that brought the reward of an overwhelming victory. Tiberius Caesar's family loyalty then brought him back to Rome, although the Alps were almost blocked by snow; but the protection of the empire led him back to Germany at the start of spring. On leaving, the commander had placed his winter quarters in the middle of the country at the source of the river <Julia>.

106. Heavens above, what a great volume would be required to recount our operations the following summer under Tiberius Caesar! All Germany was marched over by our armies; peoples were conquered who were barely known by name; and the submission of the tribes of the Chauci was accepted. All their warriors surrendered their arms, infinite in number though they were, huge in stature, and well safeguarded by their geographical position; and, along with their chieftains, and surrounded by a gleaming crowd of our soldiers under arms, they flung themselves down before the commander's dais.

[2] The Langobardi were crushed, a race whose fierceness surpasses even the usual German ferocity. Finally—something that had not even been hoped for, much less actually put to the test—a Roman army and its standards was led from the Rhine all the way to the river Elbe, which skirts the territory of the Semnones and Hermunduri, that is, to the 400-mile mark.[341] [3] To that same point, too, thanks to amazing good fortune and the commander's

---

winter camp to the west, probably on the Lippe, extending his campaign until December, when he returned to Rome. After his adoption (in AD 4) Velleius refers to him as Caesar.

340. On the much admired Gaius Sentius Saturninus, see 2.77.3, 2.92. The reference to "his father" alludes to Augustus.

341. Both Drusus the Elder in 9 BC and Lucius Domitius Ahenobarbus in AD 1 had reached the Elbe, and here Velleius appears to be making a blatantly false claim for Tiberius. It has been suggested that in fact the uniqueness that he claims was not simply for reaching the Elbe but for what follows, the combined land and sea operation. Similarly, Drusus was actually the first to take a fleet into the North Sea, from the Rhine. Tiberius' expedition was more ambitious, to take his fleet from the mouth of the Rhine to link up with the troops sailing up the Elbe. Augustus makes reference to the achievement (*RG* 26.4), though it is not clear whether he is referring to the campaign of Drusus or Tiberius.

attention to detail, as well as the watch he kept on the seasons, came a fleet that had circumnavigated the Ocean's winding coastline. This sailed up the Elbe from some previously unheard-of and unknown sea and, after conquering numerous peoples, joined up with Tiberius Caesar and the army, bringing with it all manner of supplies in prodigious quantities.

107. Despite the magnitude of these events I cannot resist inserting here the following apparently insignificant episode. We had established our camp on the nearer bank of the above-mentioned river, and the far bank was agleam with the armed warriors of the enemy, who fell back immediately with every <. . .> movement of our vessels. One of the barbarians, who was in his later years, tall in stature and (so his dress indicated) of high rank, boarded a canoe that was a dug-out log, commonly found among those peoples. Alone, he steered this odd kind of vessel to the middle of the river and asked to be granted safe passage to disembark on the bank that we were holding and to see Caesar.

[2] The man's request was granted, and he then brought his boat to shore and, after silently contemplating Tiberius Caesar for quite some time, said: "Our young warriors are crazy. When you aren't here they worship you as a god, but when you *are* here they fear your arms instead of accepting your assurance of protection. But I, Caesar, thanks to your kind permission, have seen the gods whom I only used to hear about before, and in all my life I have not wished for, nor experienced, a happier day than this." Granted leave to touch Tiberius Caesar's hand, he got back in his boat and sailed over to the bank occupied by his people, continually gazing back at Caesar.

[3] Conqueror of all the peoples and lands that he had visited, Tiberius Caesar led his legions back to their winter quarters and then made for Rome with the same haste as he had made the previous year.[342] His army had suffered no harm or damage, and had come under attack only once, when it was taken by surprise, and that had resulted in heavy losses for the enemy.

108. There was now nothing left to be conquered in Germany apart from the Marcomanni. These were a people who, under their leader Maroboduus, had been uprooted from their original settlements and had withdrawn into the interior of the country, where they were now living on plains encircled by the Hyrcanian forest.[343] [2] No haste on my part should let me pass over

342. After taking his army safely to its winter quarters, Tiberius returned once again to Rome, where his presence is attested early in the next year in the inscribed calendar of events of the town of Praeneste (January 27, AD 6: "*Fasti Praenestini,*" in Ehrenberg and Jones [1952], 46). Dio attributes Tiberius' frequent visits to Rome to his concern that Augustus would exploit his absence to give precedence to someone else (55.27.4–5).

343. Maroboduus, the ruler of the Marcomanni, a familiar figure in Tacitus' *Annals,* had prevailed upon his people to migrate into Bohemia from southern Germany sometime after 9 BC and

mention of this man. Maroboduus was from a distinguished background
and was possessed of physical strength and a fierce spirit. He was a barbarian
by birth but not in his mentality. It was not to meet any crisis or by chance
that he gained this leadership among his people, nor was his position an
insecure one whose continuation depended on the will of his subjects. Having his mind set on stable authority with regal powers, he had decided to
take his people far from the Romans and move forward to an area where,
after running from arms more powerful than his, he might make his own
arms the most powerful of all. And so, settling in the lands mentioned above,
he either crushed all his neighbors in battle or brought them under his control on terms that he dictated.

109. By continuous training Maroboduus brought the body of troops safe-
guarding his empire almost to the standard of Roman discipline, in a short
time raising them to such a high level that they were to be feared even by
our empire. Toward the Romans his conduct was such as not <to provoke
us militarily while at the same time indicating> that he had at his disposal
more than enough strength and resolve to resist were he himself provoked.
[2] The representatives that he sent to the Caesars would sometimes com-
mend him to them as being a suppliant, but on other occasions they spoke
for him as though he were their equal. Tribes and individuals revolting from
us would find refuge with him, and he would openly take the role of our
rival, making no real effort to conceal it. He had built up an army of 60,000
infantry and 4,000 cavalry, and by training it in interminable wars against
his neighbors he was preparing it for greater operations than those in which
he was then involved. [3] He was formidable for the following reason, too.
He had Germany to his left and on his front, Pannonia to his right, and the
Norici to the rear of his settlements, and he was feared by all of them since
he always appeared to be on the point of invading them. [4] He did not
allow Italy to feel secure in the face of his growing power, either, since his
territory started at a point not much farther than two hundred miles from
the peaks of the Alps, which form Italy's boundary.
[5] Such was the man and such the area on which Tiberius Caesar decided to launch an offensive from opposite directions the following year.
Sentius Saturninus was assigned the task of bringing his legions through the
lands of the Chatti to Boiohaemum (such being the name of the region that
Maroboduus inhabited), by hewing his way through the forests adjoining
those of Hyrcania. Tiberius himself proceeded to lead against the Marcomanni

had established a powerful kingdom, which Rome saw as a serious threat to its interests in the
region, especially given its important strategic location.

the army then in service in Illyricum, starting from Carnuntum, a place in the kingdom of Noricum that was the closest to them in that direction.[344]

[While Tiberius prepares to crush Maroboduus, a rebellion breaks out in Pannonia and Dalmatia in AD 6. Tiberius concentrates his initial efforts on Pannonia and achieves success by the end of 8.]

110. The projects of humans are sometimes shattered and sometimes delayed by Fortune. Caesar had already prepared his winter quarters on the Danube, and he had advanced his army to a point no more than five days' march from the first posts of the enemy. [2] He had decided that Saturninus should bring up <legions . . .> They were almost at an equal distance from the enemy and were to meet up with Caesar at a prearranged rendezvous within a few days. But then the whole of Pannonia, which the advantages of a lasting peace had rendered arrogant and which was now at the height of its power, took up arms together, after inducing Dalmatia and all the peoples of that area to support its plan. [3] At that point necessity took precedence over glory, and it did not seem safe to have the army hidden away in the interior and to leave Italy unprotected before an enemy that was so close.[345]

The total number of the peoples and tribes that had rebelled exceeded 800,000; some 200,000 infantry experienced in the use of arms were assembled, and 9,000 cavalry. [4] This huge gathering took its orders from dynamic and experienced commanders. One section had decided to head for Italy, their link to which lay through Nauportus and Tergeste on their common border; another had streamed into Macedonia; a third had assigned itself the task of defending the home territories. Supreme command lay with the two Batos and with Pinnes.

[5] All the Pannonians had a knowledge not only of the discipline of the Romans but also of our language (many of them even of our writing), and

---

344. Tiberius devised a simple pincer movement, whereby he would advance from the southeast from Carnuntum (in modern Austria) with the army of Illyricum, and Sentius Saturninus would advance from Moguntiacum (Mainz) in the west.

345. Maroboduus was saved by the Pannonian revolt, which lasted from AD 6 to 9. The revolt occasioned panic in Rome, and led to the conscription of a large army, part of which was taken to the front by Velleius himself.

Before AD 9 the area between the Middle Danube and Macedonia was generally called Illyricum, but by the end of the rebellion it was divided into southern and northern provinces known as Dalmatia and Pannonia, respectively. Rome's tribute in 9 BC caused much resentment in an area that had never been properly subdued. Moreover, when Messalinus (2.112), legate in Illyricum, tried to raise forced levies, a revolt broke out under Bato, leader of the tribe of the Daesitiates, which spread through all of Dalmatia (Dio 55.29). The Pannonians joined the rebellion under their ruler Pinnes while the Breuci, a tribe within Pannonia, under a leader also called Bato, rebelled and marched against Sirmium (modern Mitrovica).

they were familiar with our armed training. And so, truly, no tribe was ever as swift at making war follow plans for it and at putting decisions into effect. [6] Roman citizens were assassinated; traders were butchered; a large detachment of veterans was totally wiped out in the area farthest removed from their commander in chief; Macedonia was occupied by troops; there was destruction of everything everywhere by fire and the sword. In fact, the fear aroused by this conflict was even great enough to shake and daunt the spirit of Caesar Augustus, toughened though that was by his experience of such great wars.

111. Troop levies were therefore held and there was also a general recall of veterans from all areas.[346] Men and women were obliged to provide freedmen for military service according to their incomes. And in the senate the voice of the princeps was heard declaring that, unless precautions were taken, the enemy could come within sight of the city of Rome within ten days. The services of Roman senators and equestrians were requested for the war, and they all promised them. [2] But we would have been wasting our time on all these preparations had there not been a man to direct them; and so the state asked Augustus to give it, as its ultimate protection, a commander for the war—Tiberius.

[3] In this war, too, my modest abilities found an opportunity to render assistance of some distinction. At the end of my cavalry service I was a quaestor-designate. Though not yet a senator I was put on a level with senators and even with designate plebeian tribunes, and I brought a division of the army that was put in my charge by Augustus from the city to his son. [4] Following that, during my quaestorship, I waived my right to the provincial sortition and was sent to Tiberius as Augustus' legate.

What armies of the enemy did we see that first year! What great opportunities our leader's foresight granted us to escape the fury of their united forces <and then defeat them> separately. With what circumspection as well as <. . .> utility did we see affairs conducted under the commander's authority! What prudence went into the organization of the winter camp! What pains were taken to see that the enemy, hemmed in by the guard posts of our army, could not break out at any point, and <that his strength would be sapped> through shortage of provisions and the onset of furious internal wrangling.

---

346. The gravity of the crisis can be gauged by the decision to recruit freedmen into the ranks, just as slaves were conscripted after Rome's defeat by Hannibal at Cannae, in the Apulian region of southeast Italy, in 216 BC. Dio (55.31.1) provides a somewhat different, and probably less convincing, version of Tiberius' status, suggesting that Augustus was afraid he was stretching out the war from self-interest and so sent out Germanicus in command of an army.

112. The first campaigning season of the war saw a feat by Messalinus, happy in its outcome and bold in its enterprise, which must be set on record.[347] [2] Messalinus was a man with a spirit even more noble than his family line, one who well deserved to have had Corvinus as his father and to leave his own cognomen to his brother Cotta. He was in command of Illyricum when there was a sudden uprising and he, with the Twentieth Legion, which was only at half strength, was surrounded by the army of the enemy, but he defeated and put to flight more than twenty thousand of them. For this he was honored with triumphal ornaments.

[3] Wherever Tiberius Caesar was to be found, the barbarians' satisfaction with their numbers and trust in their strength were not great enough for them to have confidence in themselves. The division of their army actually facing our commander we wore down as it suited us or as we wished, reducing it to a state of life-threatening starvation, so that it did not dare withstand our men's attack or engage them when they offered an opportunity for battle and deployed their line. Instead the enemy seized Mount Claudius and raised fortifications to defend themselves.[348]

[4] By contrast, another division had streamed out to meet an army that the ex-consuls Aulus Caecina and Silvanus Plautius were bringing from the overseas provinces, and had surrounded five of our legions as well as some auxiliary troops and the royal cavalry (Rhoemetalces, king of Thrace, had joined up with the generals just mentioned and was bringing with him a large detachment of Thracians to assist them in that war).[349] This division inflicted an almost deadly defeat on all of them: [5] the royal mounted troops were

347. Marcus Valerius Messalla Messalinus (consul 3 BC) was the eldest son of Messalla Corvinus, the literary patron (2.71), and brother of Marcus Aurelius Cotta Maximus Messalinus (consul AD 20).

348. Mount Claudius is generally identified as near the village of Warasdin on the right bank of the Drava River.

349. Late in AD 7 reinforcements were brought from the east, from Moesia and Galatia, by the governors Aulus Caecina Severus and Marcus Plautius Silvanus, respectively. They were taken by surprise at the Volcaean Marshes, west of Sirmium, where they narrowly escaped disaster and reached Siscia. Both men had played an important role in Illyricum in 6 BC, unmentioned by Velleius. Caecina was of Etruscan stock, a professional soldier who had by AD 15 served for forty years. In 14 he was legate in Lower Germany where he dealt with the mutiny that followed Augustus' death, and during Germanicus' campaigns he skillfully extracted his troops from disaster and led them back to the Rhine. In 21 he famously argued that governors should not be accompanied by their wives in their provinces (Tac. *Ann.* 3.33). Silvanus was the colleague of Augustus as consul in 2 BC. He was the son of Urgulania, a friend of Livia.
    Rhoemetalces of Thrace was an old ally of the Romans. He initially supported Antony but switched his loyalty to Octavian before Actium. He at first acted as regent for his nephews, but Augustus later awarded him the kingdom, in 11 BC. He proved his dependability during the Pannonian revolt and died in AD 12.

routed, the allied cavalry squadrons driven back, the cohorts repelled, and there was even panic around the legionary standards. But the courage of the Roman soldiers won more glory on that day than they left over for their officers (who, seriously deviating from their commander in chief's normal practice, fell among the enemy before ascertaining through scouts where the enemy was actually located). [6] The legions were now in a critical situation: some of the military tribunes had been slaughtered by the foe; a camp prefect and a number of prefects of cohorts had fallen; and the centurions had not avoided the carnage, with even some of the first rank killed.³⁵⁰ Nevertheless, they encouraged each other and attacked the enemy. Then, not satisfied with having stemmed their opponents' assault, they broke through their line and, though things had earlier looked hopeless, seized the victory.

[7] It was at about this time that Agrippa, his mind and character depraved to an appalling degree, turned to reckless behavior and alienated the feelings of the man who was both his father and grandfather. (He had been adopted by his biological grandfather on the same day as Tiberius, and some two years before this point had already begun to show signs of the sort of person he was.) Soon afterward, as his vices increased day by day, he met an end appropriate to his demented state.³⁵¹

113. Hear now, Marcus Vinicius, how Tiberius Caesar was as great a general in war as you see him as an emperor in times of peace. The two armies were joined up (the troops that had been under Caesar and those that had come to him), and brought together into one camp were ten legions. They comprised more than seventy cohorts, <fourteen cavalry squadrons,> and more than ten thousand veterans, and in addition, there were a large number of volunteers and a great contingent of royal cavalry. In short, it was an army of a size unparalleled anywhere or at any time since the civil wars, and they all delighted in this very fact, placing their greatest confidence of victory in their numbers.

[2] The commander, however, was the best judge of what he was doing and he preferred what was effective over what looked impressive; as I have seen him invariably do in all his campaigns, he followed expedients that *merited* approval and not those that were routinely *given* approval. He waited only a few days for the army that had arrived to get back its strength after its march and then took the decision to dismiss it, since he could see that it was too large for the maintenance of discipline and could not be easily

---

350. After the reforms of Marius, each of the ten cohorts of a legion had six centurions of equal rank, apart from the First Cohort, which was double the size of the others and whose centurions had a special status.

351. Agrippa was exiled to Planasia in AD 7 (see 2.104); Velleius skillfully evades the details of his death by the use of the ambiguous word *exitus* (end).

controlled.³⁵² [3] He escorted it on a long and extremely arduous march, the difficulties of which are barely describable, so that no one would dare attack it while it was a united force, and so that the enemy as a united force could not attack any single division of those who were leaving (since each tribe would be fearing for its own territory), and thus sent it back to the area from which it had come. At the start of a very harsh winter Tiberius himself returned to Siscia, setting his legates—and I myself was one of them—in charge of the winter quarters, which he had divided into sections.

114. Now for something that does not sound important when related, but which actually provides crucial evidence of a person's real worth and helpfulness, something very pleasant to experience and outstanding for the humanity it reveals. Throughout the entire period of the war in Germany and Pannonia, none of us, and none of those ahead of us or behind us in rank, experienced illness without having his health and recovery sustained through care provided by Tiberius Caesar. It was as though, despite the burden of all the other great responsibilities demanding his attention, this was the only matter for which he had time. [2] For those who needed it, a horse-drawn carriage was on hand, and his litter was put at everyone's disposal (and I took advantage of it, as did others). At one time his doctors, at another his cooking equipment, and at another his bathing gear (as though it had been brought exclusively for the purpose) were all made available to help anyone's infirmity. All we lacked was a house and domestic servants—but nothing that they could have provided for us or we could have wanted from them.

[3] I shall add another detail, which all those with us in those days will immediately recognize (as indeed they will recognize the other details that I have related). Tiberius was the only commander who always rode a horse, and the only one to dine seated with his invitees on most of the summer campaigns. He was tolerant of those who did not adhere to discipline, provided that no harm would come from the precedent; his admonitions were frequent, his reprimands infrequent, and his punishments very rare; and he followed the course of moderation, turning a blind eye to many things but checking certain others.³⁵³

352. The initial panic provoked by the rebellion meant that in the end more troops were levied than were needed. Velleius speaks of ten legions, plus auxiliary troops (cohorts) and the forces of King Rhoemetalces, and his statement has considerable authority, since he was there. Suetonius gives a figure of fifteen legions (*Tib.* 16.1). Tiberius led those troops to Sirmium to reinforce his position on the Save River and left them under the command of Plautius Silvanus before returning to his winter quarters in Siscia at the end of AD 7.

353. Velleius' eulogy of Tiberius the soldier may seem overwhelmingly sycophantic but is to some degree confirmed by Suetonius' account of Tiberius' campaigning style in Germany (*Tib.* 18–19) and concern for the welfare of the sick while he was in Rhodes (*Tib.* 11.2).

[4] Winter postponed the satisfaction of concluding the war, but in the following campaigning season all Pannonia sued for peace, and what was left of the war was limited to Dalmatia. I shall later, I hope, give an ordered account in a full-scale history of how these fierce warriors numbering many thousands had shortly before been threatening Italy with servitude; how they now brought together, at a river called the Bathinus, the weapons they had been using, all of them prostrating themselves before the knees of the commander; and how of their two most eminent leaders, Bato and Pinnes, one was captured and the other surrendered.[354]

[5] At the start of autumn the victorious army was marched back to winter quarters, and command of all the troops was given to Marcus Lepidus by Tiberius Caesar.[355] Lepidus is a man second only to the Caesars in reputation and fortune, one for whom a person's admiration and affection grows the more he has had the opportunity to know and understand him, and one thinks of him as actually adding distinction to the great names in his family tree.

[Tiberius subdues Dalmatia in AD 9, assisted by Germanicus. The achievements of a number of military commanders.]

115. Caesar then directed his attention and his weapons to the other weighty task, the war in Dalmatia.[356] In this region, proof of what an effective assistant and legate he found in my brother Magius Celer Velleianus is furnished by the statements made by Tiberius himself and by his father; and

---

354. At the end of the campaigning season Tiberius returned to Rome, arriving at the beginning of AD 9 (Dio 56.1.1). Plautius Silvanus was left in Sirmium.

Velleius gives a very abbreviated account of the final days of the rebellion, perhaps to avoid taking the spotlight away from Tiberius. After the Pannonians surrendered, according to Dio (55.34.4), Bato the Breucian betrayed Pinnes and was confirmed as sole ruler by the Romans but was captured and put to death by his namesake Bato, the Dalmatian, who revived the rebellion in Pannonia. It was soon suppressed by Plautius Silvanus, and Bato the Dalmatian moved south into Dalmatia.

355. Marcus Aemilius Lepidus was the great-nephew of the triumvir, consul in AD 6, and governor of Pannonia 8–10. Velleius possibly refers to him again later (see note 386). He was well connected to the imperial family, which perhaps explains the fulsome tones used here. His daughter Aemilia Lepida married Drusus, eldest son of Germanicus. His son married Drusilla, daughter of Germanicus. His elder brother Lucius Aemilius Paulus married Julia, Augustus' granddaughter.

356. Tiberius spent the beginning of AD 9 in Rome; at winter's end he returned to Dalmatia and completed the reconquest. He moved from the north with Germanicus while Lepidus and Silvanus moved up from the south. Dio (56.12.3–14) provides details of Tiberius' finally cornering Bato the Dalmatian at Adetrium near Salonae (Solin, Croatia), but during the difficult operation Bato escaped before it fell; later he surrendered. Suetonius reports that he was eventually sent to Ravenna, where he lived in considerable material comfort (*Tib.* 20).

the record of the high honors that Tiberius Caesar granted him at the time of his triumph also makes it clear. [2] At the start of summer, Lepidus led the army from its winter quarters and headed out toward the commander in chief Tiberius, passing through tribes still untouched and unimpaired by defeat in war, and consequently ferocious and savage. He struggled with the difficult terrain and a violent enemy and, after inflicting serious damage on those trying to block his way—he destroyed their lands, burned their buildings, and butchered their men—[3] he reached Caesar, exulting in his victory and laden with plunder. These were exploits for which he would have deserved a triumph had he been acting under his own auspices, and in recognition of them he was <awarded> triumphal ornaments, the wishes of the senate being in accord with the judgment of the two Caesars.

[4] That campaigning season crowned this important war with success. The Perustae and the Daesitiates, Dalmatian tribes virtually impossible to conquer because of their location in the mountains, their ferocious character, their amazing military knowledge, and especially because of the narrowness of their wooded mountain passes, were at this time finally pacified, at a point when they were all but eliminated. And this was now brought off not simply under Caesar's overall command but by his own personal military prowess.

[5] I was able to see nothing in this extensive war, nothing in Germany, more important or more admirable than the following. No opportunity to win a victory ever seemed to our commander favorable enough if he had to pay for it with a serious loss of men, and the course that always seemed to him to have the greatest glory was the one that was the safest. He paid more attention to his conscience than his reputation; and the leader's decisions were never directed by the judgment of the army, but the army was directed by the prudence of the leader.

116. In the war in Dalmatia Germanicus had been sent forward into many difficult areas where he provided great examples of his bravery;[357] [2] and the

---

357. Germanicus (initially Nero Claudius Drusus Germanicus) was the elder son of Drusus the Elder and Antonia Minor. He was born on May 24 in 16 or 15 BC and married Agrippina, daughter of Marcus Agrippa and Julia, daughter of Augustus (their children included the future emperor Caligula). Augustus saw Germanicus' marriage as part of his ambition to be succeeded by someone of his bloodline; when Tiberius was adopted by Augustus in AD 4 he was in turn required to adopt Germanicus (see note 336), who henceforth carried the name Germanicus Julius Caesar. Germanicus inherited his father Drusus' popularity and even surpassed it. He is described in the sources as courageous and handsome, universally admired, and the epitome of decency and integrity.

The actions of Germanicus were restricted essentially to AD 9. We know from Dio that he took towns identified as Spolonum and Seretium without serious problems, but perhaps through overly hasty action suffered a setback at Raetinum (Bihac), where his men were trapped inside

ex-consul Vibius Postumus, who was governor of Dalmatia, also earned triumphal ornaments for diligent service that was often in evidence.[358] (A few years earlier Passienus and Cossus, men with different <. . .> in certain respects but famed for their good qualities, had earned this distinction in Africa, but Cossus also passed on a testimonial of his victory in the cognomen of his son, a young man born to demonstrate virtue in all its forms.)[359] [3] In that campaign, too, Lucius Apronius, who participated in the achievements of Postumus, earned by his outstanding courage the honors he soon acquired.[360]

I wish that the omnipotence of Fortune had not been demonstrated by evidence provided by greater examples! But in this area, too, her power can be fully recognized. Take the case of Aelius Lamia, a man of traditional values but one whose kindness always softened his old-fashioned austerity.[361] In Germany, in Illyricum, and later in Africa his service was truly outstanding, but he failed to win the triumphal ornaments, lacking not the merit but the opportunity to do so. [4] Then there was Aulus Licinius Nerva Silianus, son of Publius Silius, for whom not even the man who appreciated him had ample admiration. <He demonstrated the qualities of an excellent citizen

---

the burning town (Dio 56.11–12.1). The news of the end of the revolt in Illyricum was soon overshadowed by the reports of the disaster of Varus in the Teutoburg Forest. To provide an intermission between the two events Velleius inserts a section of laudatory passages on a number of individuals.

358. Gaius Vibius Postumus, from Larinum, was consul in AD 5 as a new man (*novus homo*). He held the governorship of the new province of Dalmatia in 9–12 and was governor of Asia in 13.

359. Lucius Passienus Rufus was the son of the man identified by Seneca the Elder as the most eloquent of his generation (*Contr.* 2.5.17). He was himself an orator and father of Gaius Sallustius Crispus Passienus, great-nephew of the historian Sallust and a major figure in the late Augustan–Tiberian period. He was consul in 4 BC, then proconsul of Africa in AD 3–5, where his military achievements brought him the triumphal ornaments in 3.

Gnaeus Cornelius Lentulus Cossus was a close confidant of Tiberius. He was so fond of alcohol that he once fell asleep in the senate; he could not be roused and had to be carried home still slumbering (Sen. *Ep.* 83.15). His indulgence was no barrier to a successful career. Consul in 1 BC, he succeeded Passienus as proconsul of Africa, gaining the triumphal ornaments for victories over the Gaetuli in AD 6. For this he was given the cognomen Gaetulicus, which he seemed not to use but passed on to his son Gnaeus Cornelius Lentulus Gaetulicus (consul 26). The younger Gaetulicus was an apparently lax legate in Upper Germany, in 29–39, when he was executed by Caligula.

360. Lucius Apronius was consul in AD 8 as a new man (*novus homo*). He campaigned in the Dalmatian operation alongside Postumus. He won the triumphal ornaments in 15, serving under Germanicus, and again for his victories over Tacfarinas while governor of Africa, in 18–21. In 28 he became governor of Lower Germany; he was father-in-law of Gaetulicus, hence from 29 the commands of Upper and Lower Germany were held by a father- and son-in-law.

361. Lucius Aelius Lamia was consul in AD 3 as a new man (*novus homo*). He served in Germany in 10–12, Pannonia and Dalmatia in 12–14, and Africa in 15–16.

and a straightforward commander.>[362] Through his premature <death> he missed enjoying the emperor's distinguished friendship and achieving elevation in honor to the highest level that his father had reached. [5] If anyone says that I have looked for an opportunity to mention these men, he will find me acknowledging that charge; for impartial frankness free of mendacity is no crime in the eyes of decent men.

[Quintilius Varus' crushing defeat in Germany in AD 9. Tiberius is sent to deal with the crisis.]

117. Tiberius had only just put the finishing touch on the campaigns in Pannonia and Dalmatia when—within five days of his bringing such a momentous operation to completion—a grim dispatch from Germany <brought the news> that Varus was dead and three legions had been slaughtered, along with the same number of cavalry units and six cohorts.[363] It was as if Fortune was indulging us to the extent that when our leader was preoccupied elsewhere <. . .>. However, the reason for the disaster and the character of the general both call for a pause in the narrative.

[2] Varus Quintilius came from a family that had nobility rather than distinction. He was an easygoing character, quiet in his ways, and as slow to act physically as mentally; and he was more familiar with the leisurely life of the camp than the rigors of the military campaign. That he did not look

---

362. Aulus Licinius Nerva Silianus was consul in AD 7. He was the son of Publius Silius Nerva (consul 20 BC), and brother of Publius Silius (consul AD 3), under whom Velleius began his career (see 101.3), which may help account for the enthusiasm he shows here. The text is very corrupt at this point.

363. The disaster suffered by Varus in the Teutoburg Forest in the second half of September of AD 9, and the loss of Legions 17–19 along with the death of their commander, ranks second only to Cannae in the annals of Roman military setbacks. The defeat had a major and possibly lasting effect on Augustus. The site, which has long been sought by military historians, has been located fairly securely in the Kalkriese region.

Publius Quintilius Varus was a member of an old patrician family and was very well connected. Quaestor in 22 BC, he was consul with Tiberius in 13, when he was married to a daughter of Agrippa. Around 7, he married Claudia Pulchra, daughter of Claudia Marcella and granddaughter of Augustus' sister Octavia. Varus commanded in Africa, possibly in 7–6, and in Syria in 5–3. Although he might be seen as a capable administrator, suited to peaceful, if important provinces, rather than as a military commander, he showed much presence of mind. On the death of Herod the Great, for example, he moved troops south and dealt firmly with insurgents (Jos. *BJ* 2.39–79). He may have been active in the Alpine lowlands before he received his commission in Germany, in AD 7, in succession to Gaius Sentius Saturninus. In 9 he was attacked while marching back with troops from summer camp near the Weser, with disastrous consequences. Varus may have been a more competent commander than the sources suggest. He essentially became the scapegoat for the disaster; modern commentators attribute much of the blame to Augustus and his overconfidence in Rome's position in Germany.

down on money, however, was made clear by Syria, of which he had been governor: he entered a rich province poor and departed from a poor one rich. [3] When he was in charge of the army stationed in Germany, he imagined that its inhabitants possessed no human characteristics beyond speech and human limbs, and that while they could not be subdued by the sword they could be pacified by law. [4] With this as his goal, he passed into the center of Germany as if he were traveling among people delighting in the pleasures of peace, and he dragged out the campaigning season with court proceedings and well-regulated judicial processes at his tribunal.

118. Now the Germans are—to an extent that can scarcely be credited by anyone lacking experience of them—totally cunning as well as being absolutely ferocious, and they are a race of liars from birth. Concocting a series of bogus legal disputes, they alternated between challenging each other with lawsuits and thanking Roman justice for settling them, for having curbed their wild nature by means of a new form of discipline with which they had been unfamiliar, and for ending by legal means conflicts that were usually settled by warfare. This lulled Quintilius into a state of extreme carelessness, to the point where he imagined he was making legal pronouncements as an urban praetor in the Forum instead of someone commanding an army in the heart of German territory.

[2] Then a man named Arminius, a son of Sigimer, the chief of that people, capitalized on the general's indifference for his criminal purpose.[364] He was a young man of noble birth, brave in action and quick-thinking, possessed of a ready intelligence beyond that of the usual barbarian, and an expression and eyes that revealed the fire in his soul. He had been our steadfast companion on the previous campaign, and along with the right to Roman citizenship he had also been granted the right to equestrian status. He intelligently surmised that no one could be more swiftly brought down than a man who feared nothing, and that complacency was the most common starting point for catastrophe.

[3] Arminius at first brought in a few people as partners in his plan, and then he brought in more, telling them, and convincing them, too, that the Romans could be crushed. He also followed up his decisions with action and fixed a date for the treacherous attack.

---

364. Arminius, a leader of the Cherusci, was born about 19 BC. He held Roman citizenship and attained equestrian rank through his service in the auxiliaries. Velleius does not mention him after his successful battle against Varus. He went on to carry out campaigns well into Tiberius' reign. He fought successfully against Segestes, who led the pro-Roman faction in AD 15, and campaigned against Germanicus in 17. He was eventually killed by his own people in 21. He later became a symbol of German nationalism, under the name of Hermann. In the mid-nineteenth century the monumental Hermannsdenkmal was erected, supposedly near the site of his victory in the Teutoburg Forest.

[4] Information on this was passed on to Varus by Segestes, a loyal and illustrious member of that race, and Segestes even demanded <that the conspirators be arrested, but Fate obstructed his plans>, and had completely blunted Varus' mental alertness.[365] For this is how things go: a god very often destroys the reason of a man whose fortunes he is about to change and produces the most distressing result of all, namely, that accidental occurrences seem deserved and chance events become grounds for blame. So it was that Varus declared that he did not believe Segestes, and that his judgment of the goodwill that Arminius showed him was based on the man's merit. After the first disclosure there was no opportunity for a second.

119. How this frightful catastrophe moved ahead—for the Romans there had been none more serious than this among foreign peoples since the loss of Crassus in Parthia—I shall try to set out, as others have done, in a regular work; for the moment I must merely express sorrow for the whole affair.[366] [2] This was the bravest of all armies, peerless among the Roman troops in discipline, in action, and in battle experience. Falling victim to the apathy of its leader, the treachery of the enemy, and the unfairness of Fortune, it was not even given a clear opportunity that the men had wished for to fight or break out of their predicament. Some were even seriously reprimanded for using Roman weapons and showing the Roman spirit. Bottled up in forests, marshes, and the German ambush, the army was butchered like cattle to the point of extermination by an enemy it had always dealt with in such a manner that it was Roman anger or clemency that decided whether they lived or died. [3] The commander showed greater spirit for dying than for fighting: [4] heir to the example of his father and grandfather, he ran himself through.[367] There were two camp prefects, and the conduct of the one, Lucius Eggius, was as exemplary as that of the other, Ceionius, was disgraceful. When the battle had eliminated by far the greater part of the army, Ceionius was the man responsible for the surrender, preferring execution to death in battle. Varus' legate, Vala Numonius, generally a steady and upright character, also set a terrible example: leaving the infantry stripped of cavalry support, he set off in flight with his cavalry squadrons, heading

365. Segestes had a brother Sigimer, who may be the Sigimer who was the father of Arminius. Arminius married Segestes' daughter Thusnelda.

366. On Crassus' defeat at Carrhae in Syria, see 2.46.

367. Varus' grandfather is almost certainly the praetor of the same name in 57 BC who was involved in the recall of Cicero and proconsul in Spain in 56–53, but nothing is known about his death. Varus' father Sextus (quaestor 49) was among the senators besieged at Corfinium and given their freedom by Caesar afterward (Caes. *BC* 1.23.1–2). Sextus became a supporter of Brutus and Cassius and committed suicide with the help of his freedman after Philippi in 42.

for the Rhine.[368] Fortune punished his misdeed, however. He did not survive the men he abandoned but was killed as he deserted them.[369]

120. A real tribute should be paid Lucius Asprenas, who was serving as a legate under his uncle Varus.[370] By his steadfast and courageous action he saved the force of two legions under his command from being part of that great disaster, and he swiftly went down to the lower winter quarters, where he kept true to their allegiance even tribes that were wavering west of the Rhine. There are some, however, who believed that, while he was responsible for saving the survivors, he also appropriated the estates of men slaughtered under Varus' command, and that he purloined at will inheritances from the dead soldiers.

[2] Praise is also due to the courage of Lucius Caedicius, a camp prefect, and the men who were surrounded along with him at Aliso, where they were under siege from countless German troops.[371] They overcame all their difficulties, which shortage of supplies was rendering unbearable and the strength of the enemy making insurmountable, and, without adopting any foolhardy plan or slackening their caution, they watched out for an opportunity and with the sword made a way for themselves back to their comrades.

[3] From this it is clear that Varus, who was certainly a man of consequence and good intentions, brought about his own destruction and that of a magnificent army through his own shortcomings in judgment as a commander rather than because he was let down by his soldiers' courage. [4] As atrocities were being committed against the captives by the Germans, Caldus Coelius, a young man who was a great credit to his venerable family, brought off a heroic act. He grasped a part of the chain with which he was bound and smashed it against his head with such force that his death was instantaneous, with blood and brains gushing forth together.

---

368. Dio (56.21.2) indicates that the cavalry did in fact put up a fight during the battle and Gaius Numonius Vala's conduct may not have been as shameful as Velleius seems to imply. Nothing further of substance is known about Vala, except that he came from Campania and was the recipient of Horace's *Ep.* 1.15.

369. The order of events from this point to the end of chapter 120, as transmitted in the primary edition, is somewhat incoherent. Many (though not all) commentators believe that the sections were recorded in the wrong order and have accordingly rearranged them. The order followed here is the one adopted by Watt.

370. Lucius Nonius Asprenas was the son of Quintilia, sister of Varus. He was consul in AD 6 and legate of his uncle in 7.

371. Nothing further is known of Lucius Caedicius. Aliso was located on the upper Lippe, a tributary of the Rhine, and is identified by some with Haltern.

[5] Varus' corpse was partially burned and then torn to pieces by a barbarous enemy. His head was severed and taken to Maroboduus, who sent it to Tiberius Caesar. It was, however, given a decent burial in Varus' family grave.[372]

[6] On hearing of these events, Tiberius Caesar came rushing back to his father, and as the perpetual patron of the Roman empire he, as usual, took the empire's cause upon his shoulders.[373] He was sent to Germany; he secured the Gallic provinces; he made troop deployments; he strengthened garrisons; and, judging his prospects in the light of his own greatness rather than the confidence of the enemy (who were threatening Italy with a campaign on the scale of that of the Cimbri and Teutoni), he went on the offensive and crossed the Rhine with his army. [7] He was now launching an attack on an enemy that his father and fatherland had been happy just to have kept at bay. He pushed into the interior; he opened up roads; he laid waste the countryside; he burned houses; he drove off any who faced him; and, attended by the greatest glory, he returned to winter quarters with no loss incurred by any of the troops whom he had led across the river.[374]

121. When he entered Germany as commander on the second occasion, Tiberius' courage and fortunes were the same as they had been on the first. He shattered the enemy forces with his naval and infantry operations and, using constraint rather than punishment, he brought calm to a difficult situation in Gaul and to dissensions that had flared up among the inhabitants of Vienne.[375] After this, the senate and people of Rome brought it about

372. Velleius is the only source to provide the story about the head of Varus. According to Florus (2.30.38), Varus was buried by the soldiers and exhumed by the Germans.

373. Tiberius was in Pannonia when the disaster occurred and probably reached Rome about the end of AD 9, since on January 11, 10, he took part in the inauguration of the temple of Concordia in the city. Suetonius (*Tib.* 18.1) reports that Tiberius then *returned* to Germany, probably in reference to the fact that Tiberius had fought numerous previous campaigns there in the past. Some, however, see a more immediate context and suggest that Tiberius must have visited Germany immediately before reaching Rome in 9, and could thus be said to "return" there early in the following year. This latter theory seems contradicted by Velleius' words that Tiberius "came rushing back" to Augustus.

374. There is hyperbole on the part of Velleius, but Tiberius did seem to adopt tactics that were highly appropriate for the situation with a measured and thorough campaign of conquest in depth, without aiming for rapid conquest and being very careful not to put troops at risk.

375. Velleius seems to have telescoped together two years of the campaign. In AD 11 Tiberius was joined by Germanicus; the two seem to have proceeded with the same careful thoroughness that characterized the conduct in 10. Dio (56.25.2) states that in 11 they won no battles and conquered no tribes, remaining in Germany into the autumn but not advancing far beyond the Rhine. The problem in Vienne, the capital of the Allobroges, mentioned in no other source, probably belongs to 12.

by decree, in response to a request from his father, that Tiberius should enjoy equal authority to Augustus himself in all the provinces and armies. It was certainly absurd that these provinces, owing their protection to him as they did, should not be under his authority, [2] and that the man who was the first to bring them assistance not be judged equally entitled to the honor.[376]

Returning to Rome, Tiberius celebrated a triumph over the Pannonians and Dalmatians that was long overdue but had been deferred by the unbroken succession of wars.[377] [3] Who could be surprised at the magnificence of a triumph celebrated by a Caesar? On the other hand, who could not be surprised at Fortune's indulgence? For it was not a matter of word of mouth telling us of all the most eminent enemy leaders having been killed in battle—Tiberius' triumph had them on display in chains! It fell to me and to my brother to accompany him during this, along with outstanding men and men honored with outstanding gifts.

122. Who could not also admire this as one of Tiberius Caesar's conspicuous and brilliant instances of outstanding moderation, the fact that, although he beyond a shadow of a doubt earned seven triumphs, he was satisfied with three? For who can doubt that, after receiving the submission of Armenia, after setting over it a king on whose head he had with his own hand placed the royal diadem, and after settling matters in the east, he ought to have celebrated an ovation, and that after his conquest of the Vindelici and Raeti he should have entered the city in a triumphal chariot? [2] Or that, after his adoption, when he broke the strength of Germany in an ongoing three-year campaign, the same honor ought to have been conferred on him, and that he should have accepted it? And that, after the disaster that was incurred under Varus' command, a third triumph should have been arranged for the great commander for his having once more sacked Germany in a campaign that proved supremely successful? But in the case of this man, you would not know what to admire more, the fact that he invariably recognized no limits when facing hardships and danger, or that he observed limits when it came to accepting honors.

---

376. Tiberius was granted *imperium proconsulare*, which, linked to his *tribunicia potestas* already conferred, made him Augustus' theoretical equal and clearly marked him as his successor. He possibly received *imperium proconsulare* in AD 4, but its authority might have been limited to Germany on the earlier occasion.

377. Tiberius returned to Rome and held his triumph, postponed because of Varus' disaster, on October 23, almost certainly in AD 12. It was celebrated on a magnificent scale, and it is apparent from Suetonius' description of the triumph (*Tib.* 20) that one of the "eminent enemy leaders" on display was Bato the Dalmatian.

[Augustus dies and is succeeded by a reluctant Tiberius (AD 14). Mutinies in the legions quelled by Germanicus and Drusus, son of Tiberius.]

123. We come now to the time when there was the greatest fear of all. Augustus Caesar had sent his grandson Germanicus to Germany on mopping-up operations, and he was on the verge of sending his son Tiberius to Illyricum to consolidate with a peace treaty the conquests he had made in war.[378] Augustus proceeded into Campania, accompanying Tiberius, and also with the intention of attending an athletic tournament staged in his honor by the people of Naples. Although he had already felt the symptoms of illness coming on and his health starting to decline, his strong will struggled against his condition, and he continued escorting his son until he separated from him at Beneventum and he himself headed for Nola. His health continued to decline day by day and, wishing as he did that all should remain secure after his time, he was aware who must be sent for and he hurriedly recalled his son; and Tiberius came rushing back to his father, arriving earlier than expected. [2] Augustus then announced that his worries were gone and, enfolded in the arms of his own dear Tiberius, he entrusted to him all that he himself and Tiberius had achieved, and said he did not decline death if the Fates were calling for him. Though he rallied a little on first seeing and talking with the soul that was dearest to him, the Fates soon began to overpower all the care he was being given. Then, being dissolved into his original elements, he returned to heaven his heavenly spirit, in the consulship of Pompeius and Apuleius, at the age of seventy-five.[379]

124. Men's nervousness at the time, the alarm in the senate, the anxiety of the people, the apprehension in Rome, the fine line that we saw drawn between

---

378. In AD 12 Germanicus was awarded his first consulship (Dio 56.26.1) and in 13 was appointed governor of the Three Gauls with authority over the armies on the Rhine (Suet. *Cal.* 1.1, 8.3). He is described as Augustus' grandson because he had in AD 4 been adopted by Tiberius, who had already been adopted by Augustus (see note 336).

379. In August of AD 14 Augustus and Livia set out for Campania. They were accompanied part of the way by Tiberius, who was leaving Rome for service in Illyricum. Early in the journey Augustus fell ill, though he was strong enough to watch a gymnastic show in his honor. At Beneventum the party broke up, and because his health was worsening Augustus stopped at his old family estate in Nola and Livia sent an urgent dispatch to Tiberius, recalling him to Augustus' side. There is disagreement about what happened next. Suetonius claims that Augustus and Tiberius spent a whole day in serious discussions and categorically states that Tiberius reached Augustus before he died, but that the emperor's last moments were spent with Livia. Dio claims that Tiberius was in Dalmatia when Augustus died, and that Livia kept the information secret until he could get back. Tacitus says it was uncertain whether Augustus was dead or alive when Tiberius reached him (Suet. *Aug.* 98.5–99.1, *Tib.* 21.1; Tac. *Ann.* 1.5.3–4, 13.2; Dio 56.30–31.1).

safety and disaster—I have not the time in my fast-paced work to describe all this, nor could a person do so who has the time! I am satisfied with saying this one thing, reflecting the general opinion: we had feared the destruction of the world but did not even feel it shaken, and so great was the majesty of one man that there was no need of arms either to protect good men or to fight the bad. [2] The state, however, did see something that might be called a struggle, with the senate and people of Rome pitted against Tiberius Caesar, the former's goal being to have him succeed to his father's post, and the latter's that he be allowed the role of private citizen on a par with others rather than that of emperor over them. Finally he was won over, more by reason than by the honor of the position; for he could see that anything he did not undertake to protect would be lost. He turned out to be unique: a man who spent almost more time refusing the principate than others had spent fighting to gain it.[380]

[3] After his father was restored to heaven, and after his body had been granted human, and his soul divine, honors, the first of Tiberius' imperial acts was the reorganization of the voting assemblies on the pattern that the deified Augustus had left behind in his own handwriting.[381] At that time it fell to me and to my brother, who were Caesar's candidates, to be designated for the praetorship next after men of the highest families and holders of priesthoods. What this meant was that there was no candidate recommended by the divine Augustus after us, and none recommended by Tiberius Caesar before us.

125. The state soon felt the benefit of what it had hoped for and decided on, and we were not long kept in the dark as to what we would have suffered had our wish not been fulfilled, or what we had gained by its being fulfilled. The army that was on campaign in Germany under the command of Germanicus, who was present there, and along with it the legions

---

380. Using the *tribunicia potestas,* Tiberius was able to handle the pressing state problems; the consuls swore an oath of loyalty to him and administered the same oath to others. Tiberius gave commands to the praetorian guard and sent letters to the army commanders.

381. The senate met early in September of AD 14, when the only serious business was the funeral of Augustus. At a meeting on September 17, Augustus was accorded divine honors and the senate requested that Tiberius accept, or continue, the principate (it is not clear which); Tiberius expressed considerable reluctance, arguing that the burden was too great for a single person. The true significance of this maneuvering is unclear, but in the end Tiberius relented.

One of the first acts of Tiberius' principate was the transfer of the elections of magistrates from the people to the senate, in accordance with the instructions of Augustus. The precise details of the measure have been much debated. The senate asked that the number of praetors be increased, but Tiberius retained the old limit of twelve and bound himself not to exceed it (Tac. *Ann.* 1.14.4). He personally commended only four of the candidates for these twelve places, including Velleius and his brother.

in Illyricum, fell prey to some kind of madness and a profound desire to create general mayhem.[382] They wanted a new commander, a new political system, a new state. [2] They even had the effrontery to threaten to lay down the law to the senate, and to the emperor as well, and they tried to establish their own level of pay and length of service. They went as far as taking up arms, the sword was drawn, and their unchecked behavior all but exploded into an orgy of violence. What was missing was someone to lead the men against the state, not men to follow him. [3] But all this the mature approach of a seasoned commander in a short time calmed and brought to an end.[383] He checked many of their actions, made some promises where his dignity permitted it, and, while his punishments were severe for the most serious offenders, others received only mild reprimands.

[4] Drusus had been dispatched by his father straight into the conflagration of this military revolt, now ablaze with many fires, and, while Germanicus was forgiving in most cases at this time, he instead applied the old, traditional severity, <preferring to face> a situation dangerous for himself rather than <set> a ruinous precedent, and with the very swords of the soldiers by whom he had been besieged he suppressed his besiegers.[384] [5] He had remarkable assistance in this business from Junius Blaesus, in whose case one could not tell whether his usefulness in the military sphere exceeded his

---

382. Germanicus returned to the north at the end of AD 12, as governor of the Three Gauls, which would have given him overall authority over the eight legions posted on the Rhine. The death of Augustus had an unsettling effect among both the German and Pannonian legions. In both areas, harsh terms of service and unmet commitments had caused major problems in morale. Velleius tactfully alludes to differences in the handling of the problems. Drusus the Younger was sent to deal with the serious riots in Pannonia, accompanied by, among others, the newly appointed prefect of the praetorians, Sejanus. Through a judicious combination of conciliation and discipline, and aided by a nicely timed lunar eclipse and a similarly propitious heavy rainstorm, he was able to suppress the mutiny before it had taken proper hold. On the Rhine the problems were concentrated in Lower Germany. Germanicus vacillated and even resorted to bribes, producing a forged letter of Tiberius that offered concessions and using official money to pay for them. At one point he histrionically threatened to commit suicide and was met by jocular encouragement to go through with it (Tac. *Ann.* 1.35.4–5). As a final insult he had to endure the indignity of his family being taken hostage.

383. The reference is ambiguous; it could be to Germanicus and Drusus, each in his own sphere, but Drusus could hardly be called a "seasoned" campaigner at this point, and it is easier to see a reference to Tiberius as the overall commander.

384. Drusus the Younger, son of Tiberius and Vipsania, was born about 13 BC. He enjoyed close and friendly relations with Germanicus and married his sister Livilla. She bore him twin sons in AD 19, one of whom died in 23. The other, Tiberius Gemellus, was executed by Caligula in 37. On Germanicus' death Drusus was the clear prospect to succeed Tiberius and received *tribunicia potestas* after his consulship in 21. He died in 23, allegedly poisoned by his wife, who at the time was the mistress of Sejanus.

efficiency in civilian life.[385] Blaesus was a few years later proconsul in Africa where he earned triumphal ornaments along with the title of imperator.

As for the Spanish provinces and the army <. . .> with his good qualities and famous campaign in Illyricum we spoke about earlier.[386] When he had command there, he kept them in complete peace and tranquility since he had, to a large degree, the ability to see the right course and the authority to follow it. Dolabella, too, a man possessed of a noble candor, emulated his painstaking and loyal behavior in all that he did on the coast of Illyricum.[387]

[The reign of Tiberius praised.]

126. Who could give a detailed account of the achievements of the past sixteen years when they remain as a whole before everybody's eyes and in everybody's minds?[388] Caesar saw to his father's deification, not out of state duty but from personal scruple; he did not just call him a god, he made him one.[389] [2] Credit has been restored to the Forum; and sedition has been removed from the Forum, political corruption from the Campus, discord from the senate house.[390] Justice, equity, and industry, which had long lain

---

385. Quintus Junius Blaesus, uncle of Sejanus, was consul in AD 10. He was legate in Pannonia in command of Legions 3–5 when they mutinied. He responded with vigorous discipline, but the situation required the presence of Drusus for order to be restored. Blaesus was the choice of Tiberius to conduct the war against Tacfarinas in Africa in 21. In 22 he won the triumphal ornaments for his victories and became the last private individual to receive the acclamation of imperator. He seems to have disappeared in the debacle following Sejanus' downfall (in 31).

386. The abrupt reference to Spain is surprising, since the rest of the chapter is concerned with Germany and Illyricum, and most editors accept that there is a serious problem in the text, which had probably contained a reference to the governor Marcus Lepidus. It need not imply a major gap in the mss. Velleius may have awkwardly introduced Spain to make some laudatory comments on its commander. Lepidus' service in Illyricum was praised earlier (2.114.5), but this would be the only reference to his having held command in Spain, which was home to three legions.

387. Publius Cornelius Dolabella, consul in AD 10 and later governor of Africa, was currently in command in Dalmatia. Velleius' high opinion of him is not shared by Tacitus, who deems him guilty of unabashed sycophancy (*Ann.* 3.47).

388. At this point Velleius abandons the annalistic scheme and deals generally with Tiberius' reign. Tiberius' achievements in restoring time-honored virtues are couched in traditional elements of the panegyric, though it seems that, despite the hyperbolic tone, the account of his achievements is sound. Velleius intended to publish his history in AD 30 and counts back over the sixteen years to the year of Tiberius' accession, 14.

389. During the funeral of Augustus one of the mourners claimed to have witnessed him ascending to heaven, and when the senate met later in the year he was deified. A college of twenty priests was established, including Tiberius, his son Drusus, Germanicus, and Claudius. Livia was appointed priestess.

390. The Forum was where the *comitia tributa* met to elect the lesser magistrates. The *comitia centuriata* met in the Campus Martius to elect consuls and praetors. The senate normally met in the Curia. In AD 14 Tiberius put in place Augustus' plan to transfer the elections from the

buried and covered with decay, have been given back to the state. The magistrates have been invested with authority, the senate with majesty, the courts with dignity. Disorderliness in the theater has been quelled.[391] All people have been infused with the will to behave correctly, or have been obliged to do so. [3] Right is honored, wrong is punished. The lowly man looks up to but does not fear the powerful man; the powerful man has precedence over but does not despise the lowlier man.

When was grain more reasonably priced? When was there a more prosperous peace? The *pax Augusta* has spread throughout the lands of the east and the west, and to the regions bounded by the north and the south, keeping men safe from the fear of armed robbery in all corners of the world. [4] The generosity of our princeps provides restitution for accidental losses suffered not only by citizens but by cities.[392] The cities of Asia have been repaired, and the provinces have been freed from the malfeasance of magistrates; rank is readily available for the deserving, and for the evildoers there is punishment, late perhaps, but inevitable. Influence gives place to fairness, corruption to merit; [5] for our excellent princeps teaches his citizens to act correctly by doing so himself, and while he is the greatest in terms of power, he is greater still in the example he sets.[393]

[The contribution made by Sejanus. It is noted that Rome has always called on the services of the very best, whatever their initial status.

127. Eminent men rarely fail to enlist the services of great assistants in the management of their fortunes.[394] Thus, the two Scipios made use of the two Laelii, whom they placed on the same level as themselves in everything; and

people to the senate and thus eliminated the unrest that attended them (2.124.3). Caligula temporarily restored the right to the people.

391. Theatrical disturbances had been a mark of Augustus' regime, and Tiberius sought to quell them (Dio 57.14.9; Tac. *Ann.* 1.77.4; Suet. *Tib.* 37.2).

392. The most striking example of Tiberius' generosity occurred in AD 17 when an earthquake, described by Pliny (*NH* 2.200) as the worst in history, destroyed a number of cities in Asia. The tribute of all the cities was remitted for five years and Sardis received a special award of a million sesterces (Tac. *Ann.* 2.47; Suet. *Tib.* 48.2; Dio 57.17.7; Strabo *Geog.* 13.4.8; Sen. *NQ* 6.1.13). Cibyra in Asia and Aegium in Attica were damaged by earthquakes in 23 and had their tribute remitted for three years (Tac. *Ann.* 4.13.1). The damage to Ephesus was recorded in an inscription of AD 30 (*Inscriptiones Latinae Selectae* 156) and was perhaps mentioned in the missing section of Tacitus, *Ann.* 5.

393. Tiberius is the first to be referred to as "excellent princeps" or *princeps optimus* (Val. Max. 2.*praef*; *Corpus Inscriptionum Latinarum* 6.902, 6.904). The phrase is perhaps reminiscent of the titulature of Jupiter as "Optimus Maximus." Suetonius says that one of the titles acquired by Caligula was *optimus maximus Caesar* (*Cal.* 22.1).

394. At this point Velleius introduces, and heaps praise on, Lucius Aelius Seianus (Sejanus), generally considered to be one of the most sinister characters of the early imperial period.

the deified Augustus made use of Marcus Agrippa, and of Statilius Taurus right after him.[395] In these men's cases "newness of family" did not obstruct their elevation to multiple consulships, to triumphs, and to numerous priesthoods.[396] [2] For great affairs stand in need of great assistants, and it is important to the state that what is necessary for its functioning should have high political rank, with its utility bolstered by authority. [3] Following these examples, Tiberius Caesar has had, and still has, Aelius Sejanus as a peerless assistant in all his onerous imperial tasks.[397] Sejanus was born to a father who was a leading member of the equestrian order, but he is also on his mother's side connected to very illustrious and venerable families that enjoy distinction for their public offices. He has, moreover, brothers, cousins, and an uncle who are former consuls. Sejanus himself has a great capacity for work and loyal service, and his physique matches his mental vigor. He is a man who combines old-time gravity with cheery lightheartedness, and one who, when he is in action, seems to be at ease. He claims nothing for himself and so attains everything; and his assessment of himself is always lower than other people's estimate of him. In appearance and lifestyle he is relaxed, but his mind never sleeps.

128. In appraising this man's virtues there has long been competition between the judgment of the citizen body and that of the princeps; and the tendency of the senate and people of Rome to think that the greatest nobility lies in what is best is nothing new.[398] For those men of old who lived before the First

---

395. The career and quasi-constitutional position of Sejanus, an equestrian, was remarkable, and Velleius first goes out of his way to emphasize that in the past great men had called upon the assistance of individuals with no distinguished lineage. Gaius Laelius Maior (c. 235–c. 183 BC) was praetor in 196 and attained the consulship in 190. He served in Spain 209–206, then in Africa under Publius Cornelius Scipio Africanus, in 205–202. He conducted negotiations with Masinissa and commanded the cavalry at Zama. Valerius Maximus (4.7.7) similarly compares their friendship with that between Augustus and Agrippa. Gaius Laelius (c. 190–c. 115 BC) was the son of the above and consul in 140. He was the friend of Publius Cornelius Scipio Aemilianus and his lieutenant in Africa when Carthage fell in 146, and later at Numantia. He was an orator of some distinction (see 1.17.3, 2.9.1). Velleius also included two contemporaries, Agrippa (2.59.5) and Statilius Taurus (2.85.2), both close confidants of Augustus.

396. The word that Velleius uses here, *novitas* (newness), is clearly meant to echo the expression *novus homo* (new man).

397. Sejanus came from an equestrian family of Volsinii in Etruria. His mother was the sister of Quintus Junius Blaesus (see 2.125.5). His father Lucius Seius Strabo was appointed one of the prefects of the praetorian guard by Augustus and in that capacity swore an oath of allegiance to Tiberius on his accession (Tac. *Ann.* 1.7.2).

398. Velleius continues the train of thought introduced in 2.127 and extols the merits of the new man (*novus homo*), the man who, despite having no consuls in his family background, succeeds in holding that office, and Velleius enumerates those who have demonstrated noble qualities through their virtues, rather than through their lineage.

Punic War (three hundred years ago) raised Tiberius Coruncanius, a "new man," to the topmost position in the state, according him all the offices, including even that of *pontifex maximus*.[399] [2] They elevated to consulships, censorships, and triumphs Spurius Carvilius, who was of equestrian background, and soon after him Marcus Cato, who was not only "new" but also came from Tusculum and was a newcomer to Rome, and after these Mummius Achaicus, too.[400] [3] There were men who regarded Gaius Marius, who was of obscure origin, as being unquestionably the leading citizen of the Roman nation, right down to his sixth consulship, and men who had so much respect for Marcus Tullius that he could virtually procure the top offices for anyone he liked by his recommendation alone. And then there were those who refused Asinius Pollio nothing that even those from the most noble families had to struggle to obtain, with much sweat of the brow. These people certainly had this same feeling, that the greatest honor should go to whosoever possessed outstanding personal qualities. [4] It was the perfectly natural adherence to these precedents that impelled Caesar to put Sejanus to the test, and Sejanus to lighten the burdens of the princeps; and it also led the senate and people of Rome to the point of willingly calling upon what they understood to be their best practical asset to take charge of their security.

[Specific accomplishments of Tiberius. Prayer to the gods to protect him and his achievements.]

129. But now that I have more or less given a general picture of Tiberius Caesar's principate, let us review a number of specific items. What foresight he displayed in summoning to Rome Rhascupolis, murderer of his own brother's son Cotys, who shared his throne! (In this matter Tiberius availed himself of the outstanding services of the ex-consul Pomponius Flaccus, a man with a natural aptitude for all things needing to be done correctly, and one possessed of straightforward integrity who invariably deserved glory rather than sought it.)[401] [2] With what seriousness does he listen attentively to

---

399. Tiberius Coruncanius was consul in 280 BC, in fact 310 years before, when Pyrrhus reached Tarentum; he had the task of preventing the Samnites from rallying to Pyrrhus' side. He was the first plebeian to be *pontifex maximus*, in 254. He was dictator (for the purpose of elections) in 246 and died in 243.

400. Spurius Carvilius was the first consul to be identified in the sources as a new man (*novus homo*). He was consul in 293 BC when he suppressed the Samnites and again in 272 when he reduced Tarentum. Other examples cited have already appeared in Velleius' narrative: Marcus Porcius Cato the Elder (2.35), Lucius Mummius Achaicus, conqueror of Corinth (1.12), Marius (2.11.1), Marcus Tullius Cicero (2.34.3), and Asinius Pollio (2.63.3).

401. On the death of the king of Thrace, Rhoemetalces (see 2.112.4), in AD 12, Augustus had split the kingdom between Rhoemetalces' son Cotys and his brother Rhascupolis (also

legal cases, as a senator and judge, not as princeps and <Caesar>! How swiftly did he crush the ingrate <. . .> and stirring up sedition.[402] With what precepts did he furnish his dear Germanicus, and how well he instructed him in the rudiments of war when he was on campaign with him—with the result that he later welcomed him back as the conqueror of Germany! Such honors he piled on him, despite his young years, making the splendor of his triumph match the magnificence of his achievements![403] [3] How often has he honored the people with gifts and, when he could do so with the senate's approval, how willingly has he supplemented the census ratings of senators without encouraging extravagance but also without permitting an honorable poverty to be stripped of dignity![404] With what great honors did he send his dear Germanicus into the overseas provinces![405] What forceful diplomacy was his when Maroboduus (and may I say this without offense to the emperor's majesty) was sticking to the boundaries of the kingdom he had usurped just like a snake hidden in the earth and he <. . .>, employing his son Drusus as his intermediary and assistant, forced him out by the curative properties of his planning![406] How respectfully, and yet how securely, he keeps the man detained!

---

spelled Rhescuporis). Following Augustus' death the latter invaded Cotys' kingdom and on the pretense of negotiations murdered him. Rhascupolis was taken prisoner by Lucius Pomponius Flaccus (consul AD 17, governor of Moesia 18–19) and sent to Alexandria where he was executed following an escape attempt.

402. The reference to sedition is obscure. Some believe that Velleius is alluding to Marcus Drusus Libo, the great-grandson of Pompey and great-nephew of Scribonia, wife of Augustus. He was tried before the senate in September of AD 16 on a charge of planning to assassinate Tiberius, his sons, and other leading citizens. He committed suicide during the course of the trial. Others argue that the corrupt text contained the name of Clemens, the slave of Agrippa Postumus who, after his master's death, impersonated him and gained a following (Tac. *Ann.* 2.39). Others see a reference to Archelaus, the last king of Cappadocia, tried in 17 for plotting rebellion.

403. Germanicus was appointed to his position in Gaul and Germany in AD 13. His triumph was decreed in 15 but not celebrated until May 26, 17. Tacitus describes its splendid scale (*Ann.* 2.41.2–3).

404. The sources mention Tiberius' gifts (donatives). In AD 17 he distributed 300 sesterces each to the people in the name of Germanicus (Tac. *Ann.* 2.42.1); in 20 he distributed a largesse, when he presented Germanicus' sons Nero and Drusus to the senate (Suet. *Tib.* 54.1; Tac. *Ann.* 3.29.1); in 33 he made a public interest-free loan for three years (Suet. *Tib.* 48.1); also, he indemnified the victims of a fire on Mount Caelius (see 2.130). As a result of Augustus' reforms, membership in the senate had required a property qualification of one million sesterces.

405. Tiberius bestowed on Germanicus command over the provinces of the east (Tac. *Ann.* 2.43.1).

406. Tiberius was engaged against Maroboduus in AD 7–9 (see 2.108–10). Maroboduus at first refused to join Arminius in rebellion after Varus' debacle but was defeated by Arminius in 17; not receiving the aid he sought from Rome, he rebelled and was eventually forced to surrender to Drusus. He was placed under house arrest in Ravenna, where he died eighteen years later.

What a mighty war it was that the Gallic chieftain Sacrovir and Julius Florus were stirring up!⁴⁰⁷ And yet he suppressed it with amazing speed and courage— so much so that the Roman people learned that they had prevailed before they knew that they were at war, and news of the victory arrived before news of their danger. [4] There was also the African War, which generated great fear and was escalating every day but was soon snuffed out under his auspices and through his planning.⁴⁰⁸

130. What great buildings he has erected in his own name, and in the name of his family!⁴⁰⁹ With what dutiful generosity, a generosity beyond human belief, is he now constructing a temple to his father! With what magnificent forbearance has he also restored Gnaeus Pompey's public buildings after they were destroyed by fire! (For a distinguished landmark should, in his opinion, be protected as if he had a family connection with it.) [2] What munificence he has shown in general, and especially recently after the fire on the Caelian Hill when he used his personal funds to make good the losses of men of all classes.⁴¹⁰ What calm prevails among the people when he sees to raising reinforcements (something that generates ongoing and extreme dread), without the fears usually attending a troop levy!

[3] If nature permits, or man's humble status allows it, then I take the liberty of making a complaint to the gods. What did this man do to deserve, first, having Drusus Libo embark upon his nefarious plans? And then to have Silius and Piso <so hostile to him after> he gave one his political status and raised the other's.⁴¹¹ To pass on to more serious matters (though Tiberius

407. Julius Florus, ruler of the Treveri, and Julius Sacrovir, ruler of the Aedui, rebelled in AD 21 to protest their heavy indebtedness.

408. Quintus Junius Blaesus (2.125.5) was granted a triumph during the war against Tacfarinas in Africa; Tacfarinas' rebellion broke out in AD 17 and was not finally concluded until he died in battle; his forces were crushed by Publius Cornelius Dolabella, proconsul in 23–24.

409. Tacitus and Suetonius (Tac. *Ann.* 6.45.1; Suet. *Tib.* 47.1) say that Tiberius built only two major structures in Rome: the *scaena* (stage) of the theater of Pompey that was destroyed in the fire of AD 22 and the temple of Augustus. The latter was dedicated by Caligula, and Suetonius (*Cal.* 21) claims that Caligula finished the work on the theater.

410. He indemnified the victims of the fires on the Caelian and Aventine hills in AD 27 and 36 (Tac. *Ann.* 4.64, 6.45.1; Suet. *Tib.* 48.1).

411. Gaius Silius Aulus Caecina Largus was consul in AD 13 and commander of Upper Germany in 14–21. He suppressed the rebellion of Sacrovir and Florus. He was charged in 24 with being in league with Sacrovir and having made himself wealthy. His wife Sosia Gallia was also charged. He committed suicide; she was exiled. They were in fact close friends of Germanicus and his widow Agrippina the Elder, and the charges may have been political, engineered by Sejanus as part of his campaign against Agrippina.

Gnaeus Calpurnius Piso (consul 7 BC) was appointed legate of Syria in AD 17, to offer guidance and some degree of supervision to Germanicus on his eastern mission (2.129.3 and

thought the foregoing, too, were very serious), what did he do to deserve to lose his sons at a tender age? Or his grandson from his dear Drusus?[412] [4] So far we have spoken of grievous events, but now we must come to those that are shameful. With what great sorrows, Marcus Vinicius, have the past three years tortured his soul! How his heart has burned with a flame long kept secret—the most miserable thing of all—over the pain, the indignity, and the shame that he has been forced to endure because of his daughter-in-law, and because of his grandson.[413] [5] The distress of these years has been increased by the loss of his mother, the most eminent of women, who in everything resembled the gods rather than humankind, a woman whose power none felt unless it was through seeing their danger diminished or their status raised.[414]

131. I must end the volume with a prayer. Capitoline Jupiter, and you, Mars Gradivus, originator and upholder of the Roman nation, and you, Vesta, guardian of the eternal fire, and whatever other divinities have raised up this great body that is the Roman empire to the highest point in the whole world: on you I call, and to you I pray in the name of our people. Guard, preserve, and protect these present circumstances, this peace, this emperor. And when he has served the longest possible term in his mortal post, mark out, as late as can be, successors for him, but only men whose shoulders are strong enough to bear the weight of this worldwide empire as bravely as we have witnessed his shoulders bearing it, and the plans of all the citizens, or pious <. . .>

Tac. *Ann.* 2.43.4). The two men could not collaborate, and Piso was in the process of leaving his province when he learned of Germanicus' death in 19. After his return to Rome he and his wife Plancina were charged in 20 for their conduct in the province. He committed suicide; she escaped by virtue of her friendship with Livia.

412. Tiberius' sons Germanicus and Drusus died on October 10, AD 19, and September 14, 23, respectively. Twins were born to Drusus in 19. Velleius here refers to the one who died in the same year as Drusus.

413. Agrippina, wife of Germanicus, hence Tiberius' daughter-in-law, supposedly plotted against the emperor and was banished in AD 29 or 30 to the island of Pandateria, where she died in 33 on a hunger strike. Her eldest son Nero was exiled to the island of Pontia. He died in 31. According to Tacitus they were both the victims of Sejanus' machinations (*Ann.* 4.13, 59).

414. Livia died in AD 29 at the age of eighty-six. Despite Velleius' claims, relations between mother and son had not been harmonious for a number of years, and Tiberius did not attend her modest funeral. He resisted calls in the senate for her deification, to which Velleius may be making a veiled reference here.

Appendix A

A FRAGMENT OF GREEK HISTORY AND LEGEND

[This fragment, preserved in the primary edition of Velleius' history, belongs to a very early part of the original text. The very first chapters, presumably on the Trojan War, are missing, and the fragment begins in mid-sentence with an account of the Greek heroes who returned from the war.]

1. <Epeus> founded Metapontum after being separated from his commander Nestor in a storm. Teucer, because of his inaction in avenging the injustice done to his brother, was not allowed home by his father Telamon, and so he landed on Cyprus and there founded Salamis, which was the name of his native land. Achilles' son Pyrrhus settled in Epirus, and Phidippus in Ephyra in Thesprotia. [2] The king of kings, Agamemnon, was driven ashore by a storm on the island of Crete where he founded three cities, Mycenae and Tegea named from his country, and Pergamum to commemorate his conquest.

Soon afterward Agamemnon was overpowered and murdered by the criminal act of his cousin Aegisthus (who was venting an ancestral hatred on him) and the heinous misdeeds of his wife. [3] Aegisthus held the throne for seven years. Orestes then killed him along with his own mother, acting in concert with his sister Electra, a woman with a man's courage, who was his ally in all his plans. The gods' approval for his action became clear from the length of Orestes' life and the good fortune attending his reign—he lived for ninety years and ruled for seventy. He also bravely avenged himself on Achilles' son Pyrrhus. Pyrrhus had preempted him in marrying Hermione, daughter of Menelaus and Helen, although she had been promised to Orestes, and Orestes therefore killed him at Delphi.

[4] In those days the brothers Lydus and Tyrrhenus were kings in Lydia, and they were obliged by a crop failure to draw lots to decide which of them was to leave the country with a section of the population. The lot fell to Tyrrhenus, and he sailed to Italy where he conferred upon the region, its inhabitants, and the sea his own noble name that was to last forever.

After Orestes' death his sons Penthilus and Tisamenus reigned for three years.

2. The descendants of Pelops had ruled in the Peloponnese ever since their expulsion of the Heraclidae, but at this time, some eighty years after the capture of Troy and in the 120th year after Hercules had left to join the gods, they were themselves expelled by the descendants of Hercules. The leaders in this recovery of power were Temenus, Cresphontes, and Aristodemus, to all of whom Hercules was great-great-grandfather.

At about the same time Athens ceased to be a monarchy. Its last king was Codrus son of Melanthus, a man whose history cannot be passed over. For when the Lacedaemonians were defeating the Athenians in a fierce war, and Pythian Apollo had prophesied that those whose commander would be killed by the enemy would prevail, Codrus set aside his royal garments, put on shepherd's clothing, and came into the enemy camp where he deliberately provoked a brawl with someone unaware of his identity and was killed by him. [2] With his death, undying glory came to Codrus, and victory to Athens. Who could not admire a man who sought death by the very tricks that cowards use to stay alive? Codrus' son Medon was the first archon in Athens. Those who succeeded him among the Athenians were called Medontidae after him, but Medon and the archons succeeding him, right down to Charops, held that office for life. During their withdrawal from Attic territory the Peloponnesians founded Megara, a city midway between Corinth and Athens.

[3] In that period, too, the Tyrian fleet, the most powerful on the seas, founded Gades in the farthest reaches of Spain and at the very edge of our world. It was built on an island surrounded by the Ocean and cut off from the mainland by a narrow strait. A few years later Utica in Africa was also founded by the Tyrians.

The children of Orestes were driven out by the Heraclidae and were buffeted both by various misfortunes and by fierce seas until, fourteen years later, they made a home in the area of the island of Lesbos.

3. Greece was at that time shaken by major upheavals. The Achaeans, driven from Laconia, established themselves in what are their present homelands. The Pelasgians migrated to Athens, and a young Thesprotian called Thessalus, a fierce warrior, took a large contingent of his countrymen and by force of arms seized the region that today is named Thessaly after him (formerly it was known as the city-state of the Myrmidons). [2] It is appropriate, therefore, to express surprise that those writers whose subject is the Trojan period should refer to that region as Thessaly. It is the tragedians who do this most frequently (though others do as well) and they are the last people who should be granted such latitude; they should say nothing in their own person as poets—everything should be said through their characters, people who lived at the time. And if anyone is going to claim that the

Thessalians were named after Thessalus son of Hercules, then he will have to give a reason for that race never adopting the name before the time of the second Thessalus.

[3] Shortly before this, Aletes, son of Hippotes and a sixth-generation descendant of Hercules, founded Corinth, which had formerly been Ephyre; situated on the Isthmus, it formed a barrier to the Peloponnese. Nor need we be surprised that Corinth is so named by Homer; for he is speaking in his own person as a poet, and he calls both this city and certain colonies of the Ionians, founded long after Troy was captured, by the actual names that they bore in his day.

4. The Athenians established colonies at Chalcis and Eretria in Euboea, and the Lacedaemonians established one at Magnesia in Asia. Not much later the people of Chalcis, who (as I just noted) were descended from the Athenians, founded Cumae in Italy with an expedition led by Hippocles and Megasthenes. Some claim that the course of this fleet was guided by a dove that flew ahead of it, others that it was by cymbals beating at night, like the noise typically produced at the festivals of Ceres. [2] Long afterward some of the citizens of Cumae founded Neapolis. The unswerving loyalty that both cities always showed to the Romans makes them well deserving of their high reputation and their delightful settings. However, the Neapolitans maintained the culture of their forefathers more carefully, whereas having the Oscans as neighbors brought changes to the Cumaeans. The size of their city walls today bears witness to the former power of these cities.

[3] Subsequently, overpopulation prompted large numbers of young Greeks to stream into Asia looking for homes. The Ionians, for example, led by Ion, set out from Athens and settled the most famous section of the seaboard, which is today called Ionia, and there they established the cities of Ephesus, Miletus, Colophon, Priene, Lebedus, Myus, Erythra, Clazomenae, and Phocaea. They also settled on many islands in the Aegean and Icarian seas: Samos, Chios, Andros, Tenos, Paros, and Delos, and others that are also not without fame. [4] Subsequently, the Aeolians also set out from Greece and, after being driven off course into long detours, settled in places that were no less famous, founding the prominent cities of Smyrna, Cyme, Larissa, Myrina, Mytilene, and others that lie on the island of Lesbos.

5. It was after this that the talent of Homer had its brilliant dawning, a truly great talent that is without parallel; he alone deserves the appellation "poet" for the greatness of his work and the brilliance of his verse. [2] In his case the most remarkable thing is that, before him, it would not be possible to find anyone for him to imitate and, after him, anyone who could imitate him. Nor will we find any other poet, apart from Homer and Archilochus, who was both the original founder of a genre and the one who brought it to perfection.

[3] Homer lived later than the Trojan War, his subject, by a much greater margin than some people think: his *floruit* is some 950 years ago, and he was born less than a thousand years ago. So one should not be surprised at his frequent use of the expression οἷοι νῦν βροτοί εἰσιν (the people who live now): by this the differences in people are attributed to the different historical eras. Anyone who thinks Homer was born without the sense of sight himself lacks all his senses!

6. In the years that followed, power over Asia was transferred from the Assyrians, whose rule had lasted 1,070 years, to the Medes; this was some 870 years ago. [2] The king of the Assyrians, Sardanapalus, who, awash in extravagant living and too prosperous for his own good, was—in direct succession from father to son—the thirty-third to come to the throne after Ninus and Semiramis, the founders of Babylon. The Mede Arbaces robbed him of his throne and his life.

[3] This was the time of the Lacedaemonian Lycurgus, an illustrious member of the Greek race. A man of royal blood, he was the author of very harsh but very equitable legislation and of a social system well suited to that people. As long as Sparta rigorously applied it she was highly successful.

[4] It was in this time period, sixty-five years before Rome's foundation, that Carthage was founded by Tyrian Elissa, whom some call Dido. [5] About this time, too, Caranus, who was of royal descent and belonged to the eleventh generation after Hercules, set off from Argos and seized the throne of Macedonia. Alexander the Great was in the seventeenth generation from Caranus and was thus justified in boasting of his descent from Achilles on his mother's side and from Hercules on his father's.

7. Hesiod was contemporaneous with this period, separated from the age of Homer by roughly 120 years. A man of refined intellect, well known for his smooth and sweet poetry, and a great lover of peace and tranquility, Hesiod stands next to that great poet both in time and in the prestige of his work. He avoided what happened in Homer's case in that he referred to his country and his parents, very disparagingly in the case of his country because of the punishment he received from it.

[2] While lingering over foreign history, I have come across an event in our domestic history about which there has been considerable misconception, and a great variation of opinion in the sources. Some people claim that it was in this time period that Capua and Nola were founded by the Etruscans, about 830 years ago. [3] In fact, I would agree with them—but how different is the view of Marcus Cato! Cato grants that Capua was indeed

founded by the Etruscans, and that shortly afterward Nola was as well, but he maintains that Capua had stood for some 260 years before it was taken by the Romans. [4] If that is so, then the fact that it is only 240 years since the capture of Capua means that its founding dates to roughly 500 years ago. Personally—and with due respect to Cato's painstaking scholarship—I would find it difficult to believe that a city of such importance could have so quickly grown, seen its heyday, fallen, and then risen once more.

8. Next, the most famous games of all, the ones most effective in promoting physical and mental excellence, were inaugurated by Iphitus of Elis. He established these games, and their commercial activities, 823 years before you entered your consulship, Marcus Vinicius. [2] It is said that it was Atreus who actually laid the foundation for this hallowed meeting in the same location about 1,250 years ago when he held funeral games for his father Pelops, and that in that particular competition Hercules emerged as victor in every category of event.

[3] At that time archons ceased to be appointed for life in Athens, the last appointed being Alcmaeon, and instead they began to be elected for ten-year terms. That practice remained in place for seventy years, after which the administration of the government was entrusted to magistrates with yearly terms. Of those holding office for ten years the first was Charops and the last Eryxias, and the first of the annual magistrates was Creon.

Appendix B

A LINE OF GREEK HISTORY

*[A single line of Velleius, which does not appear in the primary edition, is quoted by the grammarian Priscian (*Inst. 6.63*). It alludes to the fifth-century BC Athenian statesman Cimon and must belong somewhere in the gap between 1.8 and 1.9.]*

No less famous in this period was Miltiades' son Cimon

Appendix C

VARIATIONS FROM THE TEUBNER TEXT

Watt	This Edition
2.12.2 Malliumque	Maniliumque
2.24.4 superare	superandum (Ruhnken)
2.66.1 nuntiare	nuntiari
2.67.2 in dotem	indicium (emendation suggested by Watt in his apparatus criticus)
2.117.3 a se homines	esse homines

Glossary of Common Terms

aedile Magistrate between the ranks of quaestor and praetor. His duties generally related to city administration.

assemblies Groupings of the Roman people convened to carry out specific tasks. There were four main assemblies: (a) the centuriate assembly (*comitia centuriata*), organized in "centuries" according to wealth, convened to elect senior magistrates and pass legislation; (b) the curiate assembly (*comitia curiata*) based originally on the thirty *curiae* or parishes; in the early Republic it passed laws, elected consuls, and tried judicial cases; (c) the tribal assembly (*comitia tributa*), representing the thirty-five Roman "tribes," convened to elect junior magistrates and pass limited legislation; (d) the plebeian council (*concilium plebis*), convened to elect tribunes of the plebs and plebeian aediles, and to pass *plebiscita,* which were binding on the whole state.

auxiliaries Elements of the Roman army made up of noncitizens, distinguished from legionaries, who were citizens.

censor Magistrate charged with public morality, most importantly in supervising the citizen list and the rolls of the senate. He also had major financial responsibilities, including the leasing of public land, the letting of contracts for public works, and the collection of taxes.

centurion The commander of a legionary "century," consisting originally of a hundred men but by Velleius' time of eighty.

cognomen The final element of a Roman name, sometimes in the form of an honorific title.

cohort An operational unit of the Roman army, ten to a legion. The term is also used of independent units of the auxiliaries.

comitia See **assemblies**

colony Originally a settlement of Roman citizens, usually veterans. Later the status could be conferred on other towns as a mark of distinction.

consul The senior Roman magistrate. Two were elected, to serve for one year. The consul could convene the senate or an assembly and also, during the Republic, exercised military command. On the death or resignation of a consul, he would be replaced by a "suffect." In Velleius' time it became routine to have a number of suffects in any given year.

consultum ultimum More properly *consultum de re publica defendenda,* a decree of the senate that authorized the consuls to adopt extreme measures in times of public emergency.

dictator A magistrate elected during the Republic in an emergency. He would hold office for six months.

equestrian   An order originally related to service in the cavalry, later restricted to citizens with a property qualification of 400,000 sesterces. Although not eligible for the Roman senate, members of the order played an important part in the administration of the empire in Velleius' day and held certain key offices, such as the prefecture of Egypt and of the praetorian guard.

fasces   A bundle of rods binding an axe that symbolized the authority of senior magistrates to impose punishment. Fasces were carried by a lictor attending a magistrate, the rank of the magistrate indicated by the number of fasces.

flamen   Member of a specialized priesthood, with responsibility for a specific god. The chief flamines were those of Jupiter (the *flamen dialis*), Mars, and Quirinus, and flamines were also assigned to the cult of deified emperors.

imperator   During the Republic, strictly a magistrate vested with *imperium*. Also, a victorious general would be given the salutation of *Imperator* (Commander) by his troops and awarded a crown of bay leaves in the field. This preceded the award of a triumph. Under the empire "imperator" became part of the titulature of the emperor.

imperium   The power to command, vested for a fixed period of time in magistrates of a certain rank.

iugerum **(plural: *iugera*)**   A Roman unit of measurement equivalent to about two-thirds of an acre. According to Pliny *NH* 18.3, it was the area that could be ploughed by a *iugum* (yoke) of oxen in one day.

legate   A flexible term with several applications. Basically it refers to an individual delegated to a particular task. Under the Republic it was used of the officers, usually senators, who made up the staff of military commanders and provincial governors. Under the empire the term is regularly used of the officer in charge of a legion or the governor of an imperial province. Under Augustus the rank of *legatus Augusti,* which Velleius held, referred to a legionary commander; from Tiberius on it was used for a provincial governor, and a legionary commander was known as *legatus legionis*.

legion   The major operational unit of the Roman army. By the end of the fifth century BC it numbered approximately 6,000 men, all Roman citizens; the number was set at 4,800 under the reforms of Marius. At the time of Velleius' service each legion numbered approximately 5,400 men and had 120 cavalry attached to it.

lex   A law, identified by the attachment of an adjective derived from the proposer's name, such as the *lex Manilia,* proposed by Gaius Manilius (sometimes the names of more than one proposer will be preserved). A law had to be carried through one of the popular assemblies. Under the Republic and the first part of the imperial period, laws could not be validated in the senate, although they could originate in senatorial decrees, which were then forwarded to one of the assemblies.

new man (*novus homo*)   A man who succeeded in holding the office despite having no consuls in his family background. Tenure of the consulship tended to be restricted to a limited number of powerful families.

optimates   In the late Republic, a term applied to the senatorial party who saw themselves acting on behalf of "the best" (*optimi*) in opposition to the *populares*.

ovation   A lesser triumph. The victorious commander would wear myrtle rather than laurel, and enter the city on foot.

patrician   Member of an exclusive branch of the Roman aristocracy that controlled power in the early Republic. The rank could only be inherited for most of the republican period, but as the numbers fell new grants of patrician status were made by Julius Caesar and his successors.

plebeian tribune   Magistrate originally elected to protect the plebeians against the patricians. During the Republic the office was important because of the right to veto and initiate legislation, while the person of the holder was inviolate (*sacrosanctitas*). Consequently the role of the tribune in the political arena became a highly contentious issue. In the imperial period, however, its importance declined and the rank became a routine stage between the quaestorship and praetorship.

plebs   Originally the order of citizens who were not patrician. Later writers would often use the term broadly of the common people of Rome, those not in the equestrian or senatorial classes.

pontifex maximus   The most prominent and influential of the pontiffs.

pontiffs   Members of one of the four priestly colleges of Rome, with general oversight of the state cult.

populares   From the time of the Gracchi, leaders who worked through the people, especially through the tribunes, and challenged the traditional oligarchy. See also *optimates*.

praenomen   The first element in the name of a Roman man, the "given" name. There was a very limited number of such names.

praetor   The magistrate second in seniority after the consul. His main task was to preside over the courts. In the administration of his legal duties the *praetor peregrinus* (literally, the "foreign" praetor) had responsibility for lawsuits in which one of the parties was a foreigner, as distinct from the *praetor urbanus* (literally, the "urban" praetor), who dealt with cases involving citizens.

praetorian guard   The imperial guard, originally made up of nine cohorts, commanded by a prefect or pair of prefects. The term "praetorian" could also be used of the authority of an ex-praetor.

prefect   Basically, "the person placed in charge." This term could have a range of applications, both military and administrative, especially during the imperial period. The more significant military ones were (a) the commander of an auxiliary unit or of the fleet, (b) commander of the cavalry unit attached to a legion, (c) camp prefect, second in command to the legionary legate and commander of the troops in the legate's absence, (d) commander of the praetorian guard, and (e) commander of the fire service (*vigiles*). The more significant administrative prefects are the governor of Egypt and the prefect of the grain supply. All those prefectures were held by equestrians. A small number of prefectures were held by senators, the most significant being the ancient office of city prefect (*praefectus urbi*). By the late Republic the city prefect's duties were largely ritual, but his functions were revived by Augustus, and he was given responsibility for maintaining order in the city and commanding the city police (*cohortes urbanae*); he was granted summary justice in dealing with minor criminal cases and gradually assumed responsibility for more serious cases.

proconsul   See promagistrate

promagistrate   A magistrate (usually proconsul and propraetor, also proquaestor) whose authority was extended for a period of time beyond his regular magistracy. The first instance of such an extension (*prorogatio imperii*) occurred in 326. After 146, with the proliferation of provinces, promagistracies became a regular feature of Roman administration. Promagistrates exercised authority in a province normally defined by the senate. In principle the *prorogatio* was intended to be for one year, but in the late Republic extended terms became common. After Sulla a praetor holding a promagistracy did so as proconsul. By contrast, in Velleius' time, governors (*legati*) of imperial provinces, whether of consular or praetorian rank, held office as propraetors to avoid any challenge to the emperor's proconsular authority.

propraetor, proquaestor   See promagistrate

province   Originally the term referred to the sphere of competence of a magistrate, but it came to have a more geographical character, designating individual overseas territories governed by Rome. During the period of Velleius' career, provinces were of two types: (a) "imperial," in the less-settled part of the empire, housing elements of the Roman army; their governors were appointed directly by the emperor; (b) "senatorial," in the more stable areas, with rare exceptions not housing troops. Senatorial provinces were governed by proconsuls, men of the senatorial class elected by lot. The term "public" province is often now used by scholars for this latter group.

quaestor   The lowest of the major magistracies. From Sulla on, tenure of the office granted the holder membership in the senate.

senate   The senior governing body of the Roman state, made up of ex-magistrates of the rank of quaestor and above, or of other individuals deemed worthy by the censor or emperor. In the Augustan period the number was approximately six hundred, each with a census rating of a million sesterces. The term is used also for governing bodies outside of Rome. In the period covered by Velleius, resolutions of the senate (*consulta*) did not yet have the force of law but technically had to be enacted by the popular assembly.

sesterce (*sestertius*)   The highest value base metal Roman coin, made of an alloy of zinc and copper. It is used by the Romans as the basic unit to express monetary values, with the symbol HS. Monetary equivalence is a dubious concept, but it might be noted that the annual pay of a legionary "private" in the Julio-Claudian period was 900HS.

sortition   The taking of lots. Governors of senatorial provinces were normally chosen by lot, although the process was not totally random. The key provinces of Africa and Asia were assigned by a lot taken only among senior senators.

toga   The traditional public garb of respectable Roman men, made of fine white wool. Young boys wore the *toga praetexta,* distinguished by a purple border. At about the age of fourteen, they put it aside in favor of a plain white version, the *toga virilis,* in a ceremony that marked the transition to manhood. The wearing of the *toga praetexta* was resumed by those entering into the senior magistracies.

tribune (military)   Officers, six to a legion. Five were equestrians, professional soldiers serving long-term; one would be a young man from a senatorial family, for whom the office was a stage in a public career.

tribunician authority   A power that was, in many ways, the constitutional foundation of the imperial position. Emperors did not assume the actual office of plebeian tribune but were granted the tribunes' authority (*tribunicia potestas*) and their sacrosanctity and dated their accession from the time of its bestowal.

triumph   The procession led by a victorious commander through the streets of the city of Rome up to the temple of Jupiter on the Capitoline Hill. The procession was accompanied by war booty and prisoners of war. The triumph conferred enormous prestige on the celebrant. In Velleius' time legates of the emperor could not celebrate personal triumphs; their victories were recognized by the right to wear triumphal ornaments (*ornamenta triumphalia*).

triumphal ornaments (*ornamenta triumphalia*)   See **triumph**

triumvir   One of the three members of the triumvirate, the pact of Marcus Antonius, Aemilius Lepidus, and Octavian concluded in 43 BC. The term is also, misleadingly, sometimes applied to the less formal accord concluded between Caesar, Pompey, and Crassus in 60 (the "first triumvirate"). The *tresviri capitales* were quite different, being three officers appointed to supervise executions.

Index of People and Places in Velleius' Text

References are to book, chapter, and section numbers.
Where Velleius makes reference to the inhabitants of a location, they are listed under the location.
Reference to a year for a civic title is assumed to be BC unless otherwise indicated.
"Rome" and "Italy" are not indexed.

Atia: **2**.59.2, 60.1
Atilius Regulus, Marcus: **2**.38.2
Atilius Serranus, Gaius: **2**.53.4
Atreus: **1**.8.2
Attalus III: **2**.4.1, 38.5
Attius Varus: **2**.55.4
Attuarii: **2**.105.1
Augustus: *see* Julius
Aventine: **2**.6.6
Aurelius Cotta, Gaius: **2**.43.1
Aurelius Cotta, Lucius: **2**.32.3
Aurelius Cotta Maximus Messalinus,
    Marcus: **2**.112.2
Aurelius Scaurus, Marcus: **2**.9.1,
    12.2
Auximum: **1**.15.3
Avernus, Lake: **2**.79.2

Babylon: **1**.6.2
Bagienni: **1**.15.5
Bathinus, River: **2**.114.4
Bato: **2**.110.4, 114.4
Beneventum: **1**.14.7; **2**.123.1
Bestia: *see* Calpurnius
Bibulus: *see* Calpurnius
Bithynia: **2**.4.1, 39.2, 42.3
Bocchus: **2**.12.1
Boeotia: **2**.23.3
Boiohaemum: **2**.109.5
Bononia: **1**.15.2
Bovillae: **2**.47.4
Britain: **2**.46.1, 47.1
Bructeri **2**.105.1
Brundisium: **1**.14.8; **2**.24.3, 40.3,
    50.1, 59.5, 61.2, 76.3, 86.3
Brutus: *see* Junius
Buxentum: **1**.15.3
Byzantium: **2**.7.7

Caecilius Metellus, Marcus, consul
    115: **2**.8.2
Caecilius Metellus Caprarius, Gaius,
    consul 113: **2**.8.2
Caecilius Metellus Creticus, Quintus,
    consul 69: **2**.34.1,2, 38.6, 40.5,
    48.6

Caecilius Metellus Macedonicus,
    Quintus, consul 143: **1**.11,2,3,6,
    12.1; **2**.1.2, 5.2,3
Caecilius Metellus Numidicus,
    Quintus, consul 109: **2**.8.2, 9.1,
    11.1,2, 15.3,4, 39.2, 45.3
Caecilius Metellus Pius, Quintus,
    consul 80: **2**.15.3, 28.1, 29.5,
    30.2
Caecilius Metellus Pius Scipio, consul
    52: **2**.54.2
Caecilius Statius: **1**.17.1
Caecina Severus, Aulus: **2**.112.4
Caedicius, Lucius: **2**.120.2
Caelius: *see* Coelius
Caelian Hill: **2**.130.2
Caelius Rufus, Marcus: **2**.36.2, 68.1
Caepio: *see* Fannius, Servilius
Caesar: *see* Julius
Caesetius Flavus, Lucius: **2**.68.4
Calabria: **2**.25.1
Calatia: **2**.61.2
Cales: **1**.14.3
Calidius, Marcus: **2**.36.2
Calpurnia, wife of Antistius: **2**.26.3,
    88.3
Calpurnia, wife of Caesar: **2**.57.2
Calpurnius Bestia, Lucius: **2**.26.3
Calpurnius Bibulus, Marcus: **2**.44.5
Calpurnius Piso, Gnaeus, consul 7:
    2.130.3
Calpurnius Piso, Lucius, consul 15:
    2.98.1
Calpurnius Piso Frugi, Lucius, consul
    133: **2**.2.2
Calvus: *see* Licinius
Camelius: **2**.64.1
Campania: **1**.14.3; **2**.16.2, 20.3,
    25.1, 44.4, 45.2, 48.2, 75.1, 76.1,
    123.1
Canidius Crassus, Publius: **2**.85.2,6,
    87.3
Caninius Gallus, Lucius: **2**.100.2
Cannae: **1**.9.3
Canninefates: **2**.105.1
Cannutius: **2**.64.3

Julius Caesar, Agrippa (Agrippa
Postumus): **2.**104.1, 112.7
Julius Caesar, Drusus (Drusus the
Younger), son of Tiberius:
2.125.4, 129.3, 130.3
Julius Caesar, Gaius, dictator: **2.**30.3,
36.2, 39.1, 41.1, 44.2–5, 45.2,
46,1,2, 47.1–3, 48.1,4,5, 49.2–4,
50.1,4, 51.1–3, 52.1,4, 53.2,
54.1, 55.1–3, 56.1, 57.1, 58.2,3,
59.1,3, 60.1,2,4, 61.3, 63.1,
64.1,2, 68.1,4, 69.1,5, 87.3
Julius Caesar, Gaius, grandson of
Augustus: **2.**96.1, 99.2, 101.1,3,
102.2, 103.3
Julius Caesar, Lucius, consul 90:
2.15.1
Julius Caesar, Lucius, consul 64:
2.67.3
Julius Caesar, Lucius, grandson of
Augustus: **2.**96.1, 99.2, 102.3,
103.3
Julius Caesar, Nero, son of
Germanicus: **2.**130.4
Julius Caesar Augustus, Tiberius:
2.39.3, 75.1,3, 94.1, 95.1,
96.1–3, 97.2,4, 99.1, 100.1,5,
101.1, 103.1,3, 104.1,3, 105.1,3,
106.1,3, 107.1–3, 109.5, 110.1,2,
111.2, 112.3,7, 113.1, 114.1,5,
115.1,2,4, 117.1, 120.5,6,
121.1,3, 122.1, 123.1,2, 124.2,4,
126.1, 127.3, 128.4, 129.1
Julius Caesar Germanicus: **2.**116.1,
123.1, 125.1,4, 129.2,3, 130.3
Julius Caesar Octavianus Augustus,
Gaius (Gaius Octavius before
adoption): **2.**36.1, 38.3,4, 39.2,
59.1, 60.5, 61.1,2, 62.1,5,6,
65.1,2, 66.1,2, 69.5, 70.1, 71.1,
72.2, 74.1–4, 75.1,3, 76.2–4,
77.1, 78.1,2, 83.1,2, 84.1,2,
85.1,2,4,5, 86.2,3, 87.2, 88.1,2,
89.1,2,5, 90.4, 91.1–3, 92.2,
93.1,2, 94.1,4, 95.1, 96.1, 97.1,
98.2, 99.1, 100.2,4,5, 102.1,
103.2, 104.1, 110.6, 111.2,3,

123.1,2, 124.3,4, 126.1, 127.1
Julius Caesar Strabo Vopiscus, Gaius:
2.9.2
Julius Florus: **2.**129.3
Julius Scarovir: **2.**129.3
Junia: **2.**88.1
Junius Blaesus, Quintus: **2.**125.5
Junius Brutus, Marcus: **2.**36.2, 52.5,
56.3, 58.1,2, 62.2,3, 65.1, 69.3,6,
70.1,3,4, 71.1, 72.1,2,5 73.2,
74.1, 76.1,2, 78.1, 87.3, 88.1
Junius Brutus Albinus, Decimus:
2.56.3, 58.1,2, 60.5, 61.4, 62.4,
63.3, 64.1, 87.2
Junius Brutus Damasippus, Lucius:
2.26.2
Junius Brutus Gallaecus, Decimus:
2.5.1
Junius Iuncus, Marcus, praetor 76:
2.42.3
Junius Silanus, Marcus, consul 109:
2.12.2
Junius Silanus, Marcus, consul 25:
2.77.3
Jupiter Capitolinus: **2.**131.1

Labienus, Quintus, son of Titus:
2.78.1
Labienus, Titus: **2.**40.4, 55.4
Lacedaemonia, Laconia: *see* Sparta
Laelius, Gaius, consul 190: **2.**127.1
Laelius Sapiens, Gaius, consul 140:
1.17.3; **2.**9.1, 127.1
Laenas: *see* Popilius
Langobardi: **2.**106.2
Laodicia: **2.**69.2
Larissa: **1.**4.4
Lasthenes: **2.**34.1
Latinus: **1.**8.5
Laurentian marsh: **2.**19.1
Lebedos: **1.**4.3
Lentulus: *see* Cornelius
Lepidus: *see* Aemilius Lepidus
Lesbos: **1.**2.3, 4.4
Leucas: **2.**84.2
Liber: **2.**82.4
Libo: *see* Scribonius